WRITER
G. Willow Wilson

ARTIST
Christian Ward

LETTERER
Sal Cipriano

VOLUME 1

WALKING THE PATH

EDITOR
Karen Berger

BOOK DESIGNER
Richard Bruning

DIGITAL ART TECHNICIAN
Adam Pruett

ASSISTANT EDITOR
Rachel Boyadjis

PUBLISHER
Mike Richardson

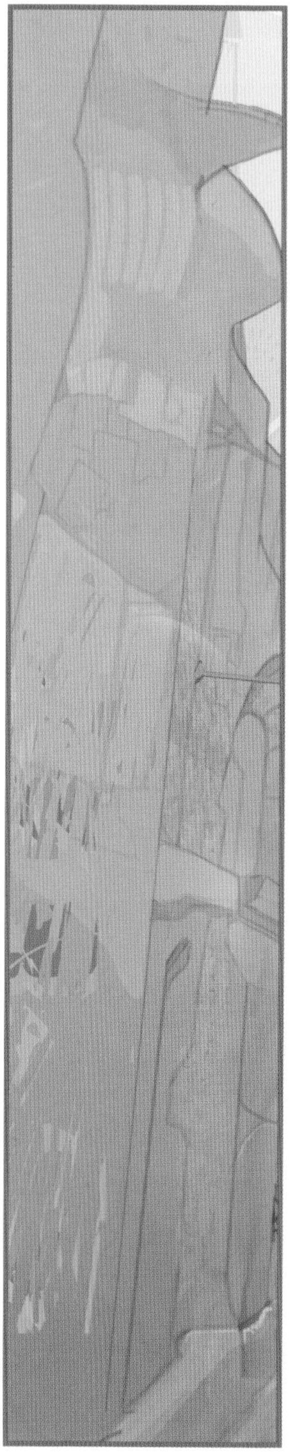

for my girls,
as always

• • •

G. Willow Wilson

for Catherine

• • •

Christian Ward

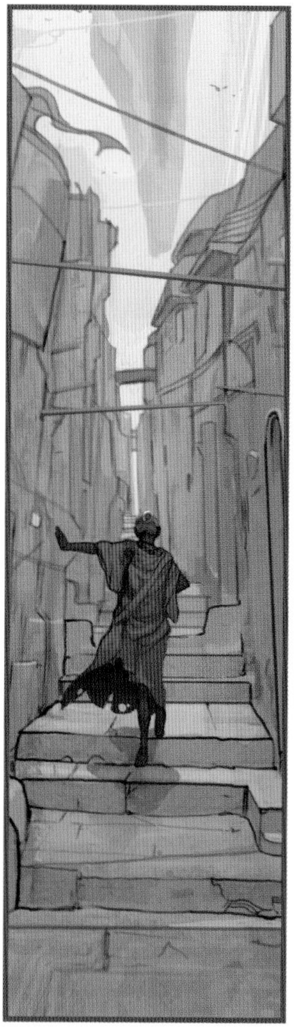

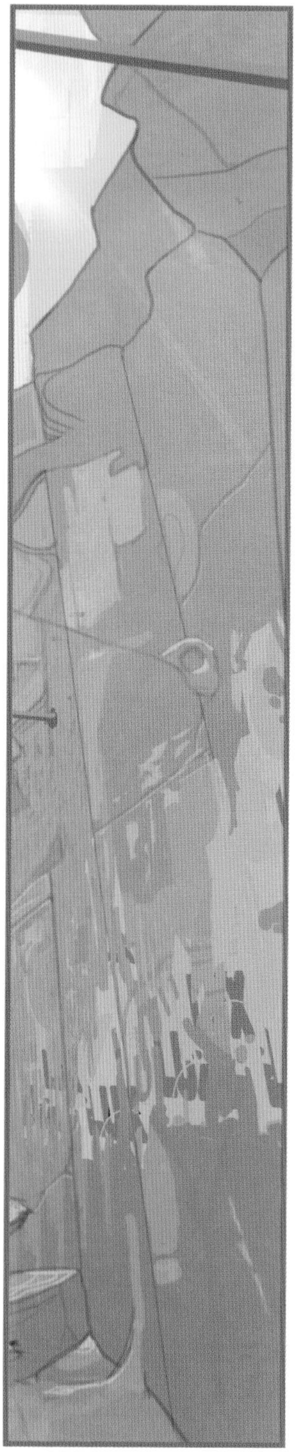

INVISIBLE KINGDOM™

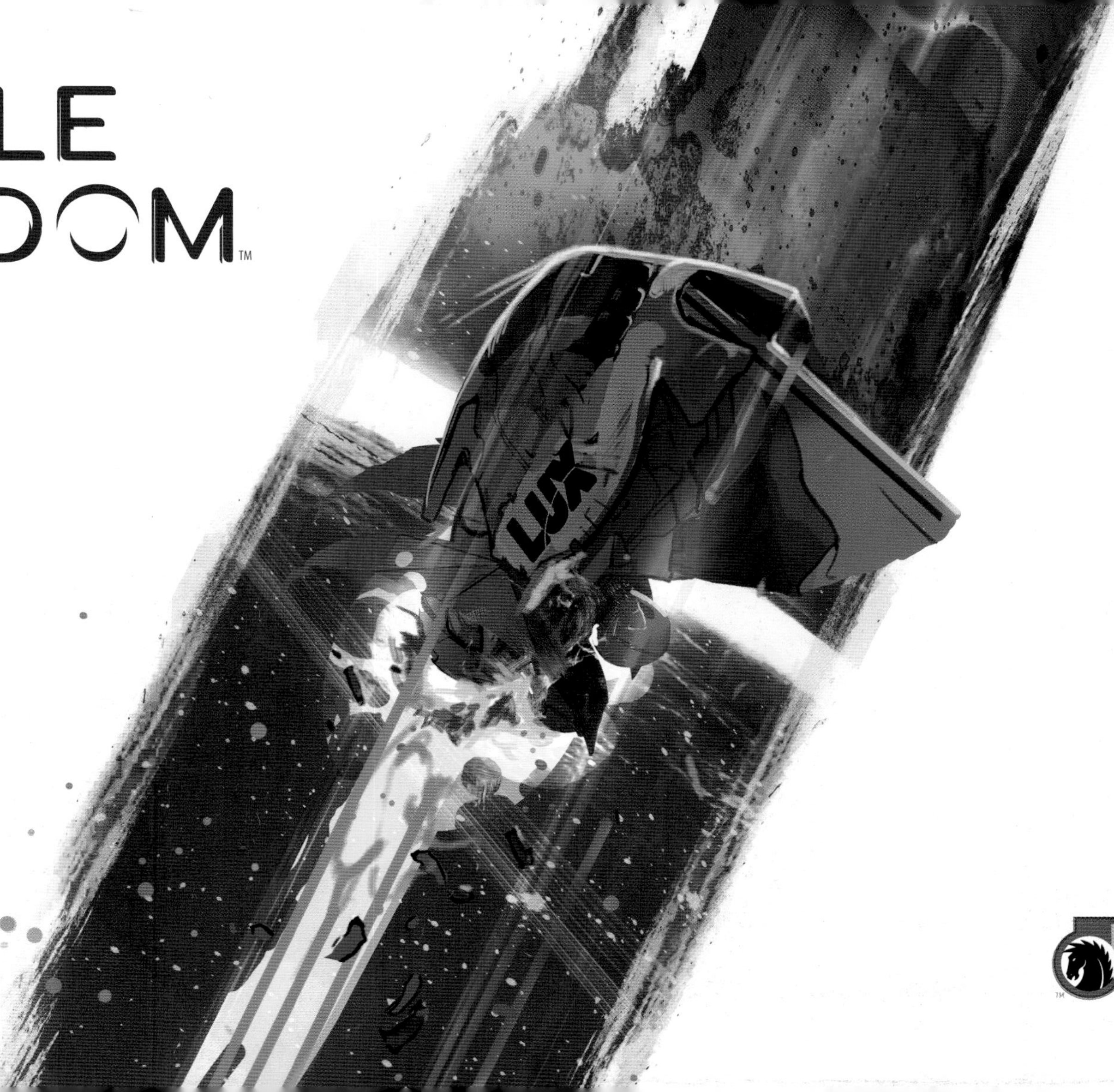
LUX

BERGER BOOKS
AN IMPRINT OF
DARK HORSE COMICS

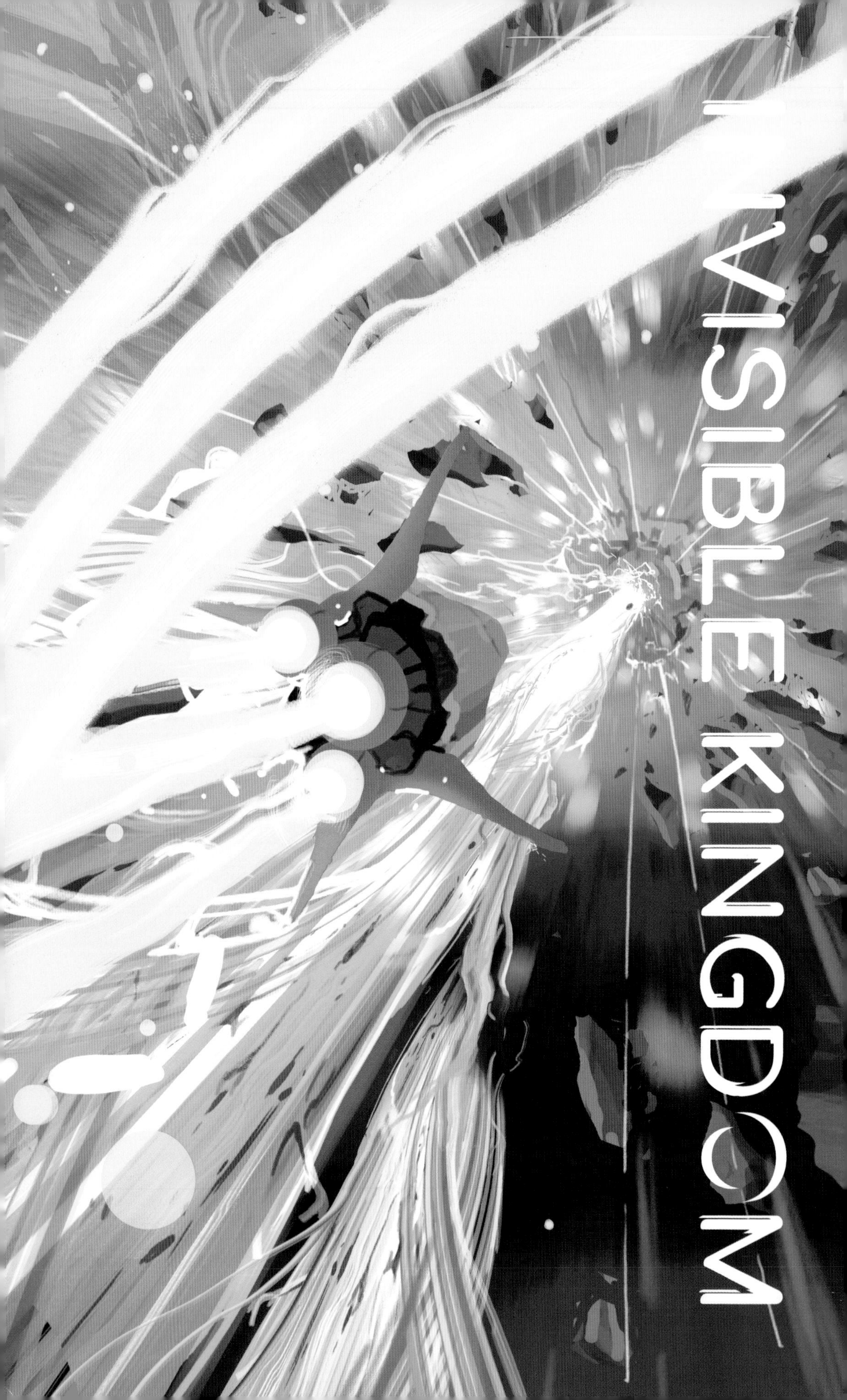
INVISIBLE KINGDOM

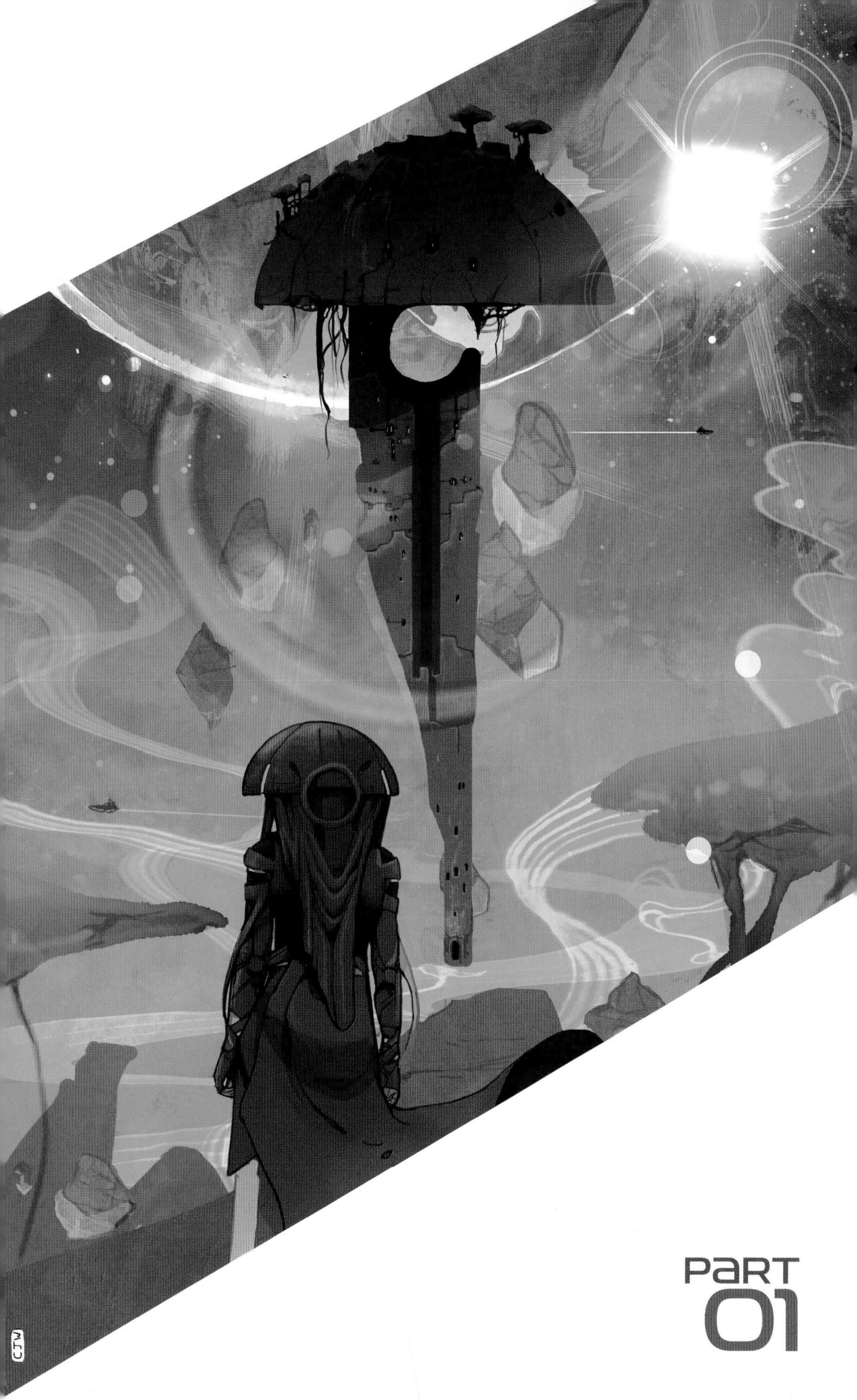

PART 01

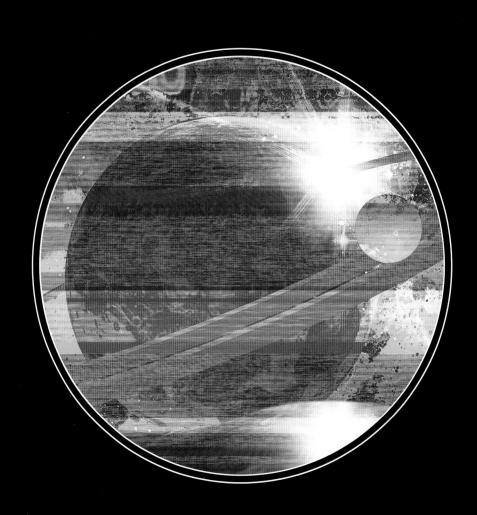

THE PLANET QARI. HIGH ORBIT.
FIVE MINUTES AGO.

DELAY NOTIFICATION 011.03.23

DEAR VALUED AND ESTIMABLE LUX CUSTOMER:

DEAR VALUED AND
ESTIMABLE LUX CUSTOMER:

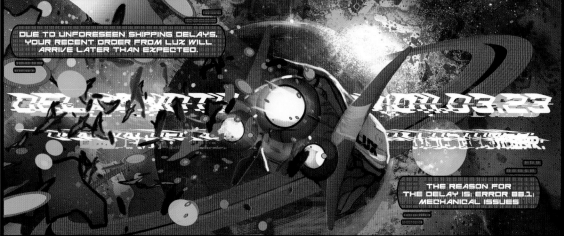

DUE TO UNFORESEEN SHIPPING DELAYS,
YOUR RECENT ORDER FROM LUX WILL
ARRIVE LATER THAN EXPECTED.

THE REASON FOR
THE DELAY IS: ERROR 88.1:
MECHANICAL ISSUES

WE UNDERSTAND YOUR TIME IS VALUABLE
AND APOLOGIZE FOR ANY INCONVENIENCE
THIS DELAY MAY CAUSE.

WE'RE AT
HALF POWER.
ATTEMPTING
TO STABILIZE
FOR LUNAR
ENTRY.

YOU
WANT TO
DITCH ON THE
MOON?!

I'M GONNA
THROW UP!

DON'T DO
IT ON MY
SHOES.

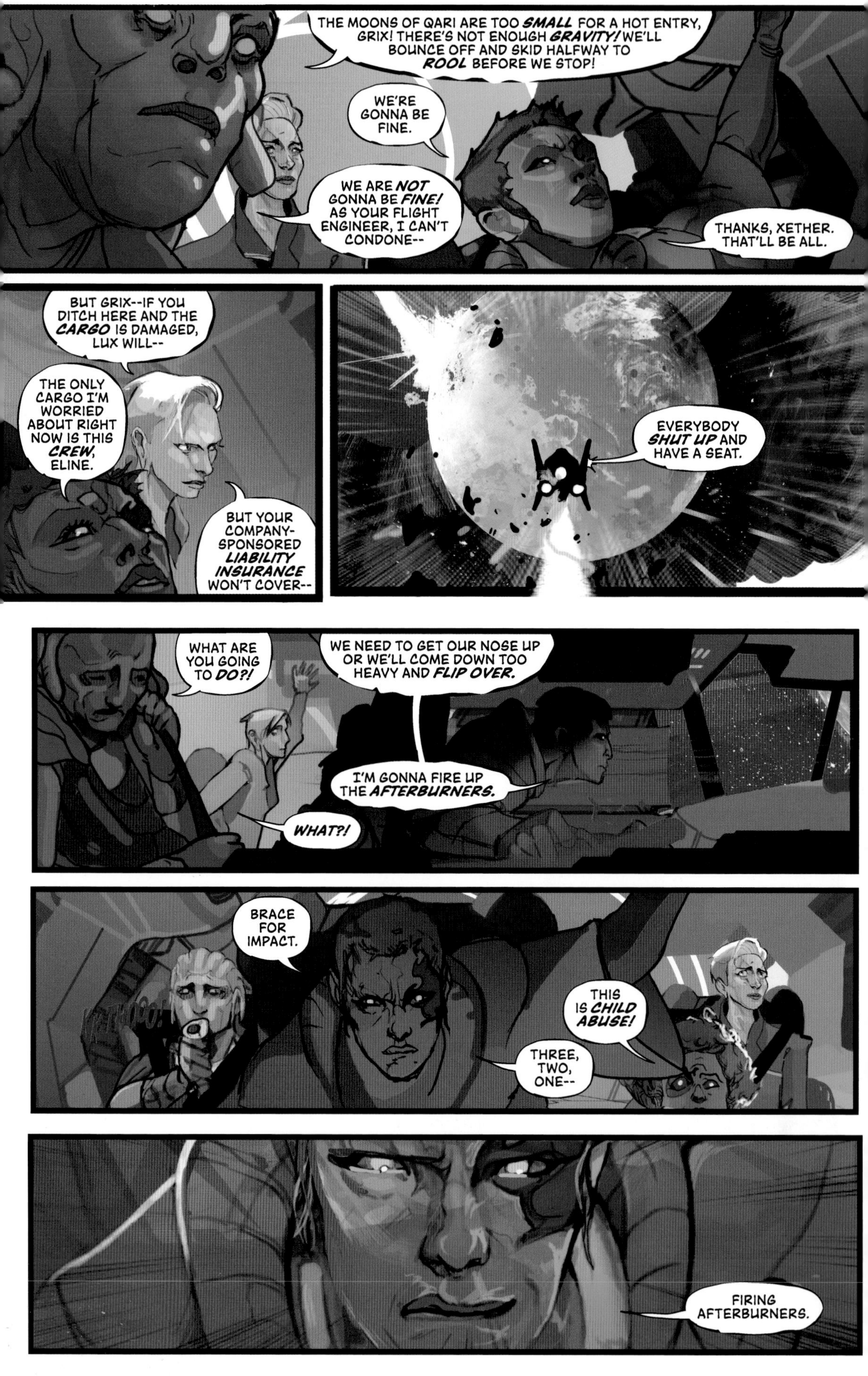
THE MOONS OF QARI ARE TOO SMALL FOR A HOT ENTRY, GRIX! THERE'S NOT ENOUGH GRAVITY! WE'LL BOUNCE OFF AND SKID HALFWAY TO ROOL BEFORE WE STOP!
WE'RE GONNA BE FINE.
WE ARE NOT GONNA BE FINE! AS YOUR FLIGHT ENGINEER, I CAN'T CONDONE--
THANKS, XETHER. THAT'LL BE ALL.
BUT GRIX--IF YOU DITCH HERE AND THE CARGO IS DAMAGED, LUX WILL--
THE ONLY CARGO I'M WORRIED ABOUT RIGHT NOW IS THIS CREW, ELINE.
BUT YOUR COMPANY-SPONSORED LIABILITY INSURANCE WON'T COVER--
EVERYBODY SHUT UP AND HAVE A SEAT.
WHAT ARE YOU GOING TO DO?!
WE NEED TO GET OUR NOSE UP OR WE'LL COME DOWN TOO HEAVY AND FLIP OVER.
I'M GONNA FIRE UP THE AFTERBURNERS.
WHAT?!
BRACE FOR IMPACT.
THIS IS CHILD ABUSE!
THREE, TWO, ONE--
FIRING AFTERBURNERS.

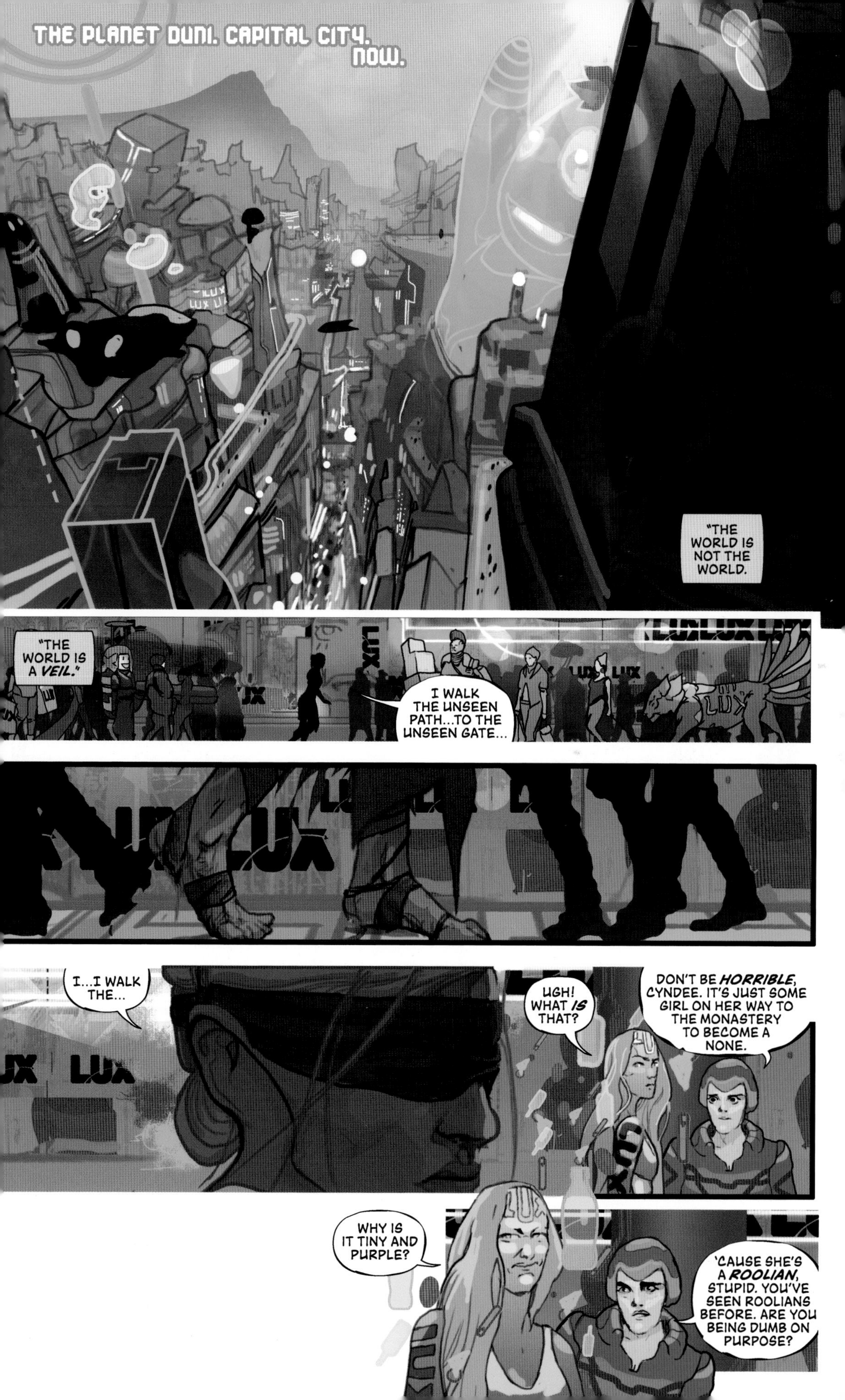
THE PLANET DUNI. CAPITAL CITY.
NOW.
"THE WORLD IS NOT THE WORLD.
LUX
"THE WORLD IS A *VEIL*."
I WALK THE UNSEEN PATH...TO THE UNSEEN GATE...
LUX
I...I WALK THE...
UGH! WHAT *IS* THAT?
DON'T BE *HORRIBLE*, CYNDEE. IT'S JUST SOME GIRL ON HER WAY TO THE MONASTERY TO BECOME A NONE.
WHY IS IT TINY AND PURPLE?
'CAUSE SHE'S A *ROOLIAN*, STUPID. YOU'VE SEEN ROOLIANS BEFORE. ARE YOU BEING DUMB ON PURPOSE?

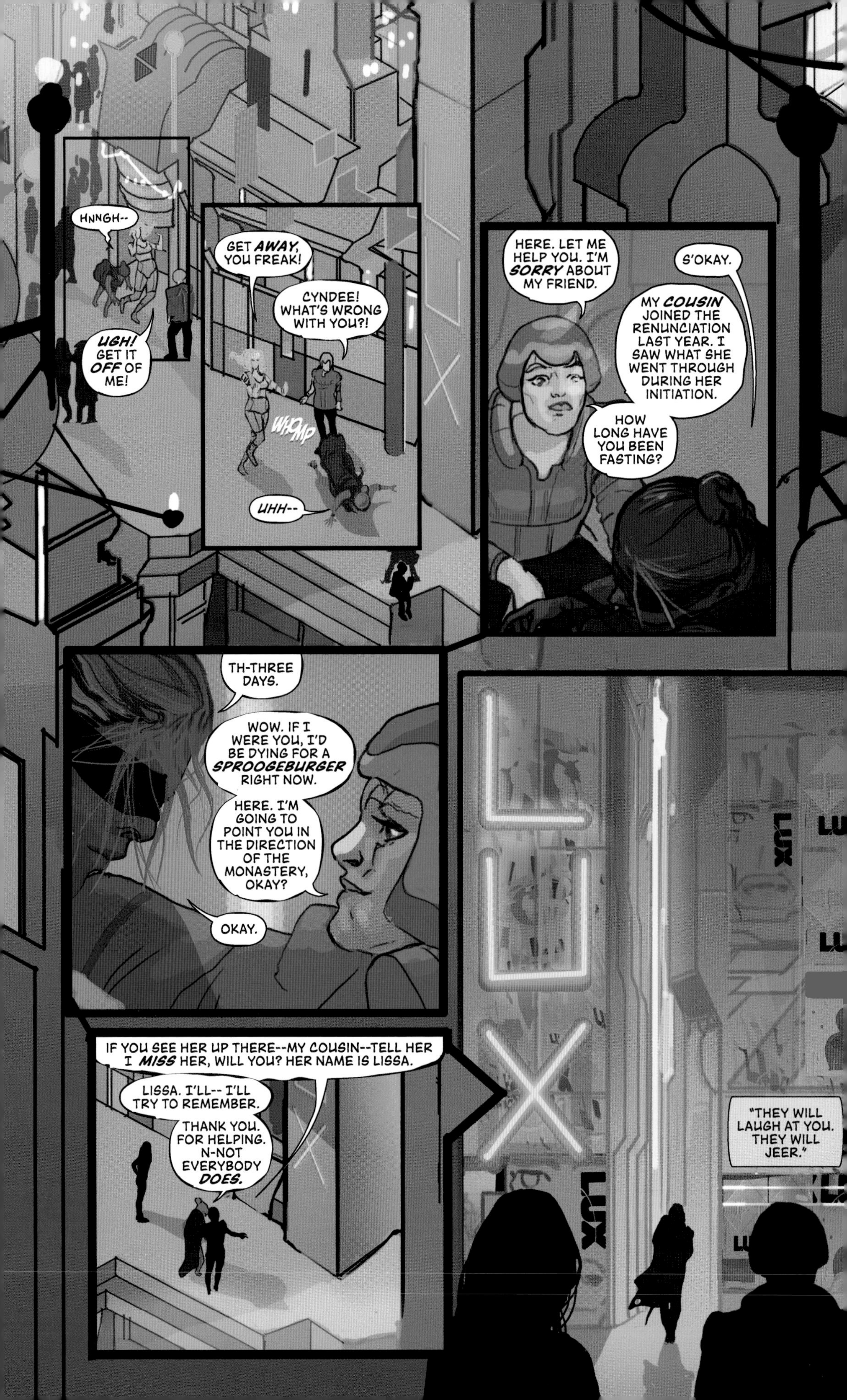
HNNGH--
UGH! GET IT OFF OF ME!
GET AWAY, YOU FREAK!
CYNDEE! WHAT'S WRONG WITH YOU?!
WHOMP
UHH--
HERE. LET ME HELP YOU. I'M SORRY ABOUT MY FRIEND.
S'OKAY.
MY COUSIN JOINED THE RENUNCIATION LAST YEAR. I SAW WHAT SHE WENT THROUGH DURING HER INITIATION.
HOW LONG HAVE YOU BEEN FASTING?
TH-THREE DAYS.
WOW. IF I WERE YOU, I'D BE DYING FOR A SPROOGEBURGER RIGHT NOW.
HERE. I'M GOING TO POINT YOU IN THE DIRECTION OF THE MONASTERY, OKAY?
OKAY.
IF YOU SEE HER UP THERE--MY COUSIN--TELL HER I MISS HER, WILL YOU? HER NAME IS LISSA.
LISSA. I'LL-- I'LL TRY TO REMEMBER.
THANK YOU. FOR HELPING. N-NOT EVERYBODY DOES.
LUX
"THEY WILL LAUGH AT YOU. THEY WILL JEER."

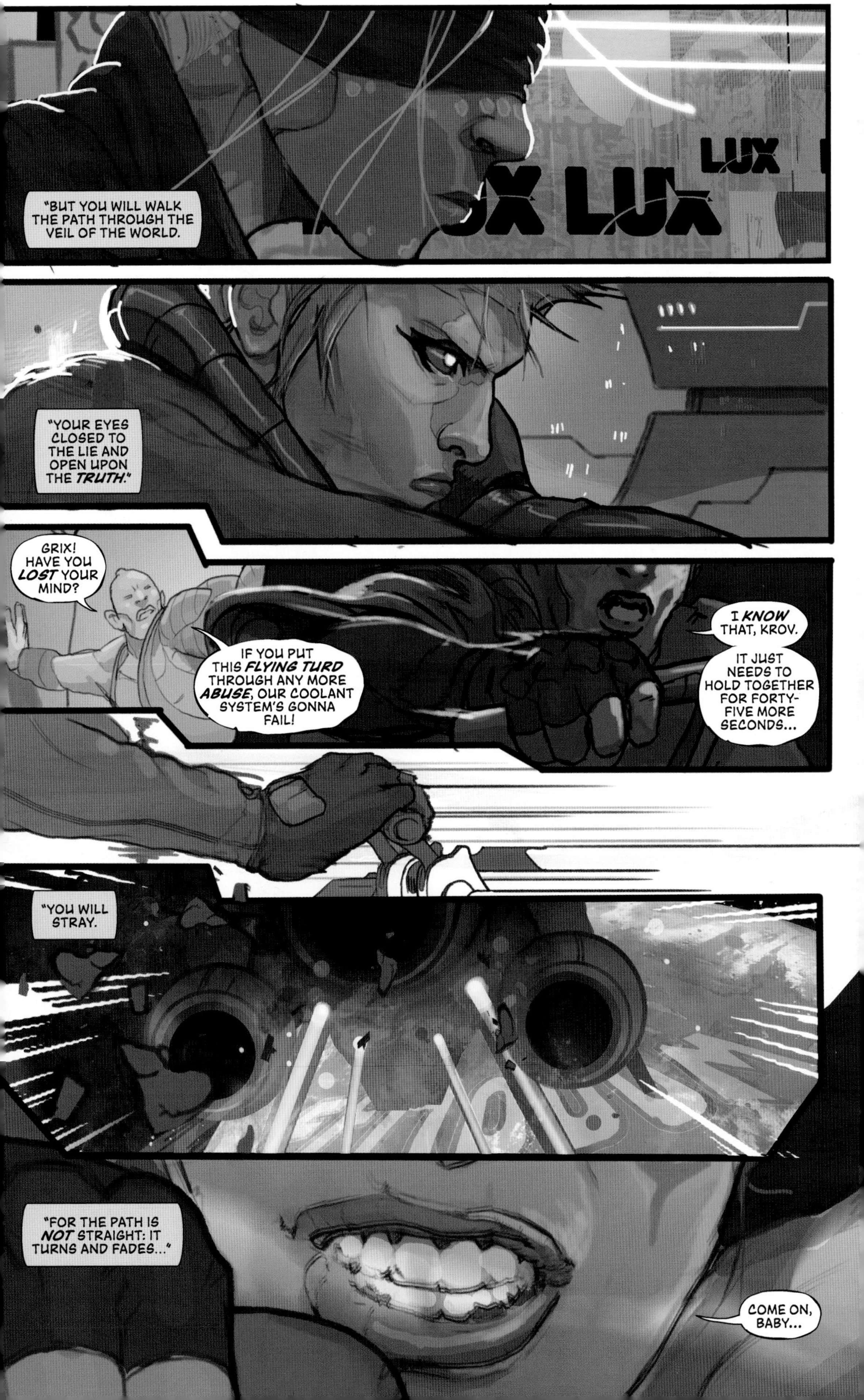
"BUT YOU WILL WALK THE PATH THROUGH THE VEIL OF THE WORLD.
LUX LUX
LUX
"YOUR EYES CLOSED TO THE LIE AND OPEN UPON THE TRUTH."
GRIX! HAVE YOU LOST YOUR MIND?
IF YOU PUT THIS FLYING TURD THROUGH ANY MORE ABUSE, OUR COOLANT SYSTEM'S GONNA FAIL!
I KNOW THAT, KROV.
IT JUST NEEDS TO HOLD TOGETHER FOR FORTY-FIVE MORE SECONDS...
"YOU WILL STRAY.
"FOR THE PATH IS NOT STRAIGHT: IT TURNS AND FADES..."
COME ON, BABY...

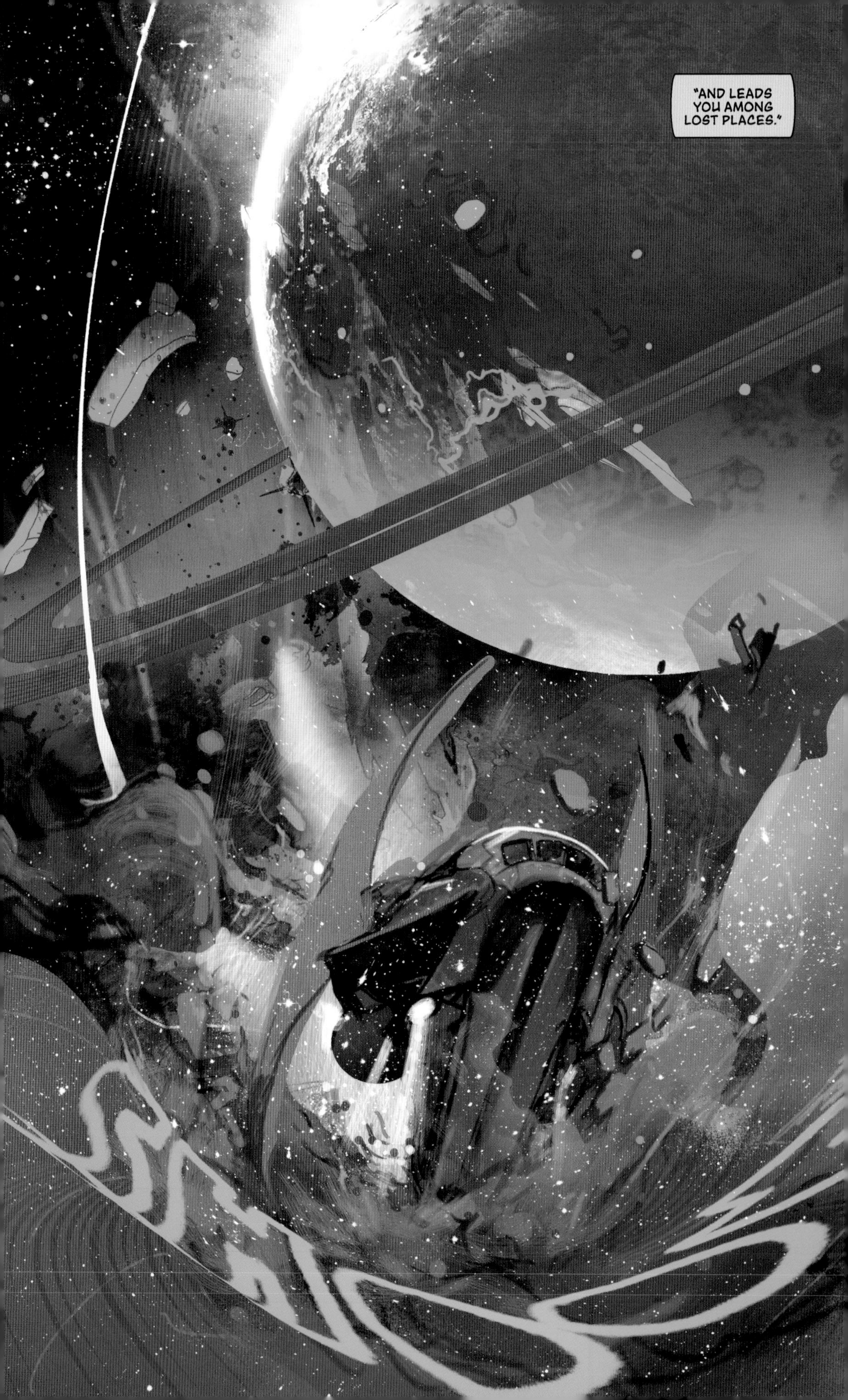
"AND LEADS YOU AMONG LOST PLACES."

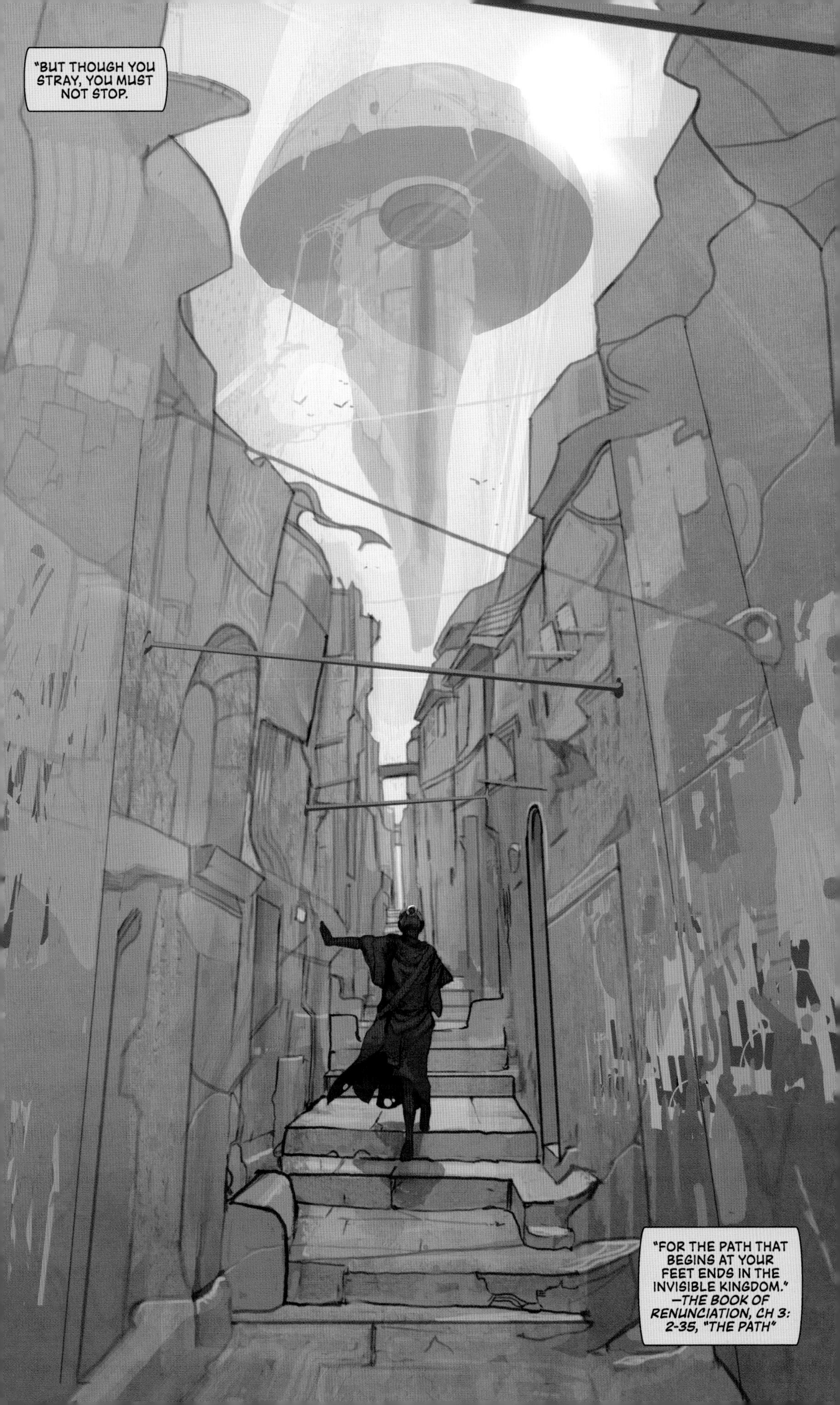
"BUT THOUGH YOU STRAY, YOU MUST NOT STOP.
"FOR THE PATH THAT BEGINS AT YOUR FEET ENDS IN THE INVISIBLE KINGDOM."
—THE BOOK OF RENUNCIATION, CH 3: 2-35, "THE PATH"

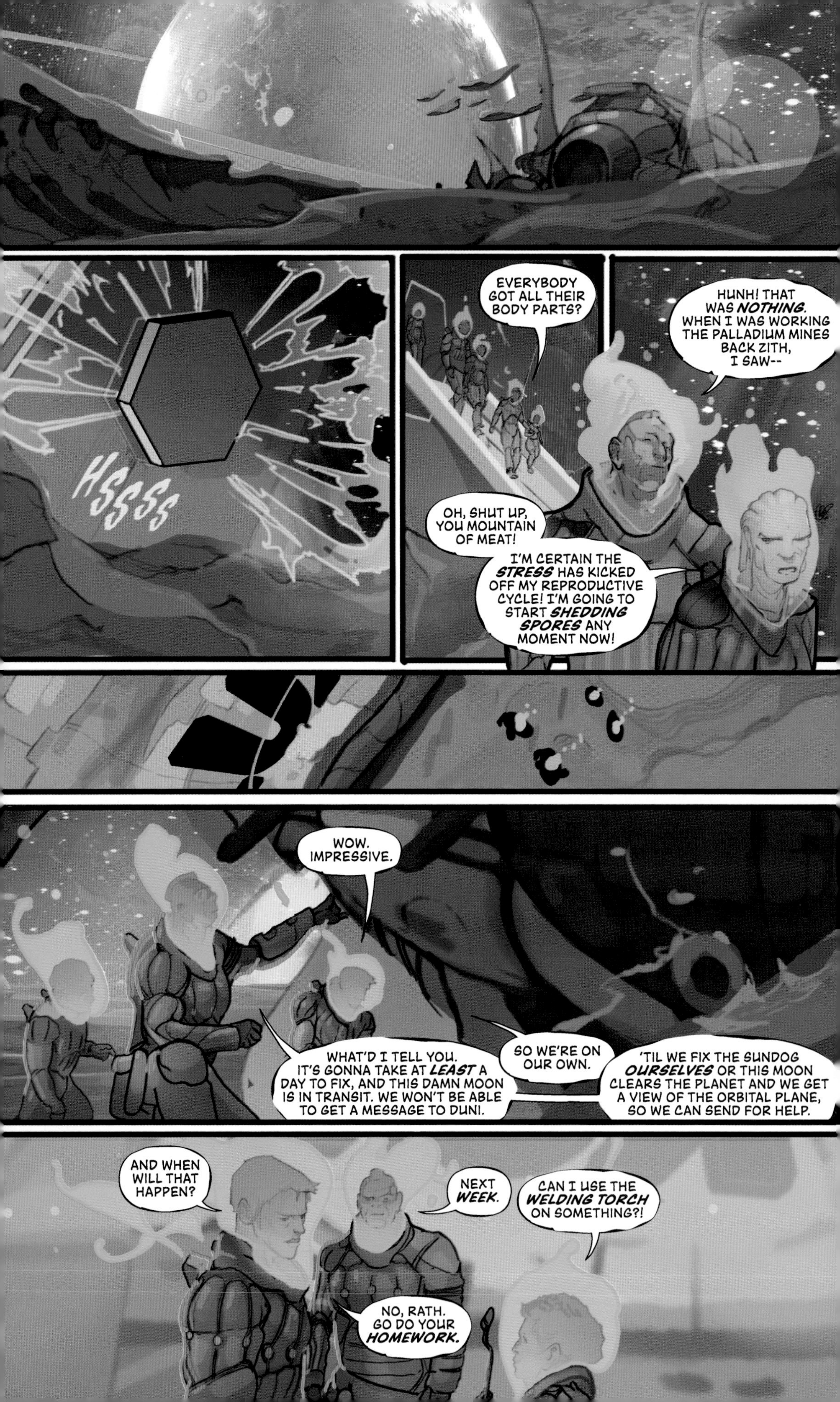
HSSSS
EVERYBODY GOT ALL THEIR BODY PARTS?
HUNH! THAT WAS NOTHING. WHEN I WAS WORKING THE PALLADIUM MINES BACK ZITH, I SAW--
OH, SHUT UP, YOU MOUNTAIN OF MEAT!
I'M CERTAIN THE STRESS HAS KICKED OFF MY REPRODUCTIVE CYCLE! I'M GOING TO START SHEDDING SPORES ANY MOMENT NOW!
WOW. IMPRESSIVE.
WHAT'D I TELL YOU. IT'S GONNA TAKE AT LEAST A DAY TO FIX, AND THIS DAMN MOON IS IN TRANSIT. WE WON'T BE ABLE TO GET A MESSAGE TO DUNI.
SO WE'RE ON OUR OWN.
'TIL WE FIX THE SUNDOG OURSELVES OR THIS MOON CLEARS THE PLANET AND WE GET A VIEW OF THE ORBITAL PLANE, SO WE CAN SEND FOR HELP.
AND WHEN WILL THAT HAPPEN?
NEXT WEEK.
CAN I USE THE WELDING TORCH ON SOMETHING?!
NO, RATH. GO DO YOUR HOMEWORK.

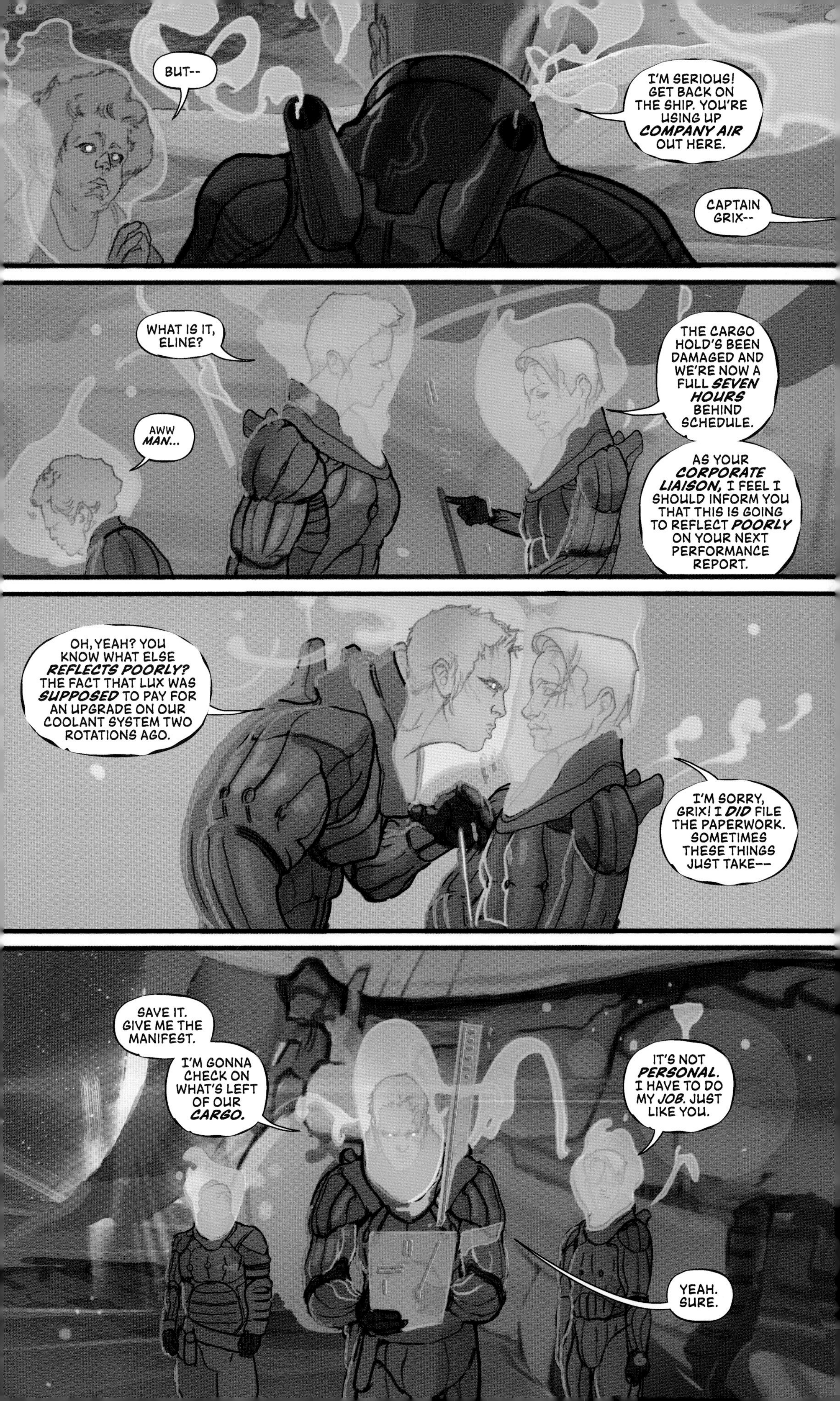

BUT--
I'M SERIOUS! GET BACK ON THE SHIP. YOU'RE USING UP COMPANY AIR OUT HERE.
CAPTAIN GRIX--
WHAT IS IT, ELINE?
THE CARGO HOLD'S BEEN DAMAGED AND WE'RE NOW A FULL SEVEN HOURS BEHIND SCHEDULE.
AWW MAN...
AS YOUR CORPORATE LIAISON, I FEEL I SHOULD INFORM YOU THAT THIS IS GOING TO REFLECT POORLY ON YOUR NEXT PERFORMANCE REPORT.
OH, YEAH? YOU KNOW WHAT ELSE REFLECTS POORLY? THE FACT THAT LUX WAS SUPPOSED TO PAY FOR AN UPGRADE ON OUR COOLANT SYSTEM TWO ROTATIONS AGO.
I'M SORRY, GRIX! I DID FILE THE PAPERWORK. SOMETIMES THESE THINGS JUST TAKE--
SAVE IT. GIVE ME THE MANIFEST.
I'M GONNA CHECK ON WHAT'S LEFT OF OUR CARGO.
IT'S NOT PERSONAL. I HAVE TO DO MY JOB. JUST LIKE YOU.
YEAH. SURE.

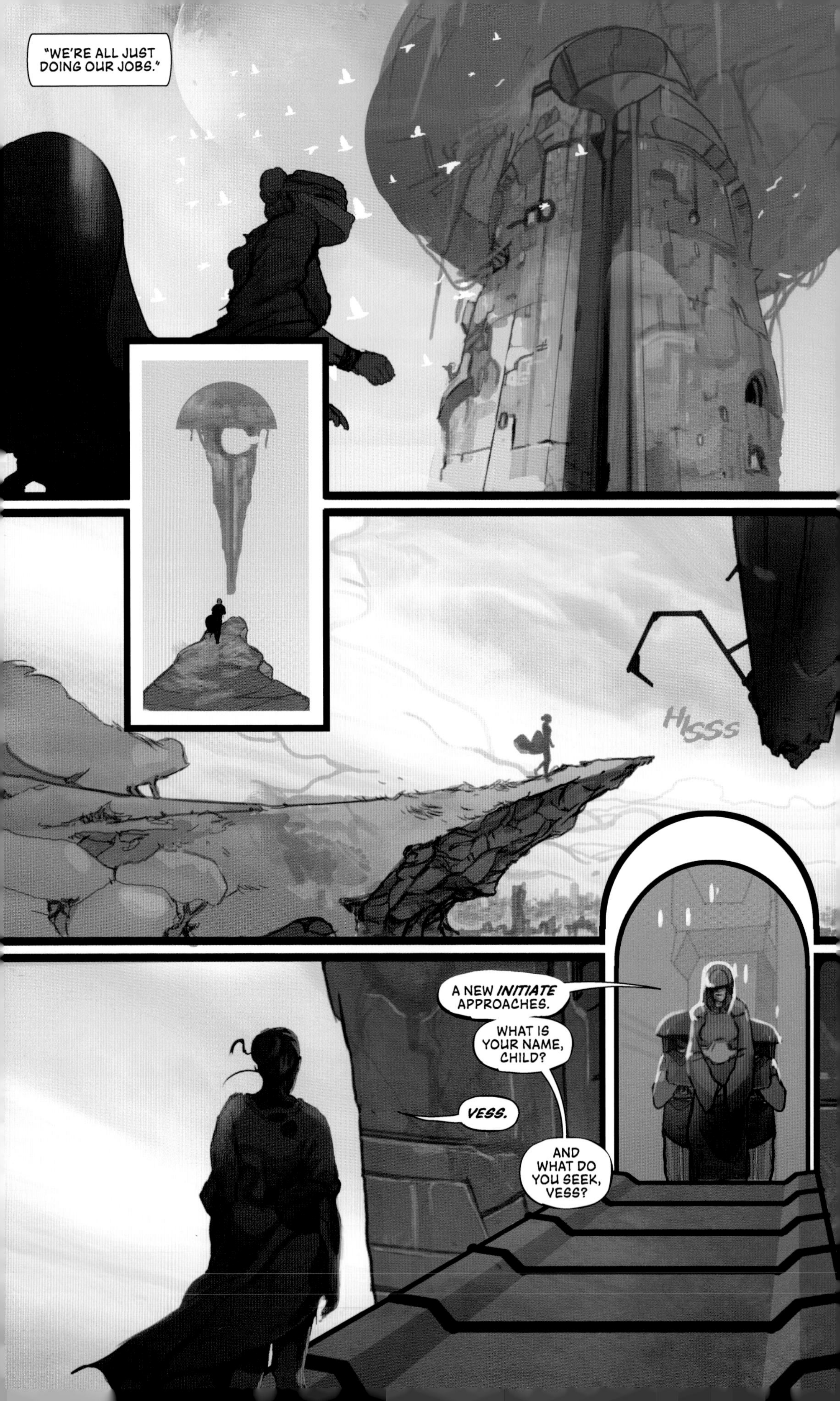
"WE'RE ALL JUST DOING OUR JOBS."
HISSS
A NEW INITIATE APPROACHES.
WHAT IS YOUR NAME, CHILD?
VESS.
AND WHAT DO YOU SEEK, VESS?

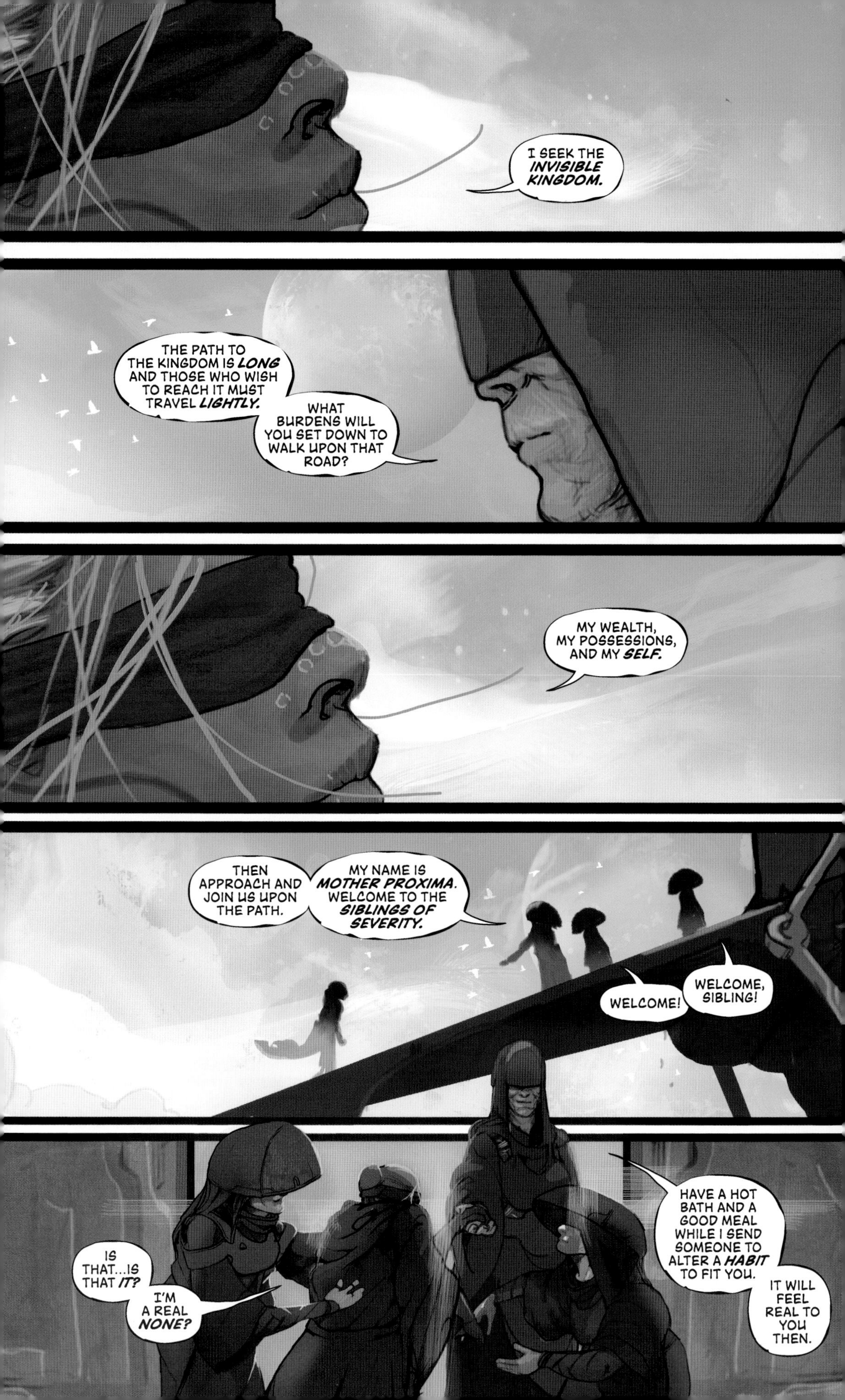
I SEEK THE INVISIBLE KINGDOM.
THE PATH TO THE KINGDOM IS LONG AND THOSE WHO WISH TO REACH IT MUST TRAVEL LIGHTLY.
WHAT BURDENS WILL YOU SET DOWN TO WALK UPON THAT ROAD?
MY WEALTH, MY POSSESSIONS, AND MY SELF.
THEN APPROACH AND JOIN US UPON THE PATH.
MY NAME IS MOTHER PROXIMA. WELCOME TO THE SIBLINGS OF SEVERITY.
WELCOME!
WELCOME, SIBLING!
IS THAT...IS THAT IT?
I'M A REAL NONE?
HAVE A HOT BATH AND A GOOD MEAL WHILE I SEND SOMEONE TO ALTER A HABIT TO FIT YOU.
IT WILL FEEL REAL TO YOU THEN.

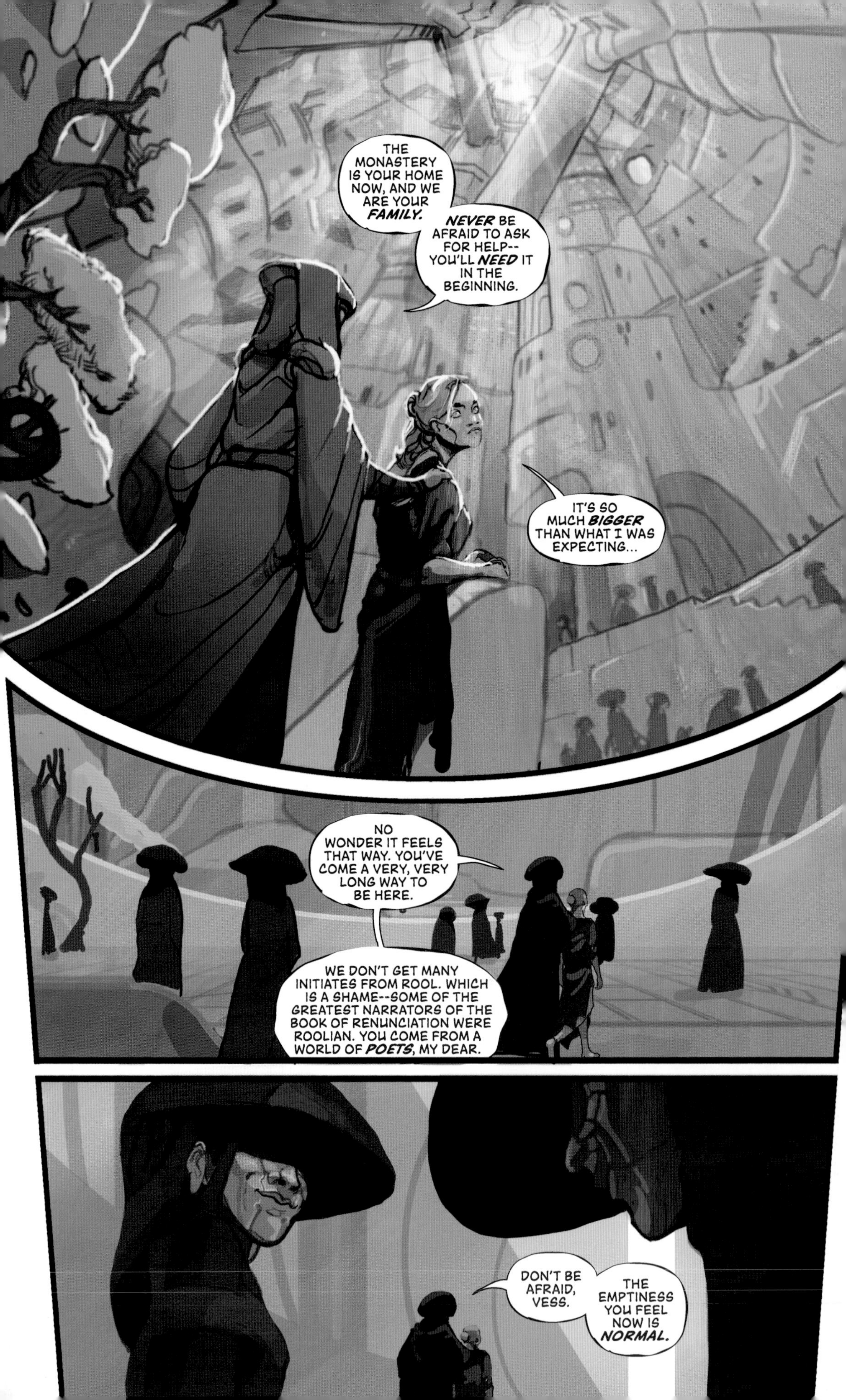
THE MONASTERY IS YOUR HOME NOW, AND WE ARE YOUR FAMILY.
NEVER BE AFRAID TO ASK FOR HELP--YOU'LL NEED IT IN THE BEGINNING.
IT'S SO MUCH BIGGER THAN WHAT I WAS EXPECTING...
NO WONDER IT FEELS THAT WAY. YOU'VE COME A VERY, VERY LONG WAY TO BE HERE.
WE DON'T GET MANY INITIATES FROM ROOL. WHICH IS A SHAME--SOME OF THE GREATEST NARRATORS OF THE BOOK OF RENUNCIATION WERE ROOLIAN. YOU COME FROM A WORLD OF POETS, MY DEAR.
DON'T BE AFRAID, VESS.
THE EMPTINESS YOU FEEL NOW IS NORMAL.

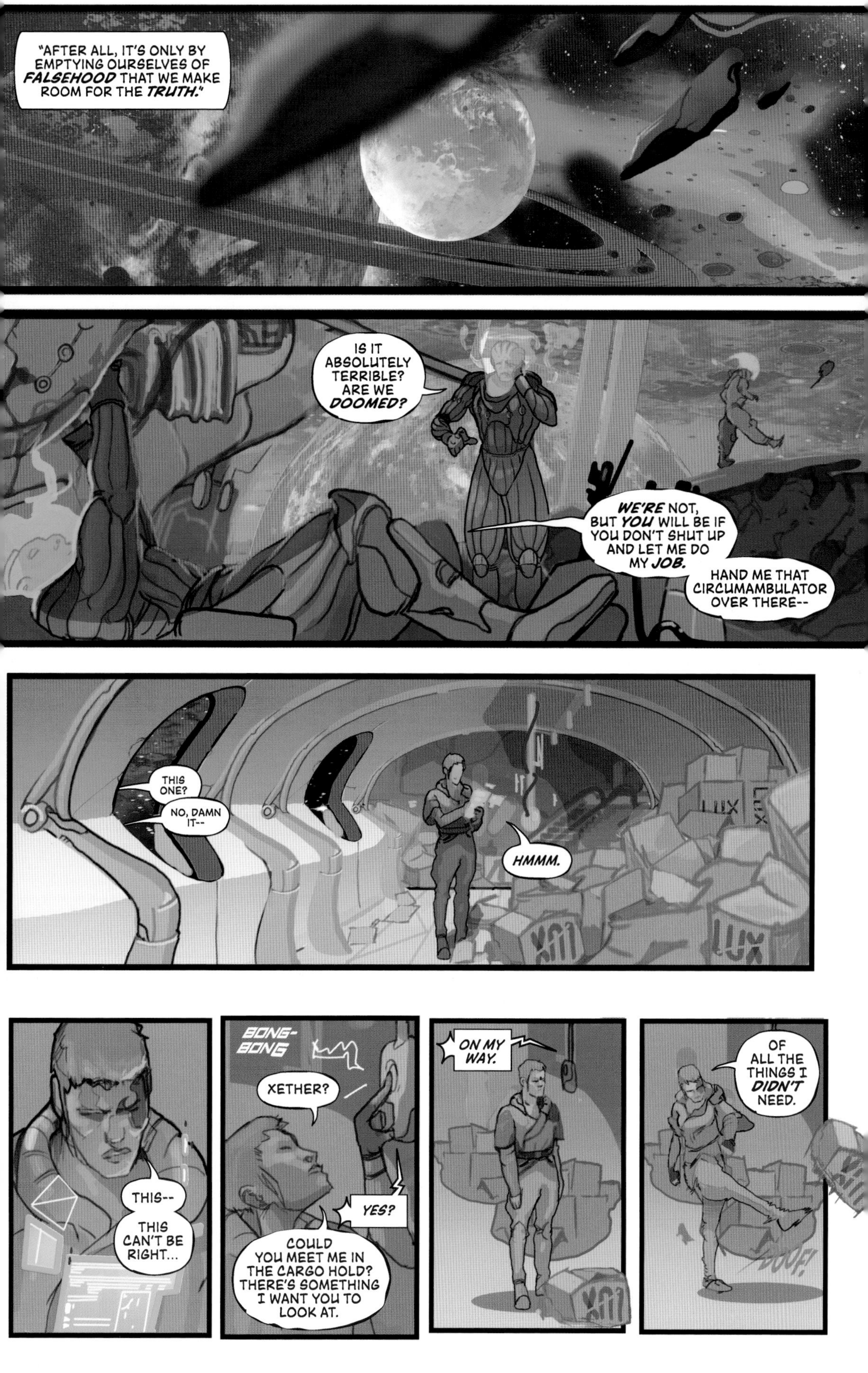
"AFTER ALL, IT'S ONLY BY EMPTYING OURSELVES OF FALSEHOOD THAT WE MAKE ROOM FOR THE TRUTH."
IS IT ABSOLUTELY TERRIBLE? ARE WE DOOMED?
WE'RE NOT, BUT YOU WILL BE IF YOU DON'T SHUT UP AND LET ME DO MY JOB.
HAND ME THAT CIRCUMAMBULATOR OVER THERE--
THIS ONE?
NO, DAMN IT--
HMMM.
LUX
THIS--
THIS CAN'T BE RIGHT...
BONG-BONG
XETHER?
YES?
COULD YOU MEET ME IN THE CARGO HOLD? THERE'S SOMETHING I WANT YOU TO LOOK AT.
ON MY WAY.
OF ALL THE THINGS I DIDN'T NEED.
DOOF!

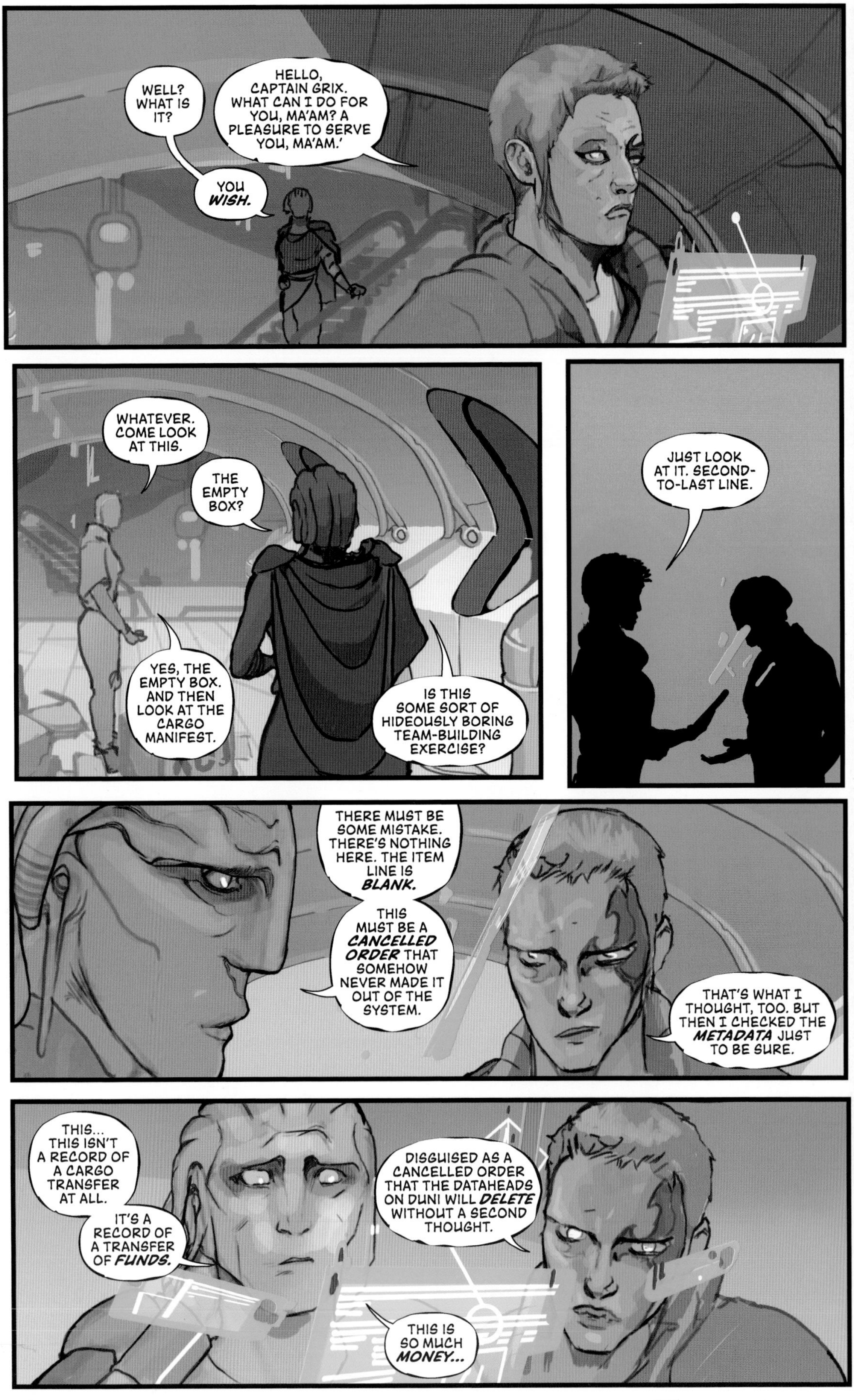

WELL? WHAT IS IT?
HELLO, CAPTAIN GRIX. WHAT CAN I DO FOR YOU, MA'AM? A PLEASURE TO SERVE YOU, MA'AM.'
YOU WISH.
WHATEVER. COME LOOK AT THIS.
THE EMPTY BOX?
YES, THE EMPTY BOX. AND THEN LOOK AT THE CARGO MANIFEST.
IS THIS SOME SORT OF HIDEOUSLY BORING TEAM-BUILDING EXERCISE?
JUST LOOK AT IT. SECOND-TO-LAST LINE.
THERE MUST BE SOME MISTAKE. THERE'S NOTHING HERE. THE ITEM LINE IS BLANK.
THIS MUST BE A CANCELLED ORDER THAT SOMEHOW NEVER MADE IT OUT OF THE SYSTEM.
THAT'S WHAT I THOUGHT, TOO. BUT THEN I CHECKED THE METADATA JUST TO BE SURE.
THIS... THIS ISN'T A RECORD OF A CARGO TRANSFER AT ALL.
IT'S A RECORD OF A TRANSFER OF FUNDS.
DISGUISED AS A CANCELLED ORDER THAT THE DATAHEADS ON DUNI WILL DELETE WITHOUT A SECOND THOUGHT.
THIS IS SO MUCH MONEY...

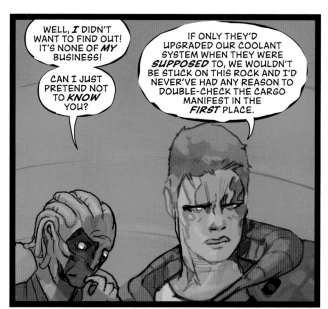

WHAT DOES IT *MEAN?*

WHAT DO YOU *THINK*, XETHER?

OBVIOUSLY SOMEBODY *INSIDE* LUX IS FUNNELING COMPANY MONEY TO SOMEBODY *OUTSIDE* LUX, AND WENT THROUGH A LOT OF TROUBLE TO MAKE SURE *NOBODY* EVER FOUND OUT.

WELL, *I* DIDN'T WANT TO FIND OUT! IT'S NONE OF *MY* BUSINESS!

CAN I JUST PRETEND NOT TO *KNOW* YOU?

IF ONLY THEY'D UPGRADED OUR COOLANT SYSTEM WHEN THEY WERE *SUPPOSED* TO, WE WOULDN'T BE STUCK ON THIS ROCK AND I'D NEVER'VE HAD ANY REASON TO DOUBLE-CHECK THE CARGO MANIFEST IN THE *FIRST* PLACE.

DAMN IT!

CLANG

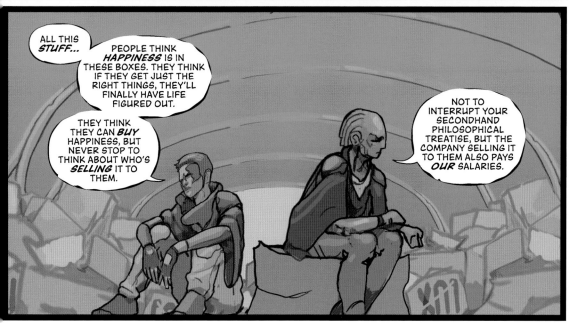

ALL THIS *STUFF...*

PEOPLE THINK *HAPPINESS* IS IN THESE BOXES. THEY THINK IF THEY GET JUST THE RIGHT THINGS, THEY'LL FINALLY HAVE LIFE FIGURED OUT.

THEY THINK THEY CAN *BUY* HAPPINESS, BUT NEVER STOP TO THINK ABOUT WHO'S *SELLING* IT TO THEM.

NOT TO INTERRUPT YOUR SECONDHAND PHILOSOPHICAL TREATISE, BUT THE COMPANY SELLING IT TO THEM ALSO PAYS *OUR* SALARIES.

SO I SUGGEST WE *FORGET* ABOUT THIS LITTLE DISCOVERY, RESEAL THE BOXES, AND BE ON OUR WAY.

I'VE CHARTED A COURSE THAT WILL SAVE US A FULL THREE HOURS ONCE THE MOON HAS TRANSITED. YOU'RE WELCOME.

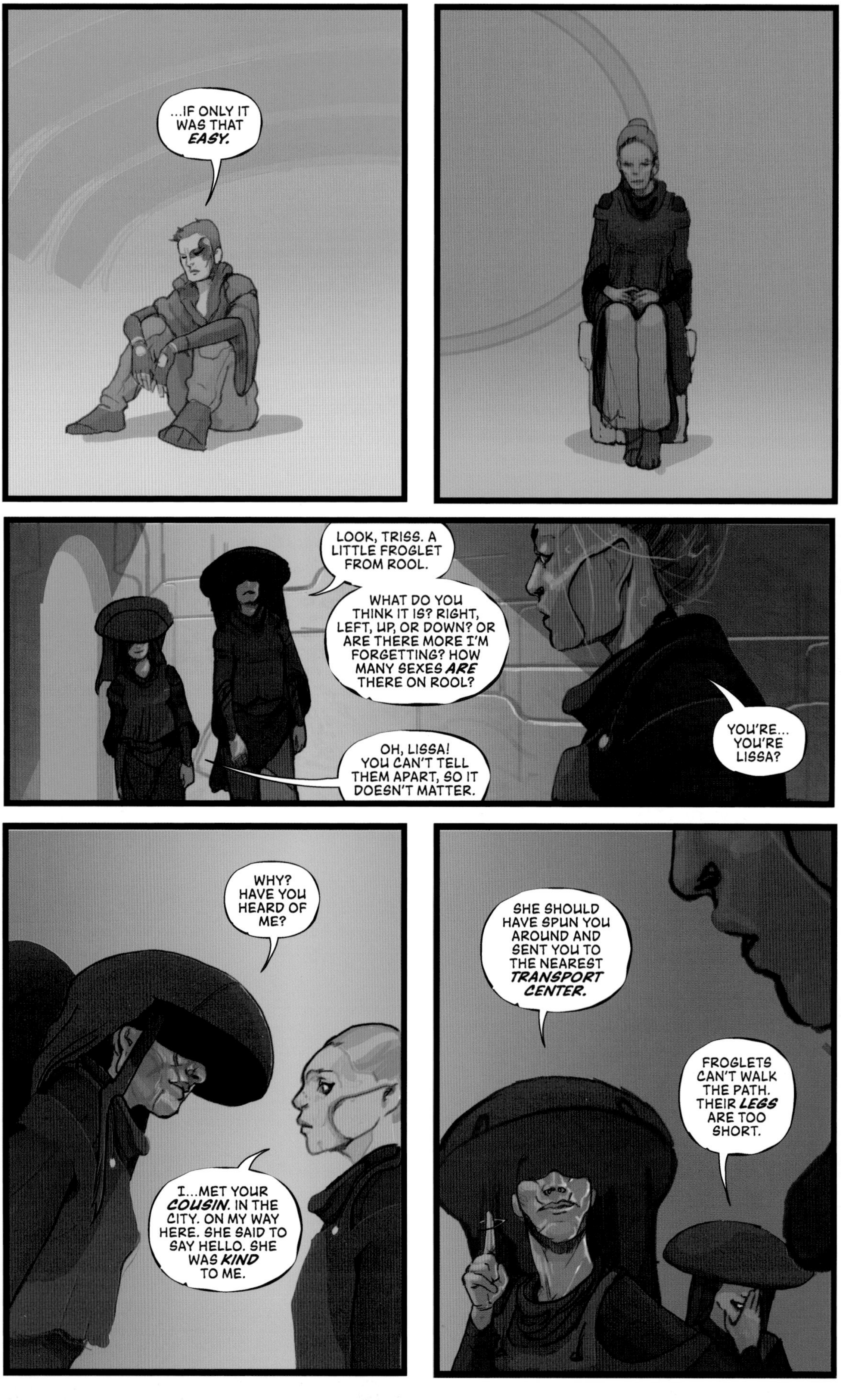
...IF ONLY IT WAS THAT *EASY.*
LOOK, TRISS. A LITTLE FROGLET FROM ROOL.
WHAT DO YOU THINK IT IS? RIGHT, LEFT, UP, OR DOWN? OR ARE THERE MORE I'M FORGETTING? HOW MANY SEXES *ARE* THERE ON ROOL?
OH, LISSA! YOU CAN'T TELL THEM APART, SO IT DOESN'T MATTER.
YOU'RE... YOU'RE LISSA?
WHY? HAVE YOU HEARD OF ME?
I...MET YOUR *COUSIN.* IN THE CITY. ON MY WAY HERE. SHE SAID TO SAY HELLO. SHE WAS *KIND* TO ME.
SHE SHOULD HAVE SPUN YOU AROUND AND SENT YOU TO THE NEAREST *TRANSPORT CENTER.*
FROGLETS CAN'T WALK THE PATH. THEIR *LEGS* ARE TOO SHORT.

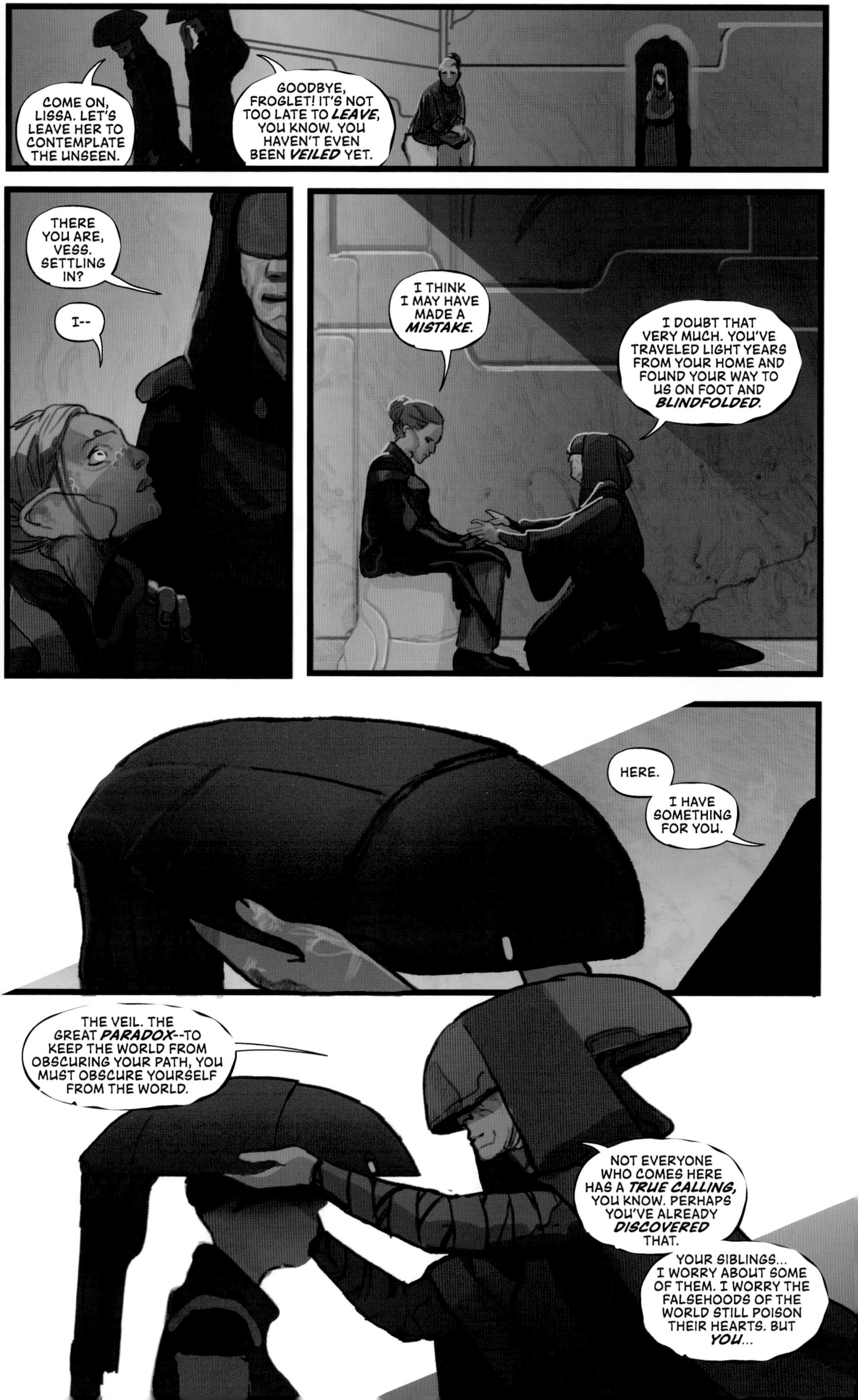
COME ON, LISSA. LET'S LEAVE HER TO CONTEMPLATE THE UNSEEN.
GOODBYE, FROGLET! IT'S NOT TOO LATE TO *LEAVE*, YOU KNOW. YOU HAVEN'T EVEN BEEN *VEILED* YET.
THERE YOU ARE, VESS. SETTLING IN?
I--
I THINK I MAY HAVE MADE A *MISTAKE*.
I DOUBT THAT VERY MUCH. YOU'VE TRAVELED LIGHT YEARS FROM YOUR HOME AND FOUND YOUR WAY TO US ON FOOT AND *BLINDFOLDED*.
HERE.
I HAVE SOMETHING FOR YOU.
THE VEIL. THE GREAT *PARADOX*--TO KEEP THE WORLD FROM OBSCURING YOUR PATH, YOU MUST OBSCURE YOURSELF FROM THE WORLD.
NOT EVERYONE WHO COMES HERE HAS A *TRUE CALLING*, YOU KNOW. PERHAPS YOU'VE ALREADY *DISCOVERED* THAT.
YOUR SIBLINGS... I WORRY ABOUT SOME OF THEM. I WORRY THE FALSEHOODS OF THE WORLD STILL POISON THEIR HEARTS. BUT *YOU*...

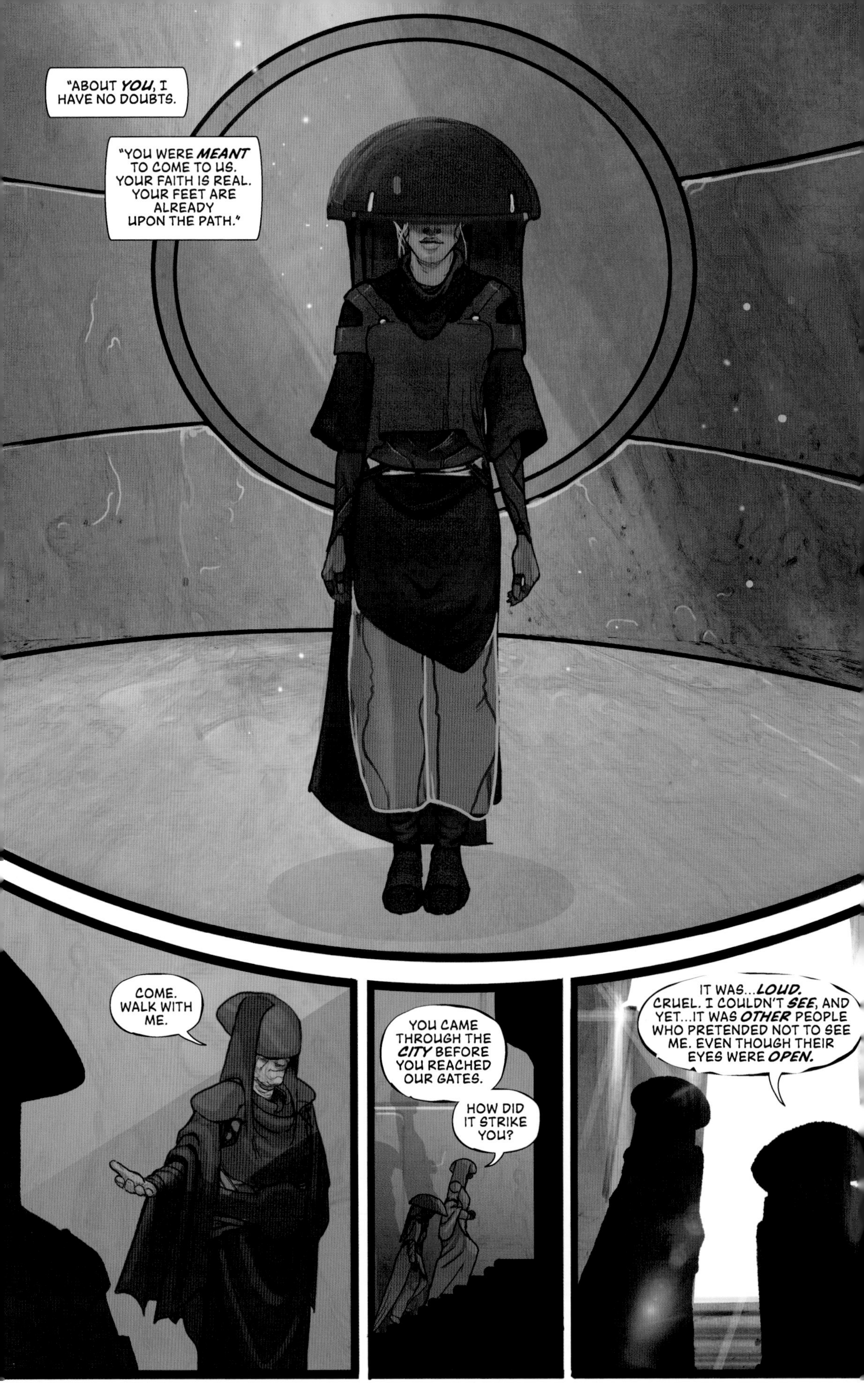
"ABOUT YOU, I HAVE NO DOUBTS.
"YOU WERE MEANT TO COME TO US. YOUR FAITH IS REAL. YOUR FEET ARE ALREADY UPON THE PATH."
COME. WALK WITH ME.
YOU CAME THROUGH THE CITY BEFORE YOU REACHED OUR GATES.
HOW DID IT STRIKE YOU?
IT WAS...LOUD. CRUEL. I COULDN'T SEE, AND YET...IT WAS OTHER PEOPLE WHO PRETENDED NOT TO SEE ME. EVEN THOUGH THEIR EYES WERE OPEN.

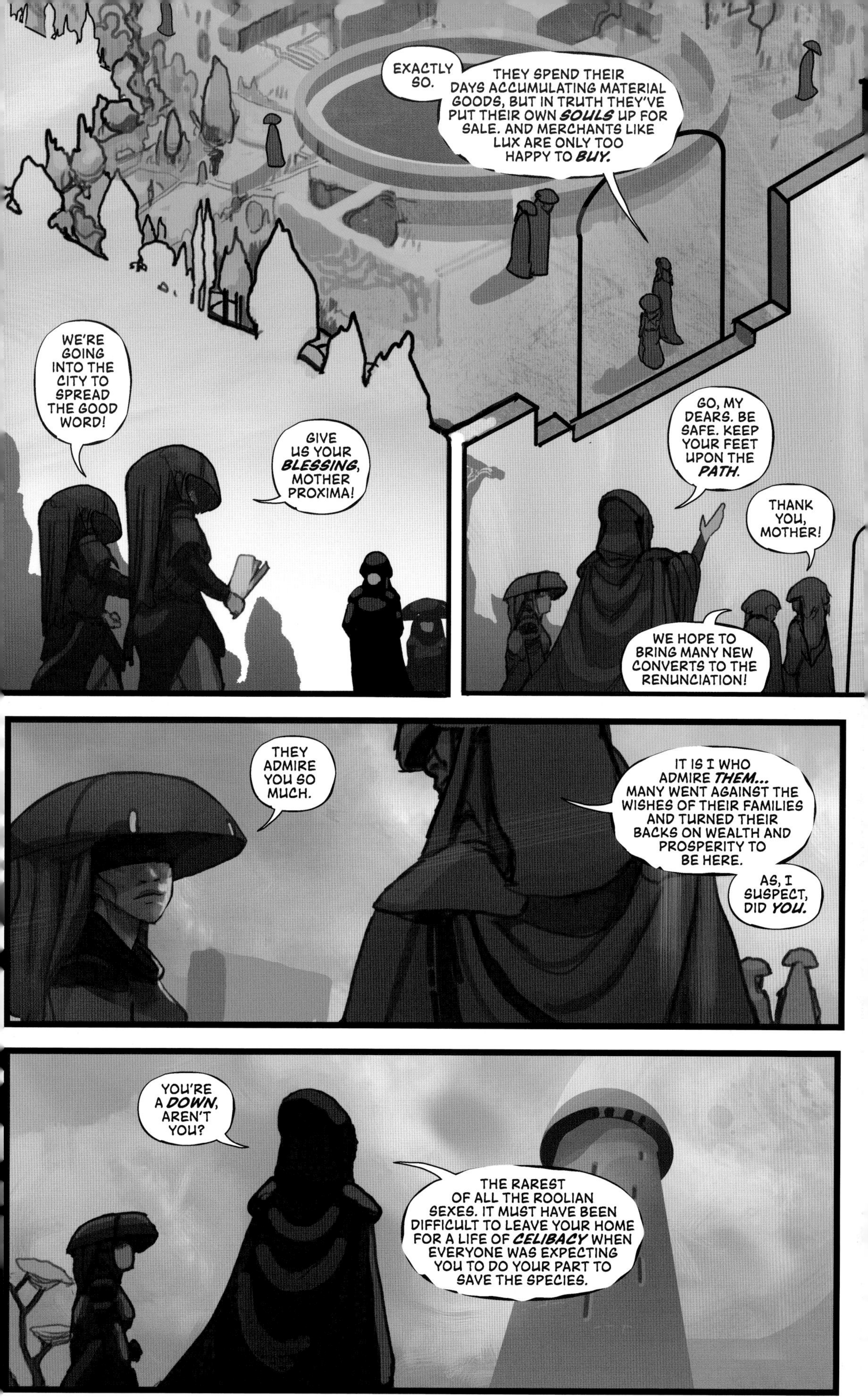
EXACTLY SO.
THEY SPEND THEIR DAYS ACCUMULATING MATERIAL GOODS, BUT IN TRUTH THEY'VE PUT THEIR OWN SOULS UP FOR SALE. AND MERCHANTS LIKE LUX ARE ONLY TOO HAPPY TO BUY.
WE'RE GOING INTO THE CITY TO SPREAD THE GOOD WORD!
GIVE US YOUR BLESSING, MOTHER PROXIMA!
GO, MY DEARS. BE SAFE. KEEP YOUR FEET UPON THE PATH.
THANK YOU, MOTHER!
WE HOPE TO BRING MANY NEW CONVERTS TO THE RENUNCIATION!
THEY ADMIRE YOU SO MUCH.
IT IS I WHO ADMIRE THEM... MANY WENT AGAINST THE WISHES OF THEIR FAMILIES AND TURNED THEIR BACKS ON WEALTH AND PROSPERITY TO BE HERE.
AS, I SUSPECT, DID YOU.
YOU'RE A DOWN, AREN'T YOU?
THE RAREST OF ALL THE ROOLIAN SEXES. IT MUST HAVE BEEN DIFFICULT TO LEAVE YOUR HOME FOR A LIFE OF CELIBACY WHEN EVERYONE WAS EXPECTING YOU TO DO YOUR PART TO SAVE THE SPECIES.

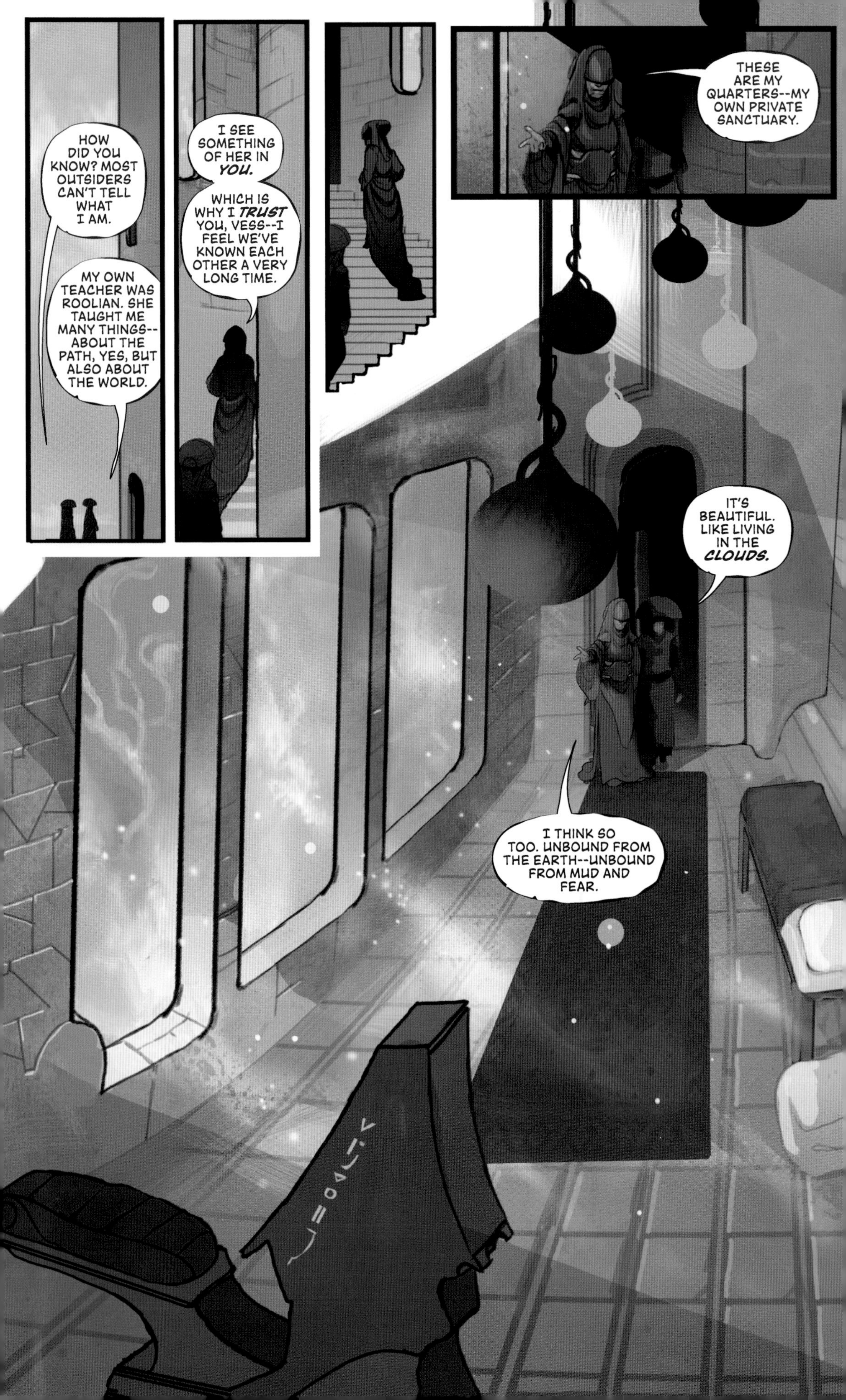
HOW DID YOU KNOW? MOST OUTSIDERS CAN'T TELL WHAT I AM.
MY OWN TEACHER WAS ROOLIAN. SHE TAUGHT ME MANY THINGS--ABOUT THE PATH, YES, BUT ALSO ABOUT THE WORLD.
I SEE SOMETHING OF HER IN *YOU.*
WHICH IS WHY I *TRUST* YOU, VESS--I FEEL WE'VE KNOWN EACH OTHER A VERY LONG TIME.
THESE ARE MY QUARTERS--MY OWN PRIVATE SANCTUARY.
IT'S BEAUTIFUL. LIKE LIVING IN THE *CLOUDS.*
I THINK SO TOO. UNBOUND FROM THE EARTH--UNBOUND FROM MUD AND FEAR.

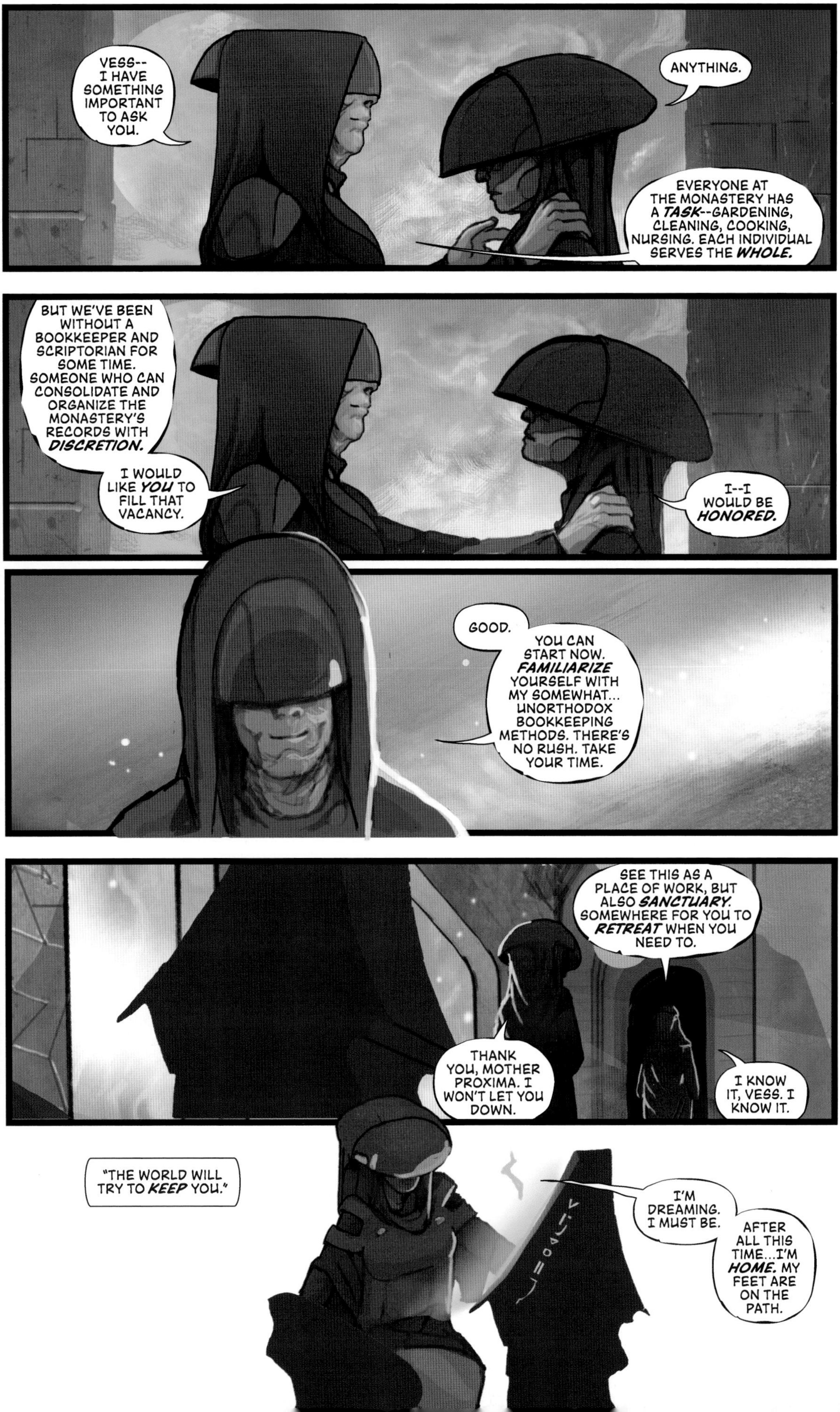
VESS-- I HAVE SOMETHING IMPORTANT TO ASK YOU.
ANYTHING.
EVERYONE AT THE MONASTERY HAS A *TASK*--GARDENING, CLEANING, COOKING, NURSING. EACH INDIVIDUAL SERVES THE *WHOLE.*
BUT WE'VE BEEN WITHOUT A BOOKKEEPER AND SCRIPTORIAN FOR SOME TIME. SOMEONE WHO CAN CONSOLIDATE AND ORGANIZE THE MONASTERY'S RECORDS WITH *DISCRETION.*
I WOULD LIKE *YOU* TO FILL THAT VACANCY.
I--I WOULD BE *HONORED.*
GOOD.
YOU CAN START NOW. *FAMILIARIZE* YOURSELF WITH MY SOMEWHAT... UNORTHODOX BOOKKEEPING METHODS. THERE'S NO RUSH. TAKE YOUR TIME.
SEE THIS AS A PLACE OF WORK, BUT ALSO *SANCTUARY.* SOMEWHERE FOR YOU TO *RETREAT* WHEN YOU NEED TO.
THANK YOU, MOTHER PROXIMA. I WON'T LET YOU DOWN.
I KNOW IT, VESS. I KNOW IT.
"THE WORLD WILL TRY TO *KEEP* YOU."
I'M DREAMING. I MUST BE.
AFTER ALL THIS TIME...I'M *HOME.* MY FEET ARE ON THE PATH.

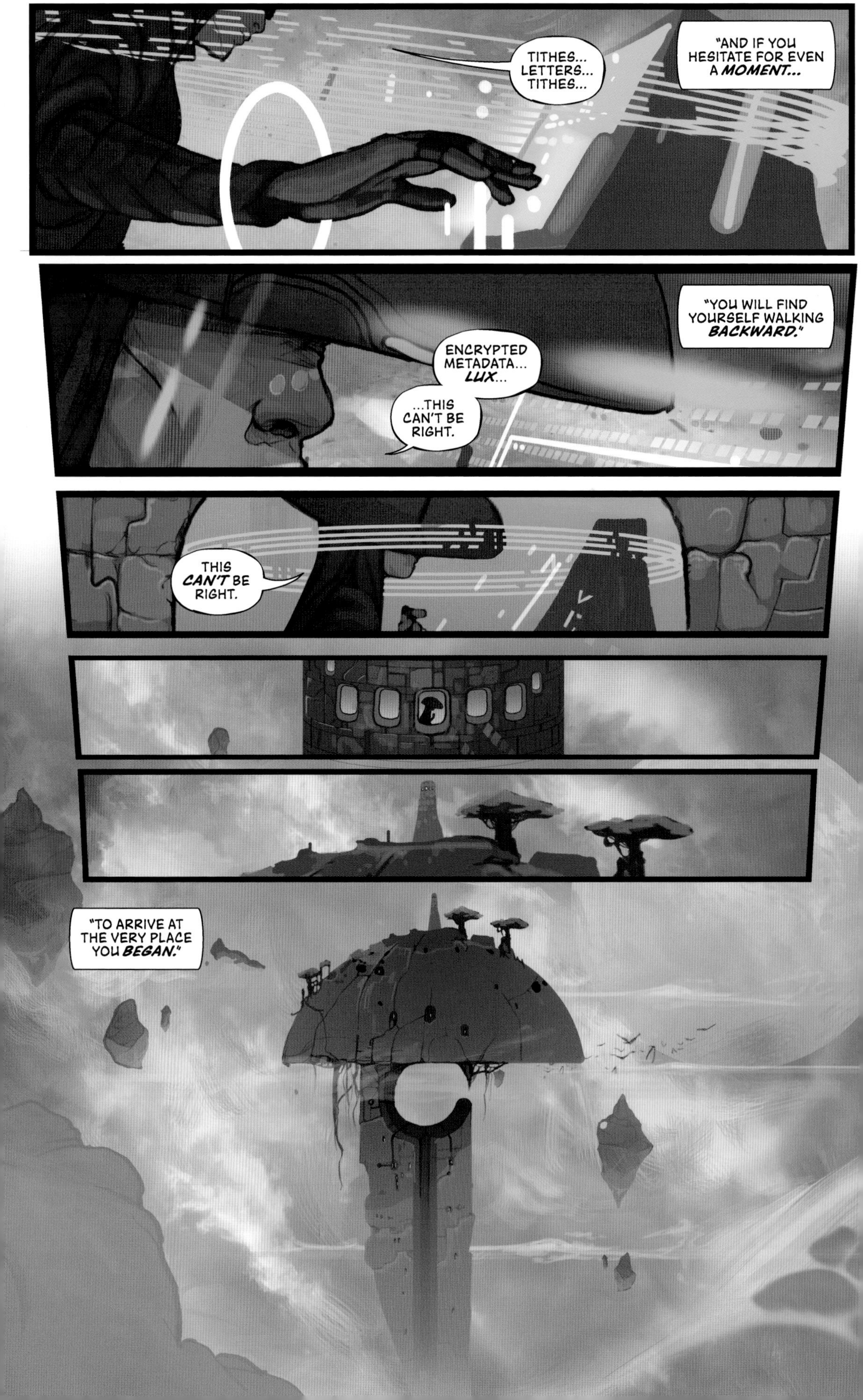
TITHES... LETTERS... TITHES...
"AND IF YOU HESITATE FOR EVEN A MOMENT...
"YOU WILL FIND YOURSELF WALKING BACKWARD."
ENCRYPTED METADATA... LUX...
...THIS CAN'T BE RIGHT.
THIS CAN'T BE RIGHT.
"TO ARRIVE AT THE VERY PLACE YOU BEGAN."

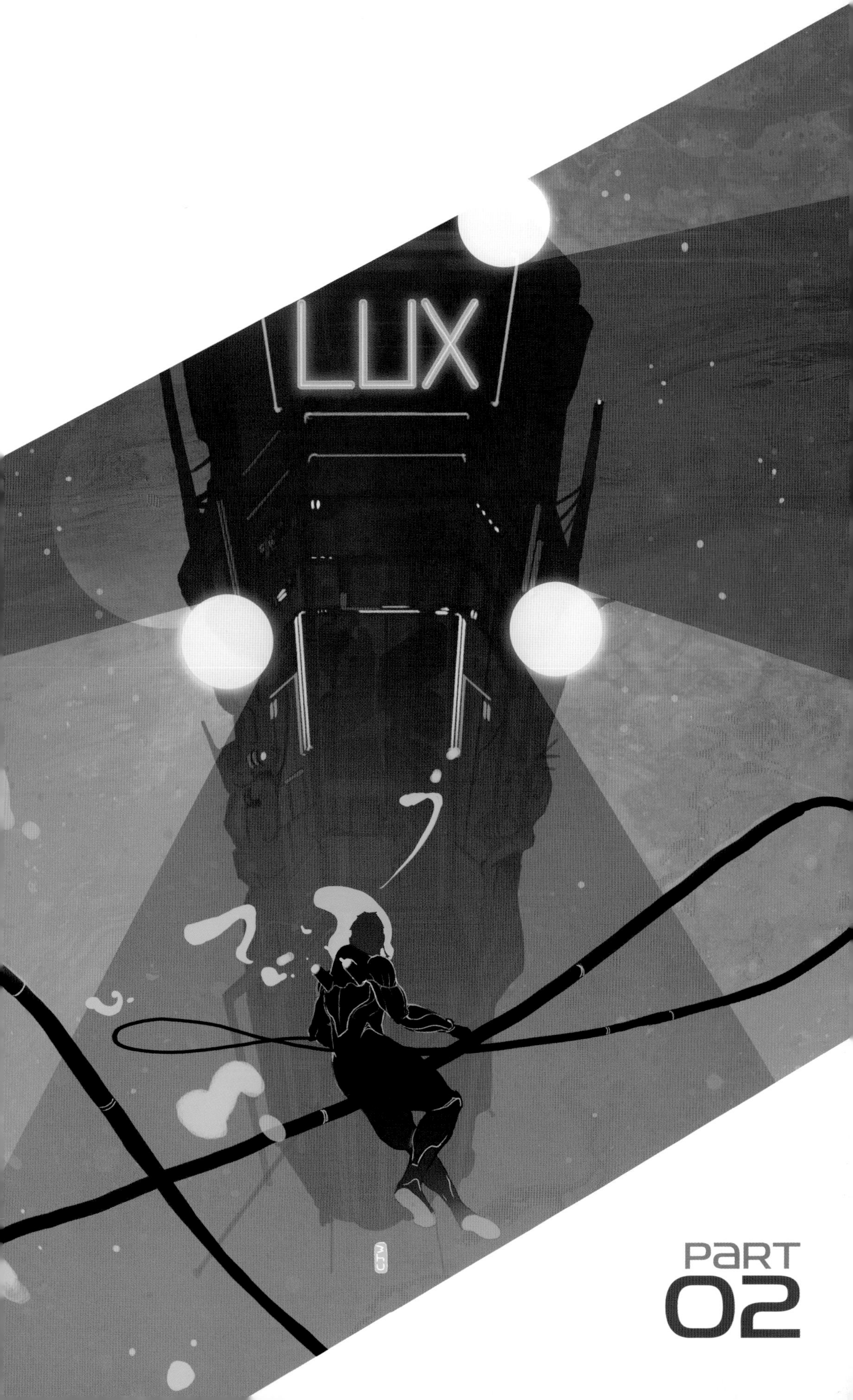
LUX

PART 02

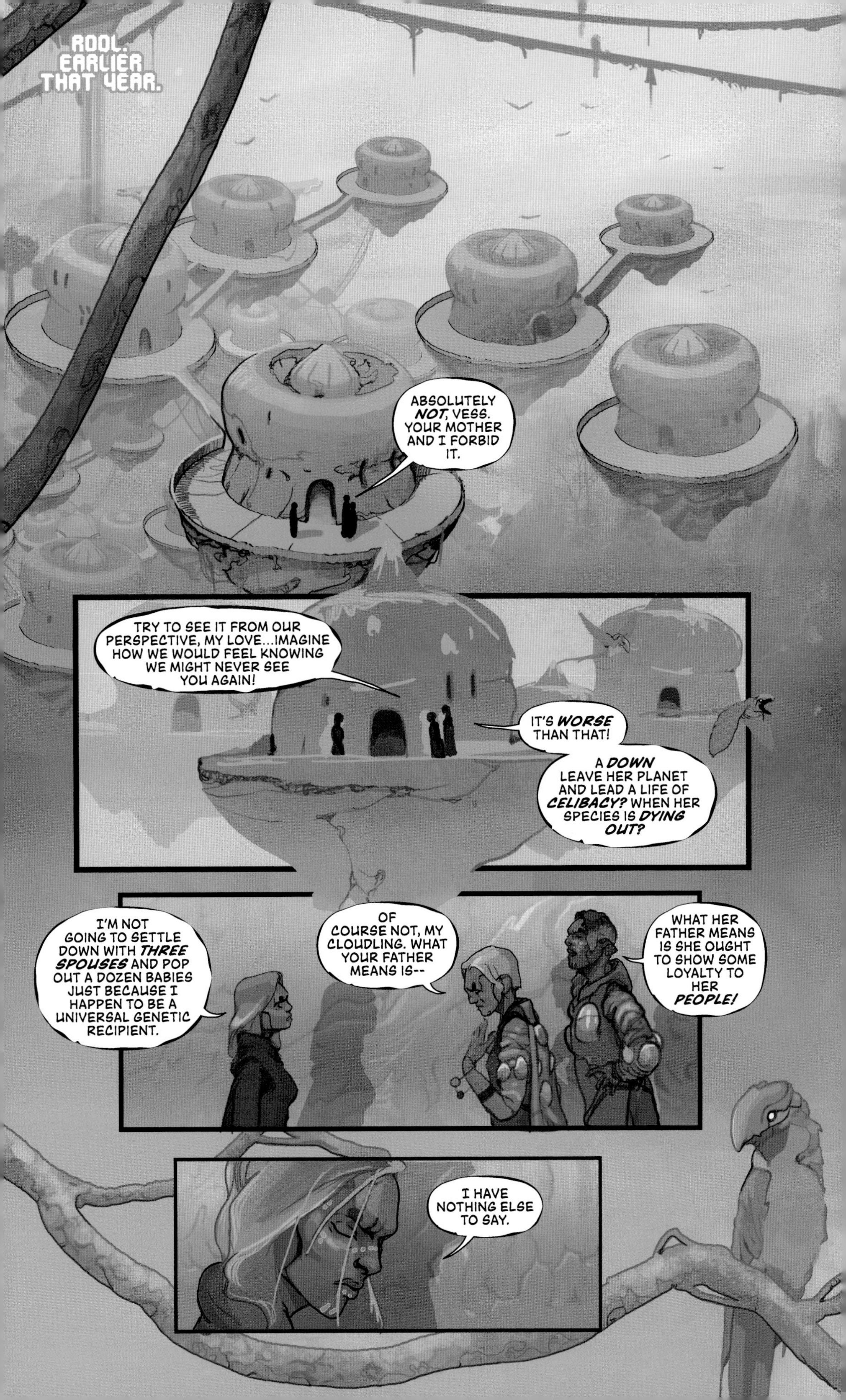
ROOL. EARLIER THAT YEAR.
ABSOLUTELY NOT, VESS. YOUR MOTHER AND I FORBID IT.
TRY TO SEE IT FROM OUR PERSPECTIVE, MY LOVE...IMAGINE HOW WE WOULD FEEL KNOWING WE MIGHT NEVER SEE YOU AGAIN!
IT'S WORSE THAN THAT!
A DOWN LEAVE HER PLANET AND LEAD A LIFE OF CELIBACY? WHEN HER SPECIES IS DYING OUT?
I'M NOT GOING TO SETTLE DOWN WITH THREE SPOUSES AND POP OUT A DOZEN BABIES JUST BECAUSE I HAPPEN TO BE A UNIVERSAL GENETIC RECIPIENT.
OF COURSE NOT, MY CLOUDLING. WHAT YOUR FATHER MEANS IS--
WHAT HER FATHER MEANS IS SHE OUGHT TO SHOW SOME LOYALTY TO HER PEOPLE!
I HAVE NOTHING ELSE TO SAY.

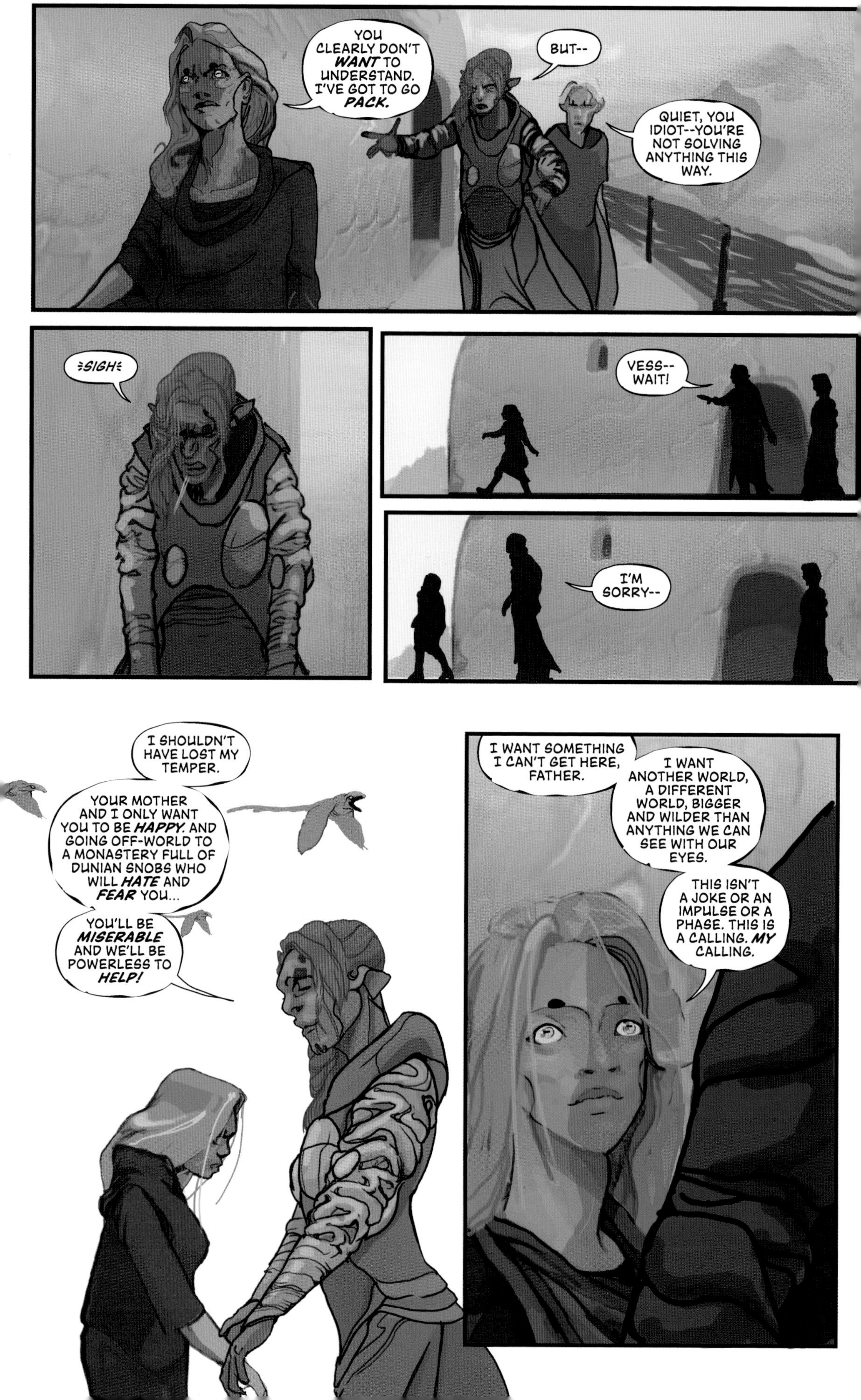
YOU CLEARLY DON'T WANT TO UNDERSTAND. I'VE GOT TO GO PACK.
BUT--
QUIET, YOU IDIOT--YOU'RE NOT SOLVING ANYTHING THIS WAY.
SIGH
VESS-- WAIT!
I'M SORRY--
I SHOULDN'T HAVE LOST MY TEMPER.
YOUR MOTHER AND I ONLY WANT YOU TO BE HAPPY. AND GOING OFF-WORLD TO A MONASTERY FULL OF DUNIAN SNOBS WHO WILL HATE AND FEAR YOU...
YOU'LL BE MISERABLE AND WE'LL BE POWERLESS TO HELP!
I WANT SOMETHING I CAN'T GET HERE, FATHER.
I WANT ANOTHER WORLD, A DIFFERENT WORLD, BIGGER AND WILDER THAN ANYTHING WE CAN SEE WITH OUR EYES.
THIS ISN'T A JOKE OR AN IMPULSE OR A PHASE. THIS IS A CALLING. MY CALLING.

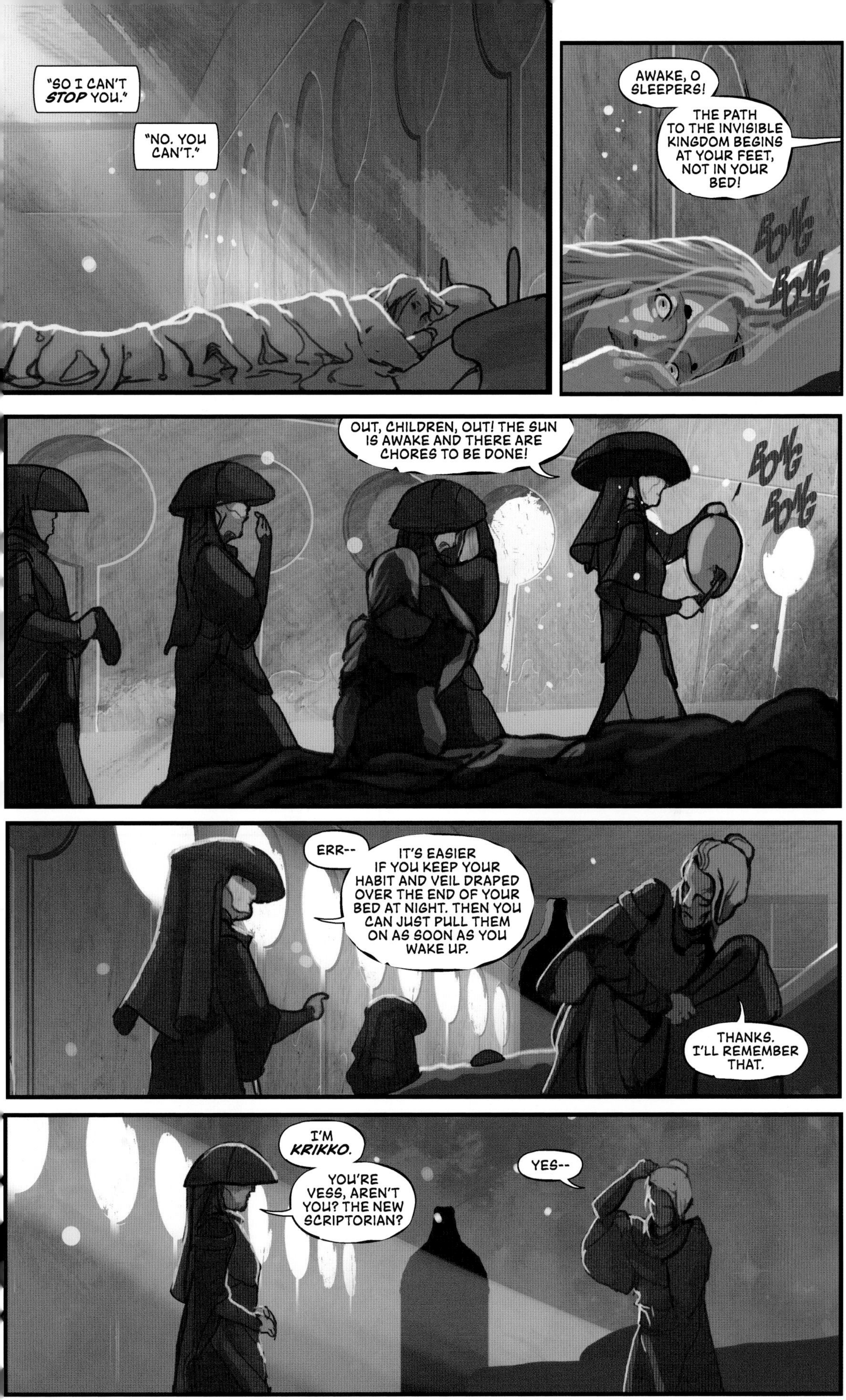
"SO I CAN'T STOP YOU."
"NO. YOU CAN'T."
AWAKE, O SLEEPERS!
THE PATH TO THE INVISIBLE KINGDOM BEGINS AT YOUR FEET, NOT IN YOUR BED!
BONG BONG
OUT, CHILDREN, OUT! THE SUN IS AWAKE AND THERE ARE CHORES TO BE DONE!
BONG BONG
ERR--
IT'S EASIER IF YOU KEEP YOUR HABIT AND VEIL DRAPED OVER THE END OF YOUR BED AT NIGHT. THEN YOU CAN JUST PULL THEM ON AS SOON AS YOU WAKE UP.
THANKS. I'LL REMEMBER THAT.
I'M KRIKKO.
YOU'RE VESS, AREN'T YOU? THE NEW SCRIPTORIAN?
YES--

WHEN I FIRST CAME HERE, MOTHER PROXIMA HAD ME MUCKING OUT THE *FLECKBIRD CAGES* FOR A MONTH TO SEE IF I WAS REALLY *SERIOUS*.

YOU'RE LUCKY SHE'S STARTING YOU OUT WITH SOMETHING SO IMPORTANT. YOU MUST HAVE DONE SOMETHING TO *IMPRESS* HER.

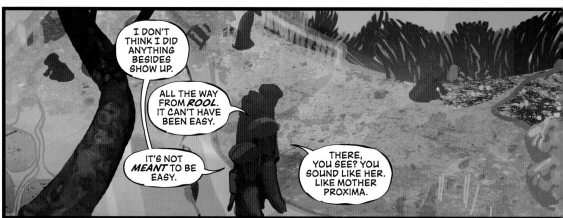

I DON'T THINK I DID ANYTHING BESIDES SHOW UP.

ALL THE WAY FROM *ROOL*. IT CAN'T HAVE BEEN EASY.

IT'S NOT *MEANT* TO BE EASY.

THERE, YOU SEE? YOU SOUND LIKE HER. LIKE MOTHER PROXIMA.

IT'S A HARD LIFE, BUT A *GOOD* LIFE.

IN MY *OLD* LIFE, I SPENT ALL DAY WAITING FOR THE NEXT BOX FROM LUX TO SHOW UP. BUT IT WAS NEVER ENOUGH. I REALIZED THAT *THINGS* CAN'T MAKE YOU HAPPY.

SO I CAME *HERE*. AND EVERYTHING JUST...FELL INTO PLACE.

BUT WHAT IF...WHAT IF YOU FOUND SOMETHING HERE THAT SEEMED *WRONG*? THAT SEEMED OUT OF PLACE?

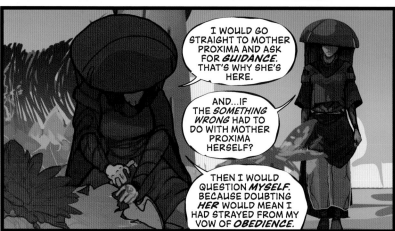

I WOULD GO STRAIGHT TO MOTHER PROXIMA AND ASK FOR *GUIDANCE*. THAT'S WHY SHE'S HERE.

AND...IF THE *SOMETHING WRONG* HAD TO DO WITH MOTHER PROXIMA HERSELF?

THEN I WOULD QUESTION *MYSELF*. BECAUSE DOUBTING *HER* WOULD MEAN I HAD STRAYED FROM MY VOW OF *OBEDIENCE*.

YES. ...OBEDIENCE.

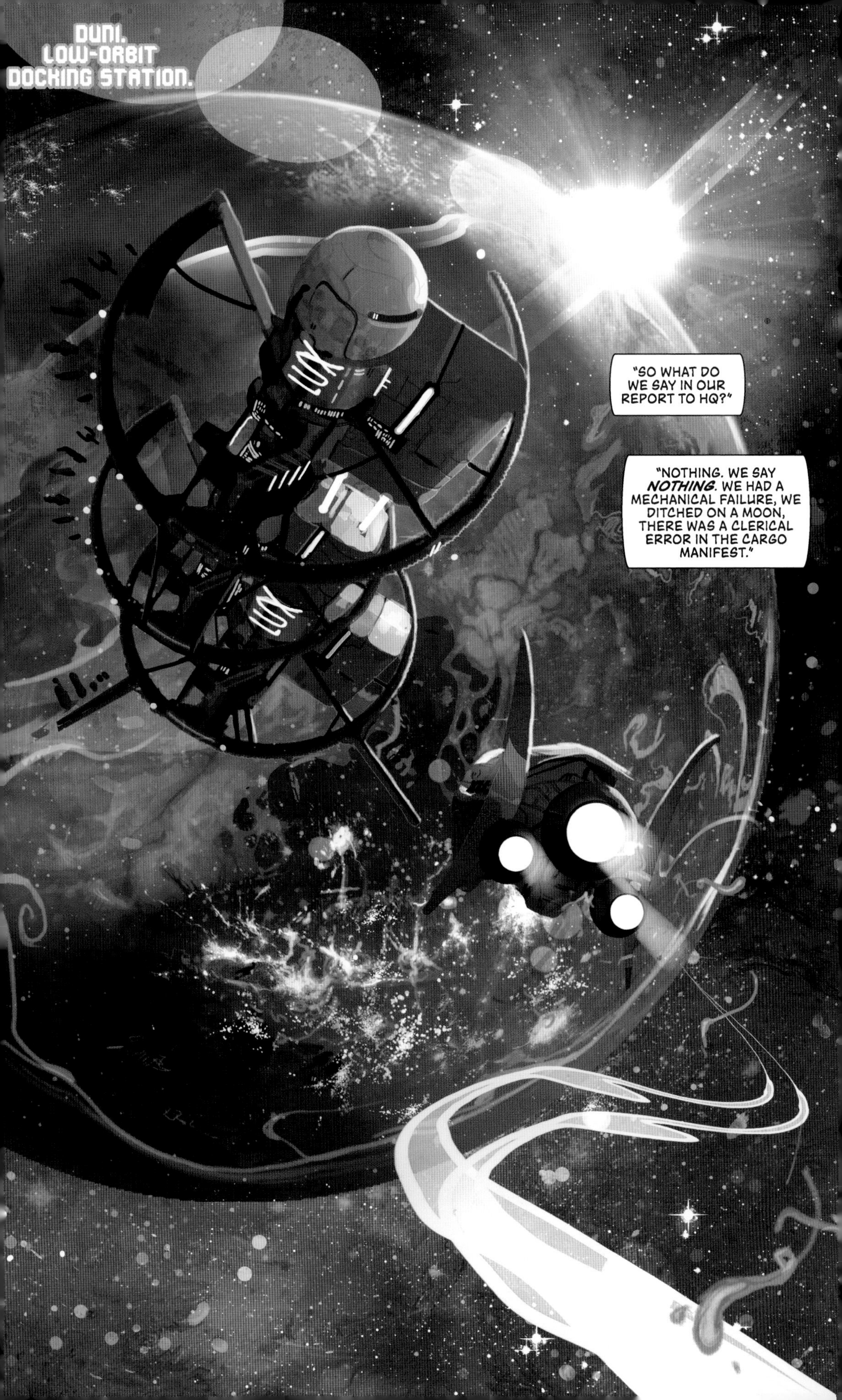
DUNI. LOW-ORBIT DOCKING STATION.
"SO WHAT DO WE SAY IN OUR REPORT TO HQ?"
"NOTHING. WE SAY *NOTHING*. WE HAD A MECHANICAL FAILURE, WE DITCHED ON A MOON, THERE WAS A CLERICAL ERROR IN THE CARGO MANIFEST."

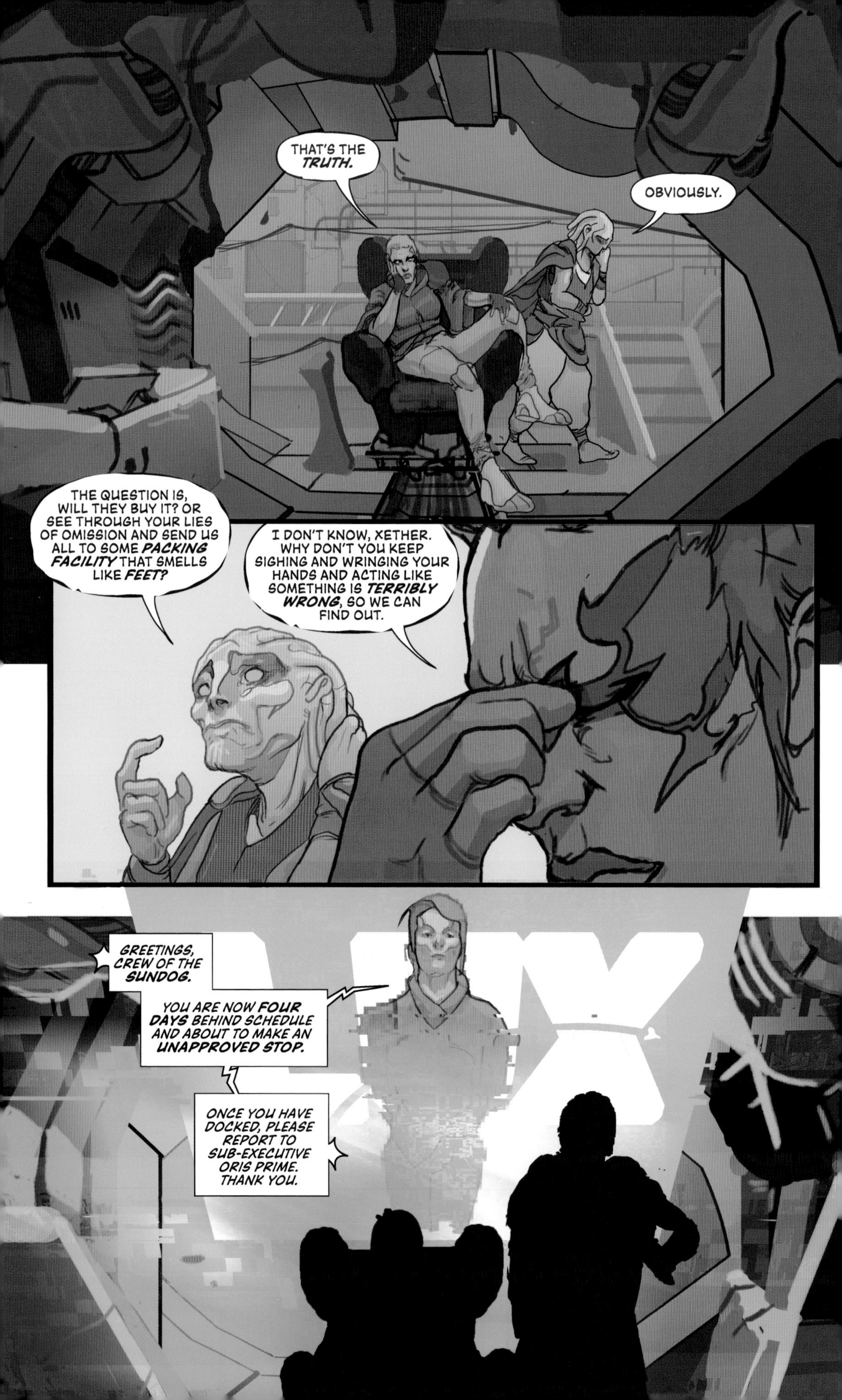

THAT'S THE TRUTH.
OBVIOUSLY.
THE QUESTION IS, WILL THEY BUY IT? OR SEE THROUGH YOUR LIES OF OMISSION AND SEND US ALL TO SOME PACKING FACILITY THAT SMELLS LIKE FEET?
I DON'T KNOW, XETHER. WHY DON'T YOU KEEP SIGHING AND WRINGING YOUR HANDS AND ACTING LIKE SOMETHING IS TERRIBLY WRONG, SO WE CAN FIND OUT.
GREETINGS, CREW OF THE SUNDOG.
YOU ARE NOW FOUR DAYS BEHIND SCHEDULE AND ABOUT TO MAKE AN UNAPPROVED STOP.
ONCE YOU HAVE DOCKED, PLEASE REPORT TO SUB-EXECUTIVE ORIS PRIME. THANK YOU.

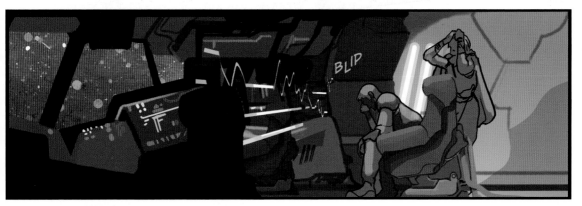

THIS OUGHT TO BE FUN.

KK-THOOO!

I JUST GOT A VERY STRANGE MESSAGE FROM HEADQUARTERS. IS SOMETHING WRONG?

ARE WE GOING DOWN TO THE SURFACE?

YES, RATH, WE'RE GOING DOWN TO THE SURFACE.

YAY!

GRIX-- I KNOW SOMETHING HAPPENED ON THAT MOON. YOU'VE BEEN ACTING SO STRANGELY EVER SINCE WE CRASHED, AND NOW THERE'S THIS...

JUST... TELL ME SO I CAN HELP.

RATH! WHY DON'T YOU GO DOWN TO THE GALLEY AND MAKE A SHOPPING LIST OF STUFF TO PICK UP ON THE SURFACE.

YES, CAPTAIN!

LOOK--IT'S NOTHING. I FOUND A MIX-UP IN THE CARGO MANIFEST. THEY PROBABLY JUST WANT TO CLEAR IT TO COVER THEIR ASSES. YOU KNOW. ROUTINE STUFF.

IF THIS WAS ROUTINE, THEY WOULDN'T BE SENDING YOU TO PRIME.

LIKE I SAID, ELINE. DON'T WORRY ABOUT IT.

DON'T BE LIKE THIS. I WANT TO HELP. I'VE SERVED ON THIS SHIP FOR FOUR YEARS-- YOUR SHIP. I'M AS MUCH A PART OF THIS CREW AS ANY OF THE OTHERS.

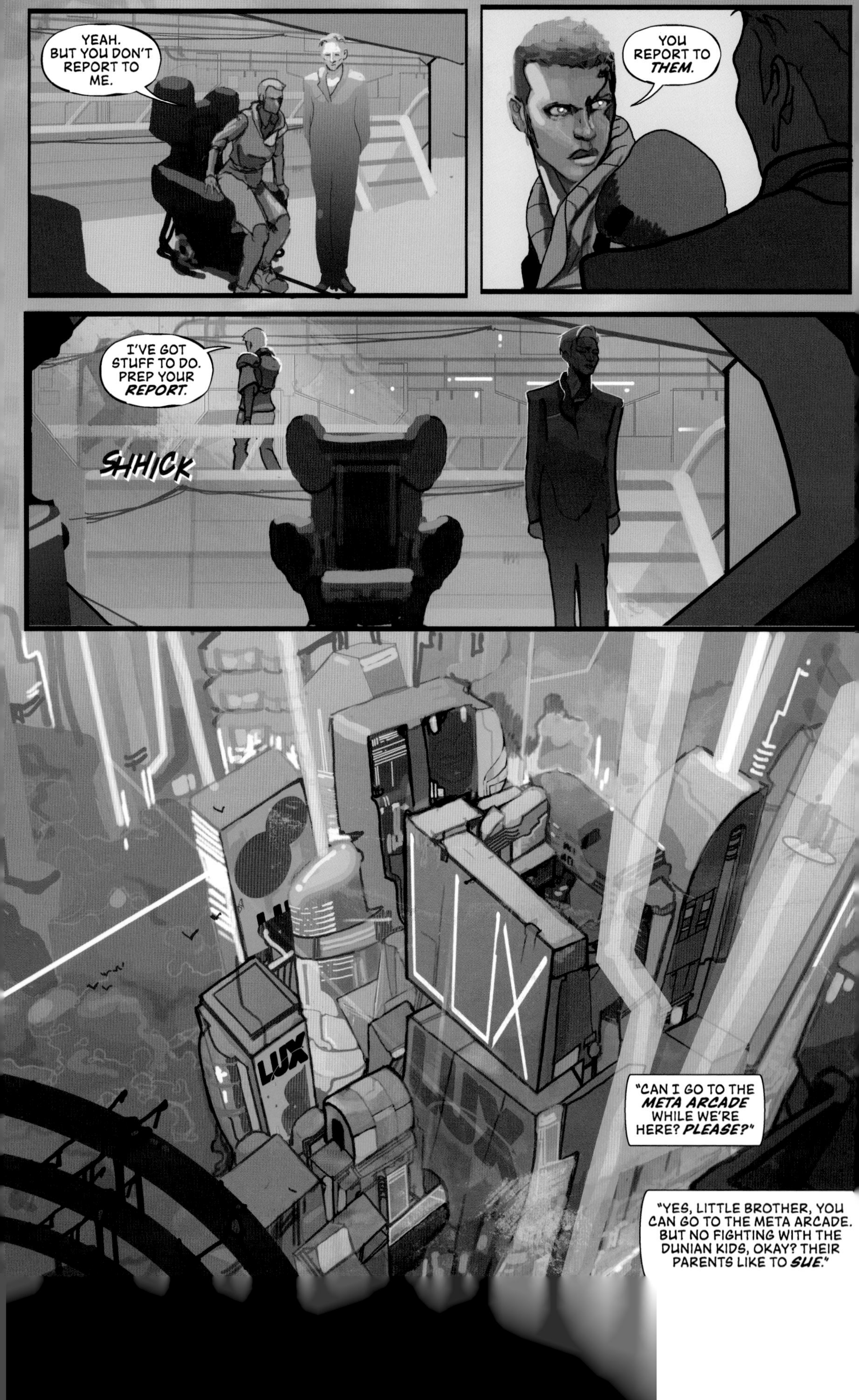
YEAH. BUT YOU DON'T REPORT TO ME.
YOU REPORT TO *THEM*.
I'VE GOT STUFF TO DO. PREP YOUR *REPORT*.
SHHICK
LUX
LUX
"CAN I GO TO THE *META ARCADE* WHILE WE'RE HERE? *PLEASE?*"
"YES, LITTLE BROTHER, YOU CAN GO TO THE META ARCADE. BUT NO FIGHTING WITH THE DUNIAN KIDS, OKAY? THEIR PARENTS LIKE TO *SUE*."

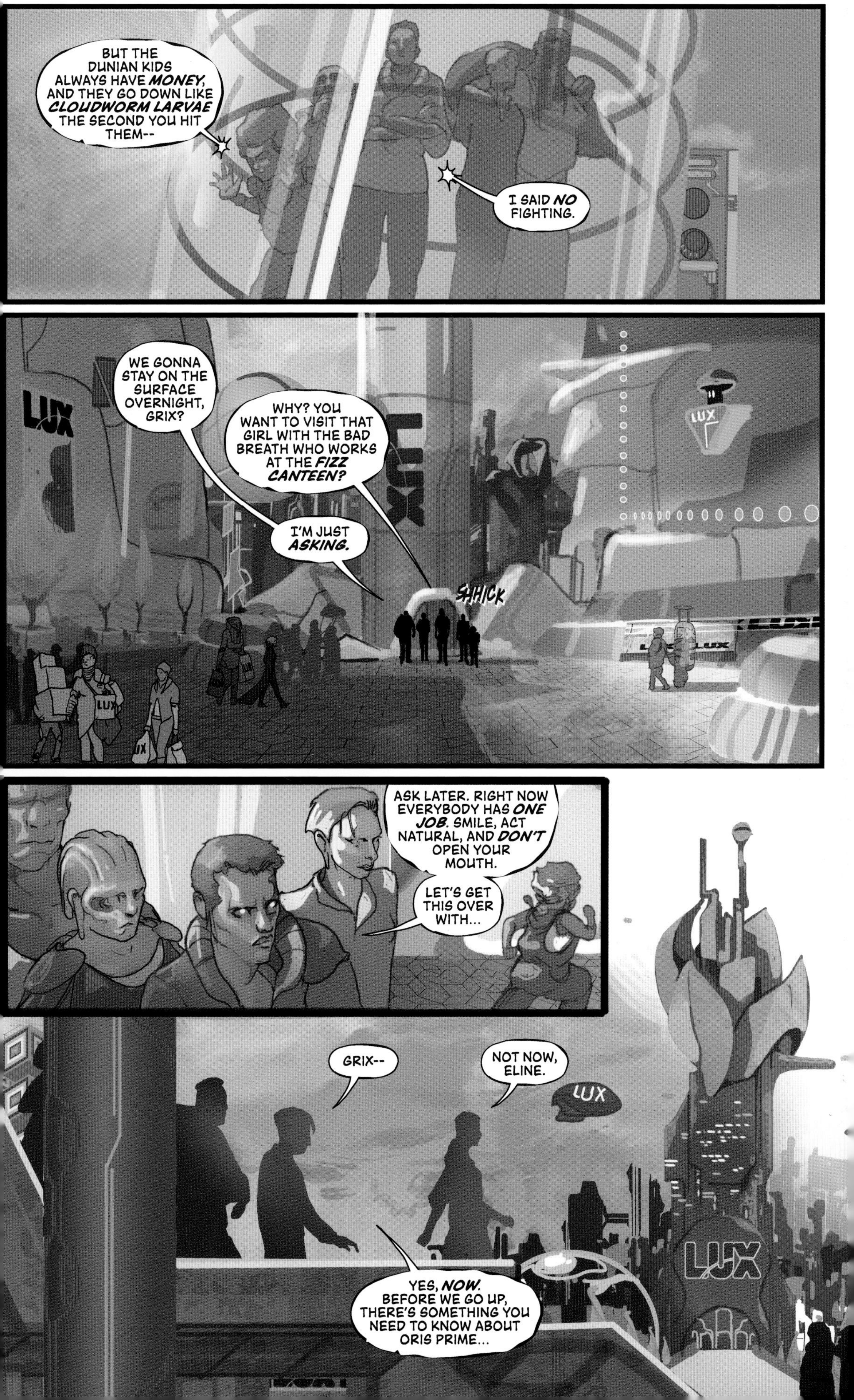
BUT THE DUNIAN KIDS ALWAYS HAVE MONEY, AND THEY GO DOWN LIKE CLOUDWORM LARVAE THE SECOND YOU HIT THEM--
I SAID NO FIGHTING.
WE GONNA STAY ON THE SURFACE OVERNIGHT, GRIX?
WHY? YOU WANT TO VISIT THAT GIRL WITH THE BAD BREATH WHO WORKS AT THE FIZZ CANTEEN?
I'M JUST ASKING.
SHHICK
LUX
ASK LATER. RIGHT NOW EVERYBODY HAS ONE JOB. SMILE, ACT NATURAL, AND DON'T OPEN YOUR MOUTH.
LET'S GET THIS OVER WITH...
GRIX--
NOT NOW, ELINE.
YES, NOW. BEFORE WE GO UP, THERE'S SOMETHING YOU NEED TO KNOW ABOUT ORIS PRIME...
LUX

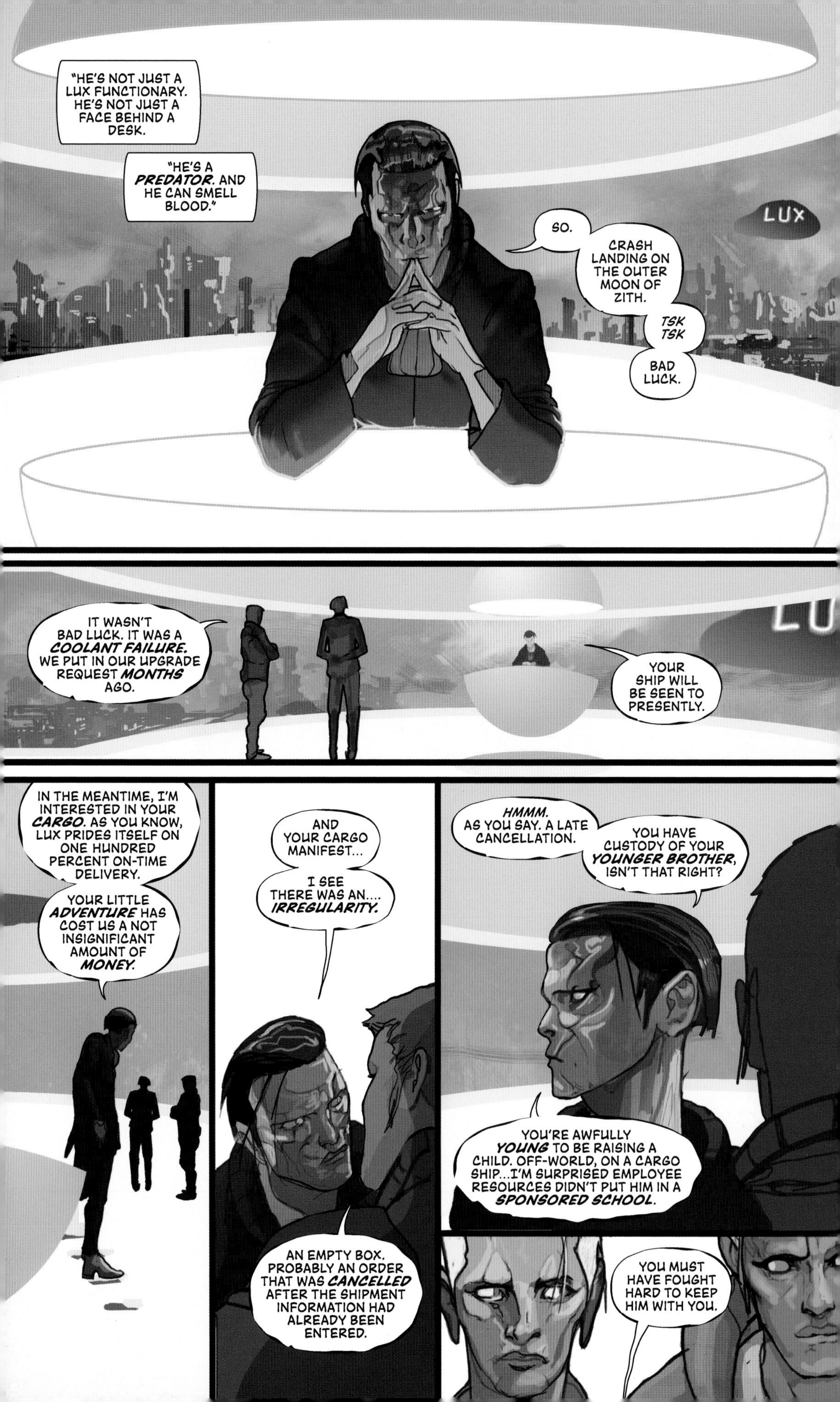
"HE'S NOT JUST A LUX FUNCTIONARY. HE'S NOT JUST A FACE BEHIND A DESK.
"HE'S A *PREDATOR*. AND HE CAN SMELL BLOOD."
LUX
SO.
CRASH LANDING ON THE OUTER MOON OF ZITH.
TSK TSK
BAD LUCK.
IT WASN'T BAD LUCK. IT WAS A *COOLANT FAILURE.* WE PUT IN OUR UPGRADE REQUEST *MONTHS* AGO.
YOUR SHIP WILL BE SEEN TO PRESENTLY.
IN THE MEANTIME, I'M INTERESTED IN YOUR *CARGO*. AS YOU KNOW, LUX PRIDES ITSELF ON ONE HUNDRED PERCENT ON-TIME DELIVERY.
YOUR LITTLE *ADVENTURE* HAS COST US A NOT INSIGNIFICANT AMOUNT OF *MONEY*.
AND YOUR CARGO MANIFEST...
I SEE THERE WAS AN.... *IRREGULARITY.*
AN EMPTY BOX. PROBABLY AN ORDER THAT WAS *CANCELLED* AFTER THE SHIPMENT INFORMATION HAD ALREADY BEEN ENTERED.
HMMM. AS YOU SAY. A LATE CANCELLATION.
YOU HAVE CUSTODY OF YOUR *YOUNGER BROTHER*, ISN'T THAT RIGHT?
YOU'RE AWFULLY *YOUNG* TO BE RAISING A CHILD. OFF-WORLD, ON A CARGO SHIP...I'M SURPRISED EMPLOYEE RESOURCES DIDN'T PUT HIM IN A *SPONSORED SCHOOL*.
YOU MUST HAVE FOUGHT HARD TO KEEP HIM WITH YOU.

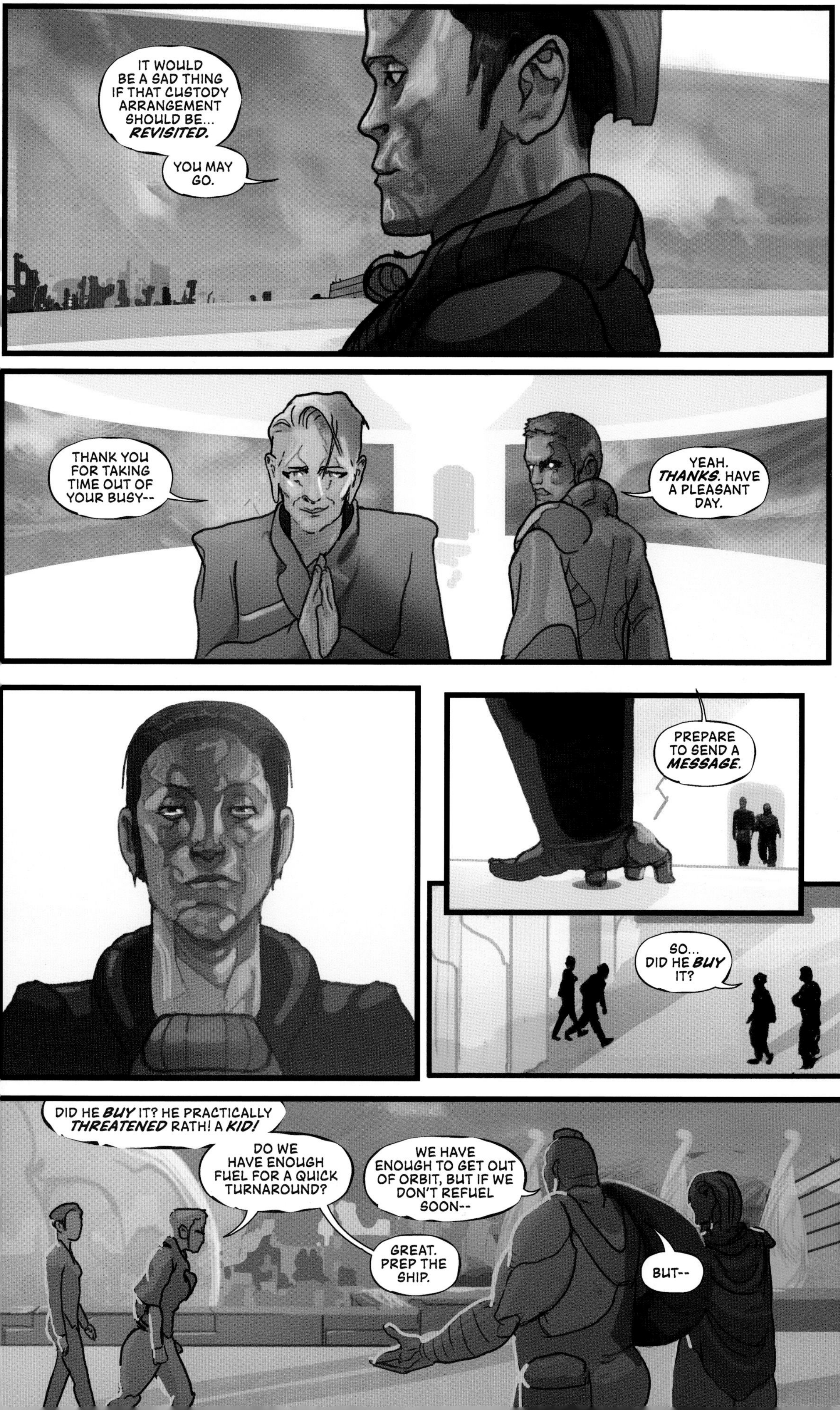
IT WOULD BE A SAD THING IF THAT CUSTODY ARRANGEMENT SHOULD BE... *REVISITED.*
YOU MAY GO.
THANK YOU FOR TAKING TIME OUT OF YOUR BUSY--
YEAH. *THANKS.* HAVE A PLEASANT DAY.
PREPARE TO SEND A *MESSAGE*.
SO... DID HE *BUY* IT?
DID HE *BUY* IT? HE PRACTICALLY *THREATENED* RATH! A *KID!*
DO WE HAVE ENOUGH FUEL FOR A QUICK TURNAROUND?
WE HAVE ENOUGH TO GET OUT OF ORBIT, BUT IF WE DON'T REFUEL SOON--
GREAT. PREP THE SHIP.
BUT--

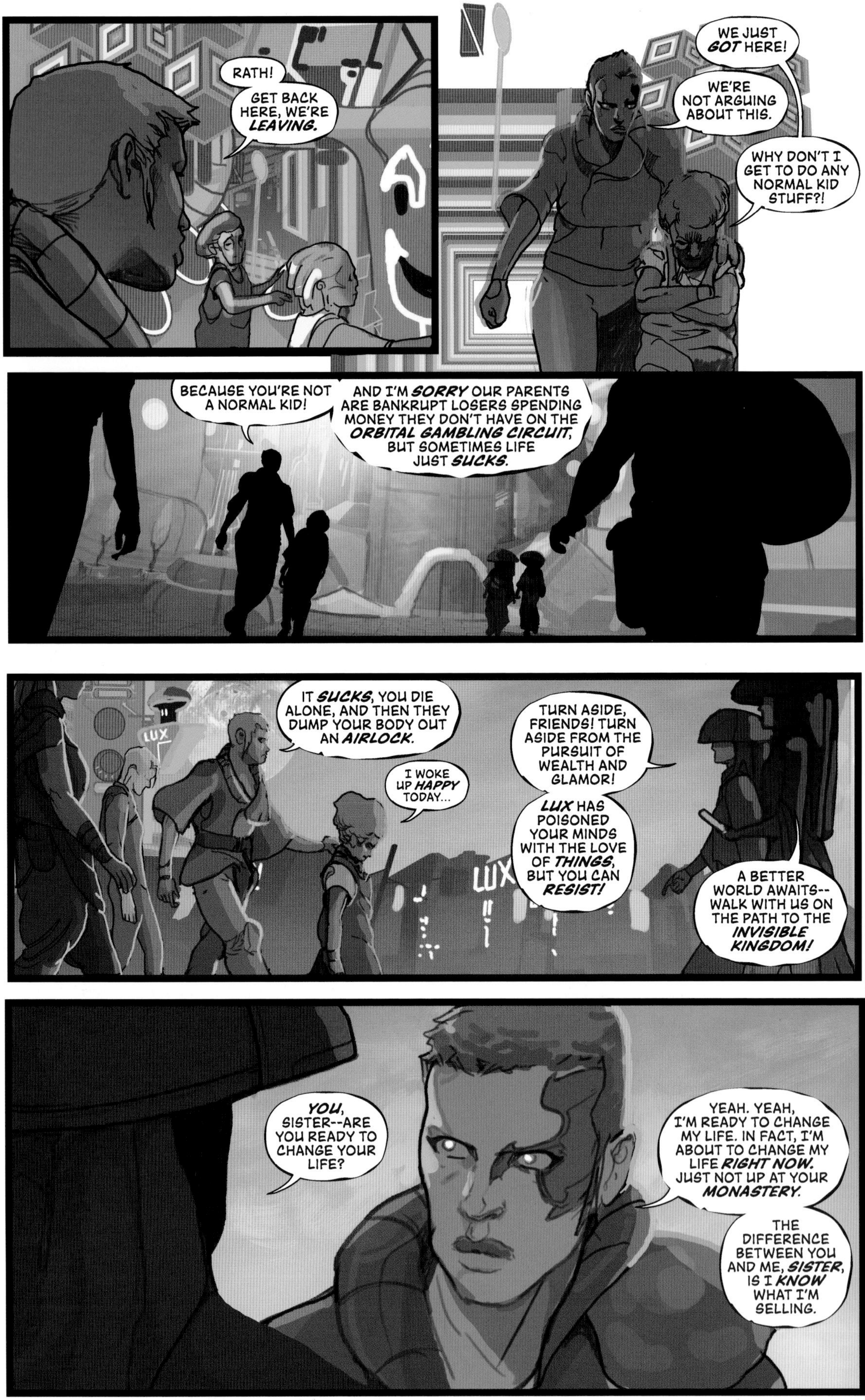
RATH!
GET BACK HERE, WE'RE *LEAVING.*
WE JUST *GOT* HERE!
WE'RE NOT ARGUING ABOUT THIS.
WHY DON'T I GET TO DO ANY NORMAL KID STUFF?!
BECAUSE YOU'RE NOT A NORMAL KID!
AND I'M *SORRY* OUR PARENTS ARE BANKRUPT LOSERS SPENDING MONEY THEY DON'T HAVE ON THE *ORBITAL GAMBLING CIRCUIT,* BUT SOMETIMES LIFE JUST *SUCKS.*
IT *SUCKS,* YOU DIE ALONE, AND THEN THEY DUMP YOUR BODY OUT AN *AIRLOCK.*
I WOKE UP *HAPPY* TODAY...
LUX
TURN ASIDE, FRIENDS! TURN ASIDE FROM THE PURSUIT OF WEALTH AND GLAMOR!
LUX HAS POISONED YOUR MINDS WITH THE LOVE OF *THINGS,* BUT YOU CAN *RESIST!*
LUX
A BETTER WORLD AWAITS-- WALK WITH US ON THE PATH TO THE *INVISIBLE KINGDOM!*
YOU, SISTER--ARE YOU READY TO CHANGE YOUR LIFE?
YEAH. YEAH, I'M READY TO CHANGE MY LIFE. IN FACT, I'M ABOUT TO CHANGE MY LIFE *RIGHT NOW.* JUST NOT UP AT YOUR *MONASTERY.*
THE DIFFERENCE BETWEEN YOU AND ME, *SISTER,* IS I *KNOW* WHAT I'M SELLING.

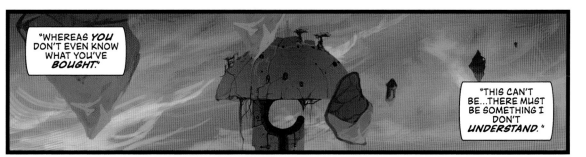

"WHEREAS *YOU* DON'T EVEN KNOW WHAT YOU'VE *BOUGHT*."

"THIS CAN'T BE...THERE MUST BE SOMETHING I DON'T *UNDERSTAND.*"

VESS.

MOTHER PROXIMA!

I--I WAS JUST REVIEWING THE MONASTERY'S *ACCOUNTS* FOR THE LAST TWO YEARS.

TO FAMILIARIZE MYSELF WITH THE SYSTEM.

THERE'S NO NEED TO LOOK GUILTY--I'M *PLEASED* TO SEE YOU TAKING YOUR WORK SO SERIOUSLY.

BUT SOMETHING'S *TROUBLING* YOU.

I'M... CONFUSED.

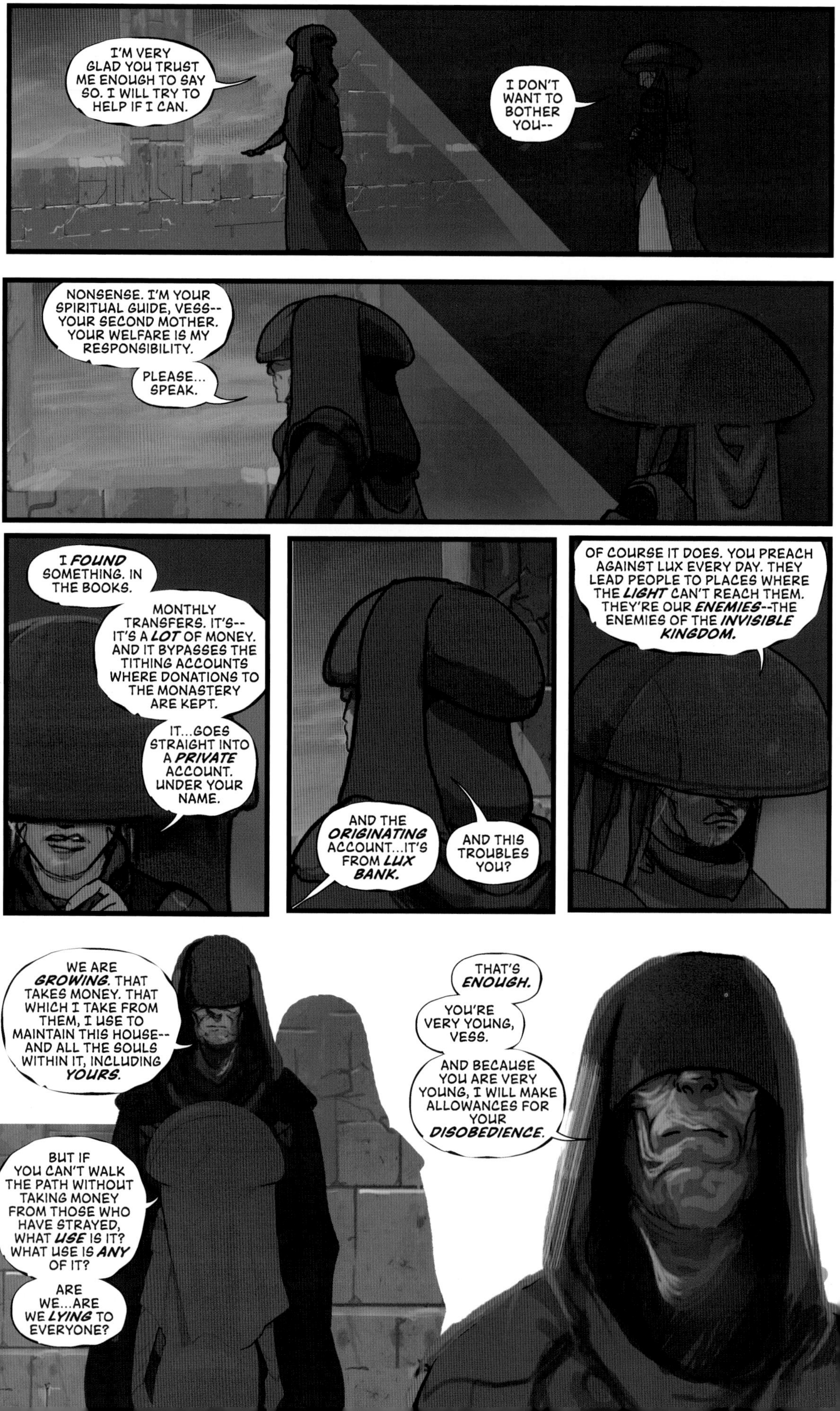
I'M VERY GLAD YOU TRUST ME ENOUGH TO SAY SO. I WILL TRY TO HELP IF I CAN.
I DON'T WANT TO BOTHER YOU--
NONSENSE. I'M YOUR SPIRITUAL GUIDE, VESS-- YOUR SECOND MOTHER. YOUR WELFARE IS MY RESPONSIBILITY.
PLEASE... SPEAK.
I *FOUND* SOMETHING. IN THE BOOKS.
MONTHLY TRANSFERS. IT'S-- IT'S A *LOT* OF MONEY. AND IT BYPASSES THE TITHING ACCOUNTS WHERE DONATIONS TO THE MONASTERY ARE KEPT.
IT...GOES STRAIGHT INTO A *PRIVATE* ACCOUNT. UNDER YOUR NAME.
AND THE *ORIGINATING* ACCOUNT...IT'S FROM *LUX BANK.*
AND THIS TROUBLES YOU?
OF COURSE IT DOES. YOU PREACH AGAINST LUX EVERY DAY. THEY LEAD PEOPLE TO PLACES WHERE THE *LIGHT* CAN'T REACH THEM. THEY'RE OUR *ENEMIES*--THE ENEMIES OF THE *INVISIBLE KINGDOM.*
WE ARE *GROWING.* THAT TAKES MONEY. THAT WHICH I TAKE FROM THEM, I USE TO MAINTAIN THIS HOUSE-- AND ALL THE SOULS WITHIN IT, INCLUDING *YOURS.*
BUT IF YOU CAN'T WALK THE PATH WITHOUT TAKING MONEY FROM THOSE WHO HAVE STRAYED, WHAT *USE* IS IT? WHAT USE IS *ANY* OF IT?
ARE WE...ARE WE *LYING* TO EVERYONE?
THAT'S *ENOUGH.*
YOU'RE VERY YOUNG, VESS.
AND BECAUSE YOU ARE VERY YOUNG, I WILL MAKE ALLOWANCES FOR YOUR *DISOBEDIENCE.*

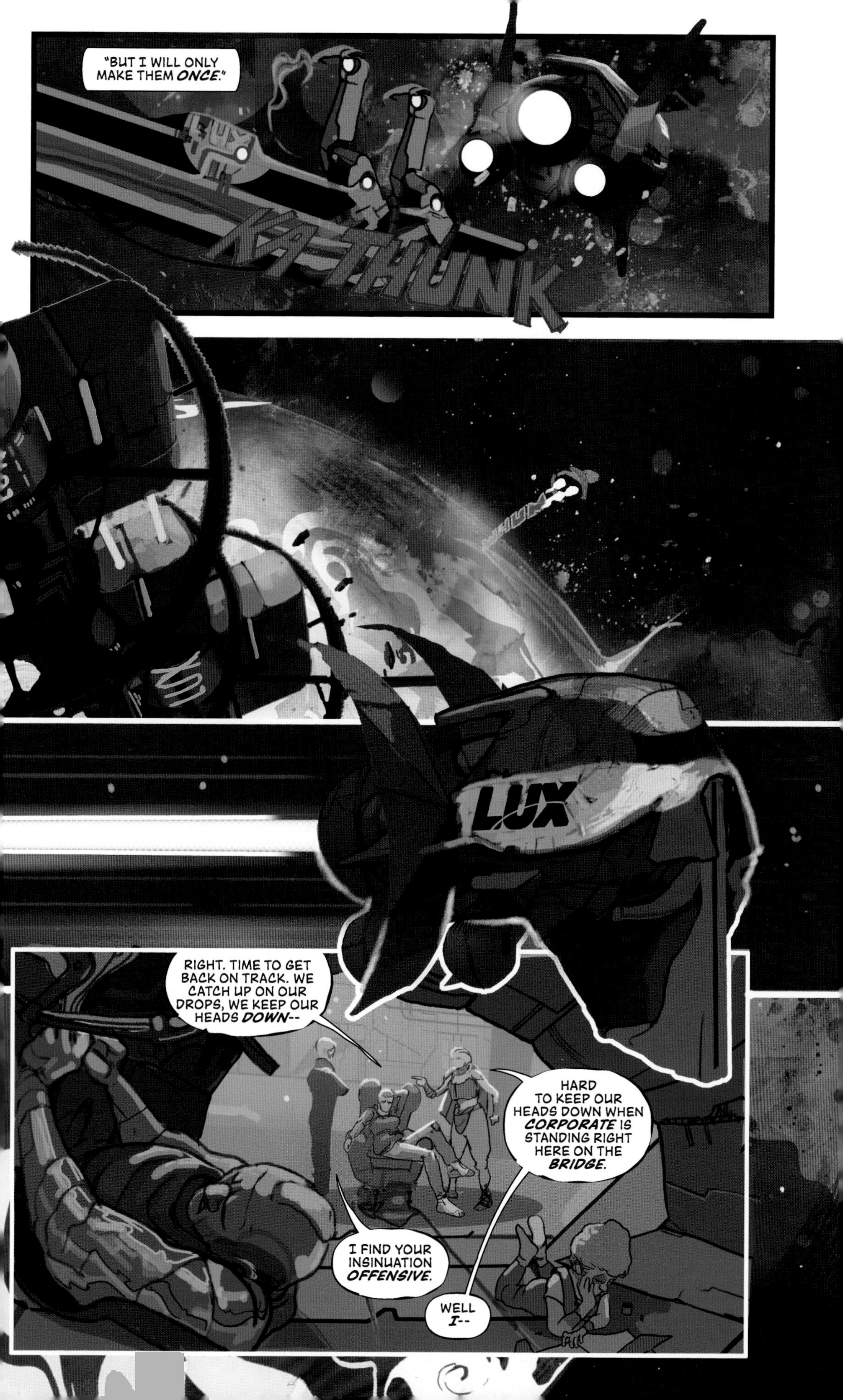
"BUT I WILL ONLY MAKE THEM *ONCE*."
KA-THUNK
RIGHT. TIME TO GET BACK ON TRACK. WE CATCH UP ON OUR DROPS, WE KEEP OUR HEADS *DOWN*--
HARD TO KEEP OUR HEADS DOWN WHEN *CORPORATE* IS STANDING RIGHT HERE ON THE *BRIDGE*.
I FIND YOUR INSINUATION *OFFENSIVE*.
WELL *I*--

ENOUGH. WHAT'S THE SCHEDULE?

THE DROP ON QARI THAT WE MISSED, THEN DOUBLING BACK TO ZITH--

DOUBLING BACK TO ZITH WHILE QARI IS OUT OF ALIGNMENT, MEANING WE'LL BE HITTING THOSE AFTERBURNERS, EXACERBATING THE COOLANT ISSUE.

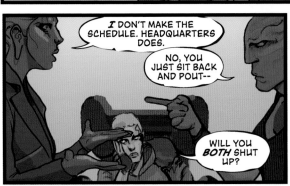

I DON'T MAKE THE SCHEDULE. HEADQUARTERS DOES.

NO, YOU JUST SIT BACK AND POUT--

WILL YOU BOTH SHUT UP?

WHY IS THAT FREIGHTER SO CLOSE?

OH.

PERHAPS IT MISCALCULATED ITS FLIGHT PATH. THOSE BIG SHIPS DO.

THAT'S NOT A LUX SHIP.

I'M HAILING THEM.

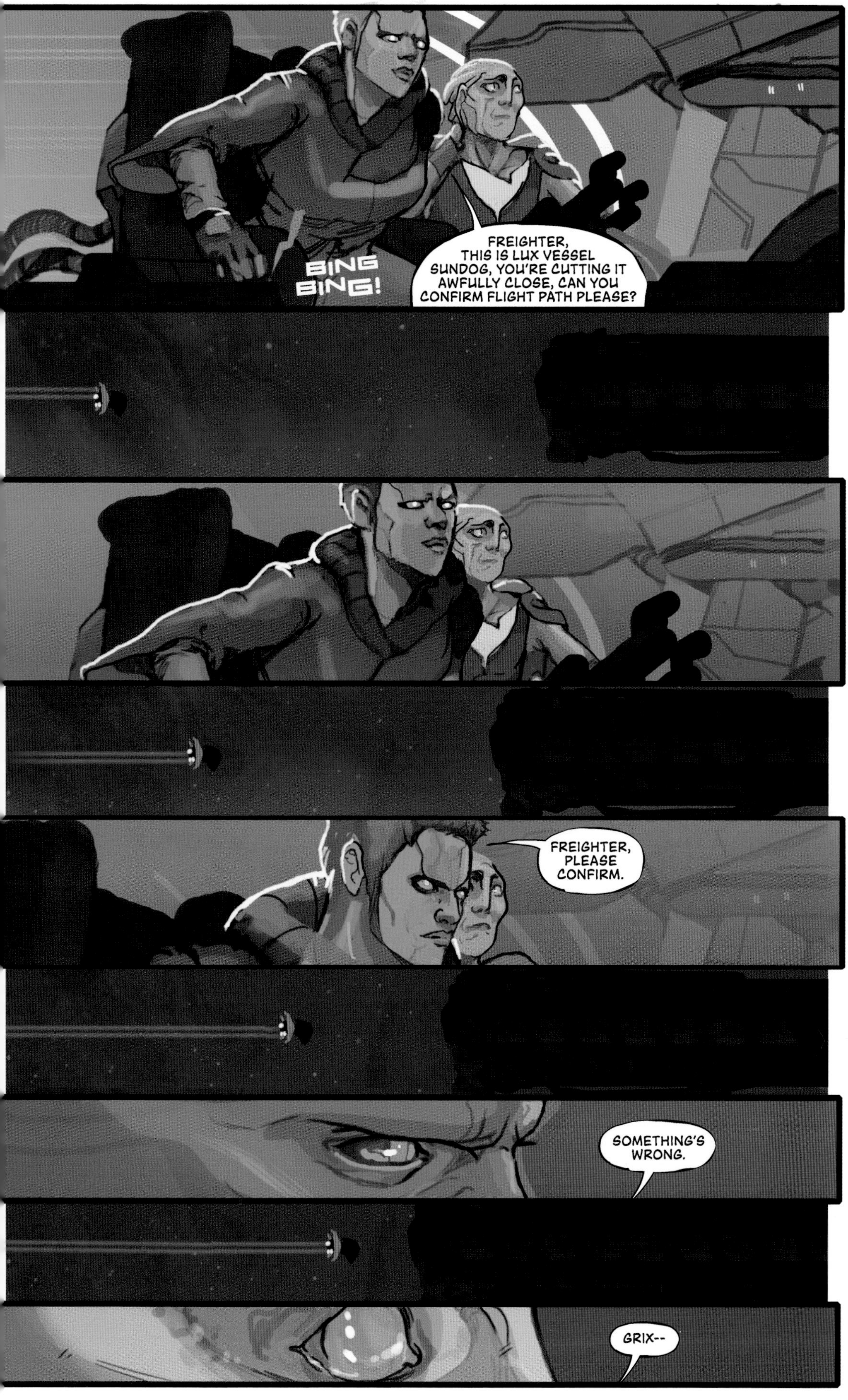
BING BING!
FREIGHTER, THIS IS LUX VESSEL SUNDOG, YOU'RE CUTTING IT AWFULLY CLOSE, CAN YOU CONFIRM FLIGHT PATH PLEASE?
FREIGHTER, PLEASE CONFIRM.
SOMETHING'S WRONG.
GRIX--

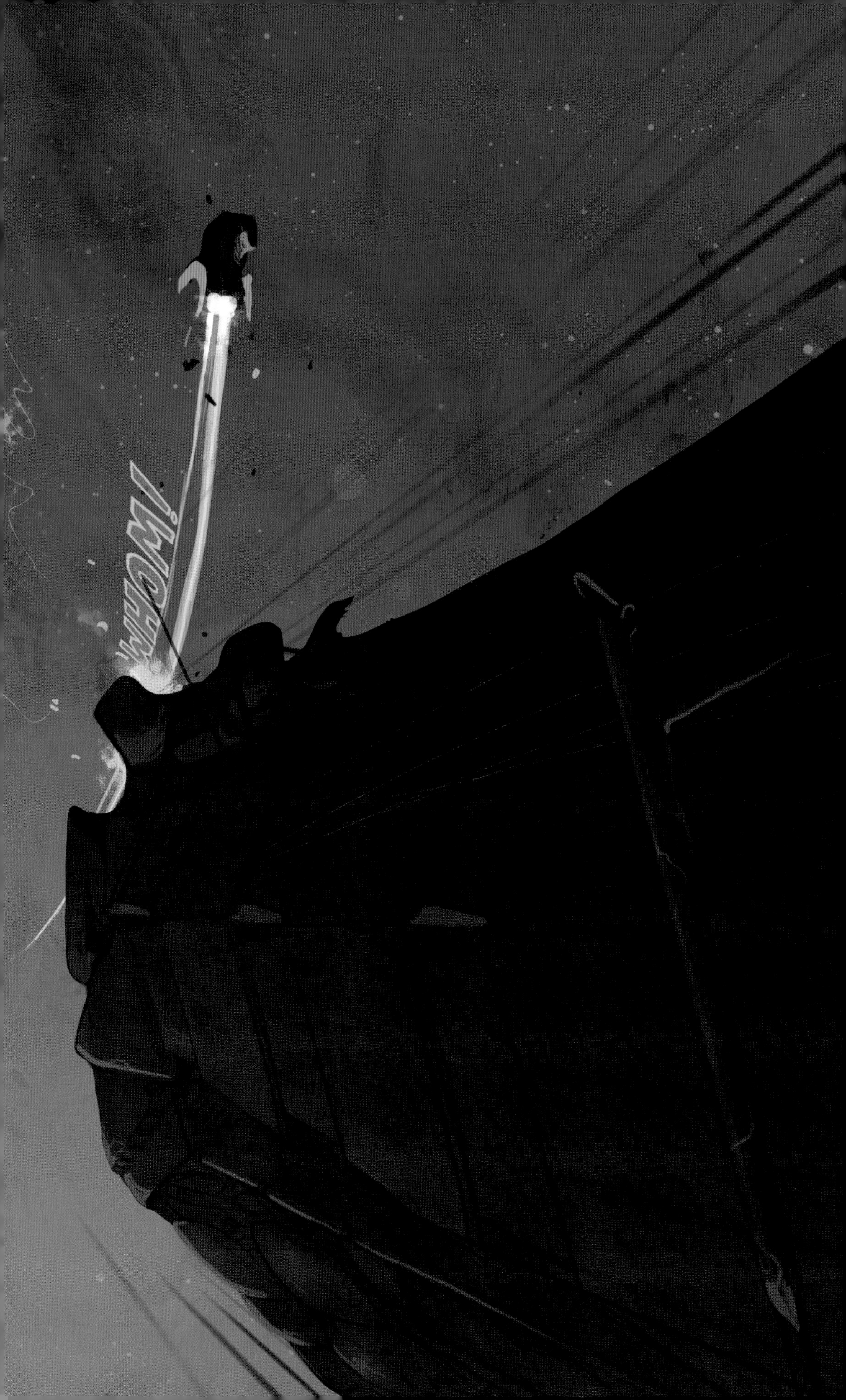
WHOM!

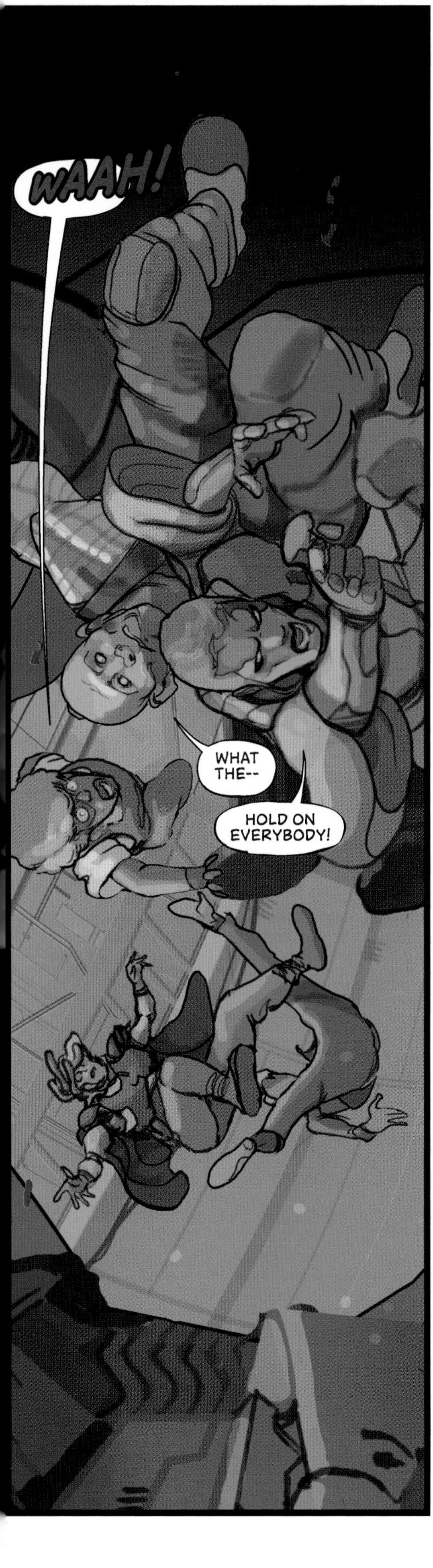
WAAAH!
WHAT THE--
HOLD ON EVERYBODY!

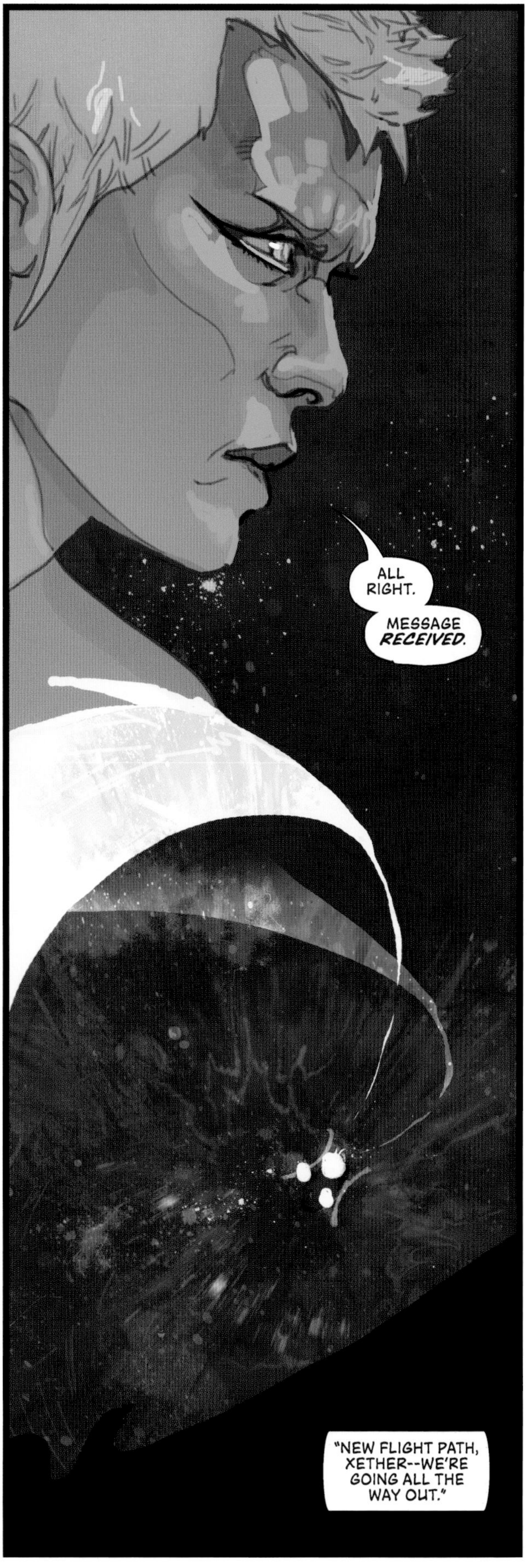
ALL RIGHT.
MESSAGE *RECEIVED*.
"NEW FLIGHT PATH, XETHER--WE'RE GOING ALL THE WAY OUT."

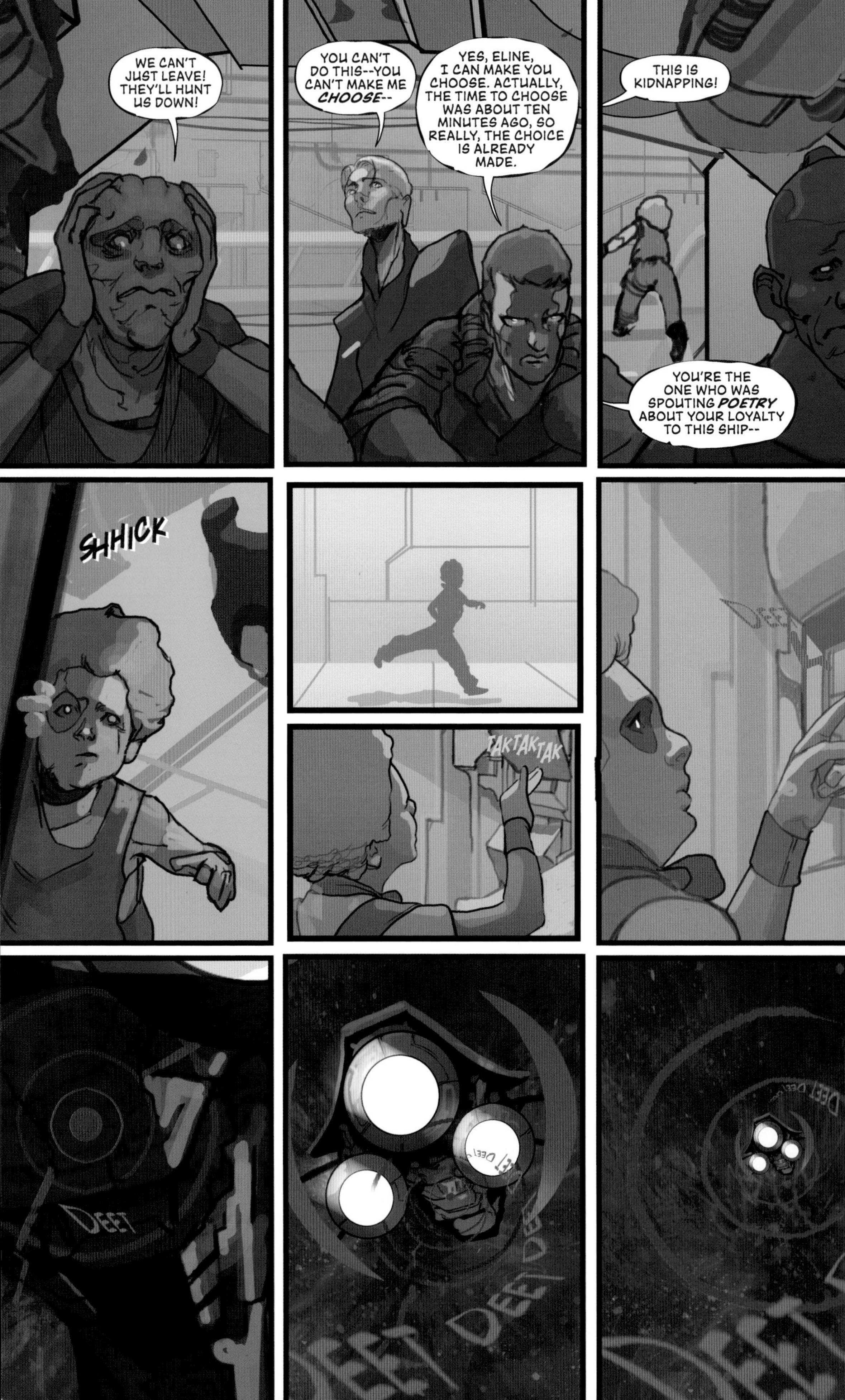
WE CAN'T JUST LEAVE! THEY'LL HUNT US DOWN!
YOU CAN'T DO THIS--YOU CAN'T MAKE ME *CHOOSE*--
YES, ELINE, I CAN MAKE YOU CHOOSE. ACTUALLY, THE TIME TO CHOOSE WAS ABOUT TEN MINUTES AGO, SO REALLY, THE CHOICE IS ALREADY MADE.
THIS IS KIDNAPPING!
YOU'RE THE ONE WHO WAS SPOUTING **POETRY** ABOUT YOUR LOYALTY TO THIS SHIP--
SHHICK
TAKTAKTAK
DEET

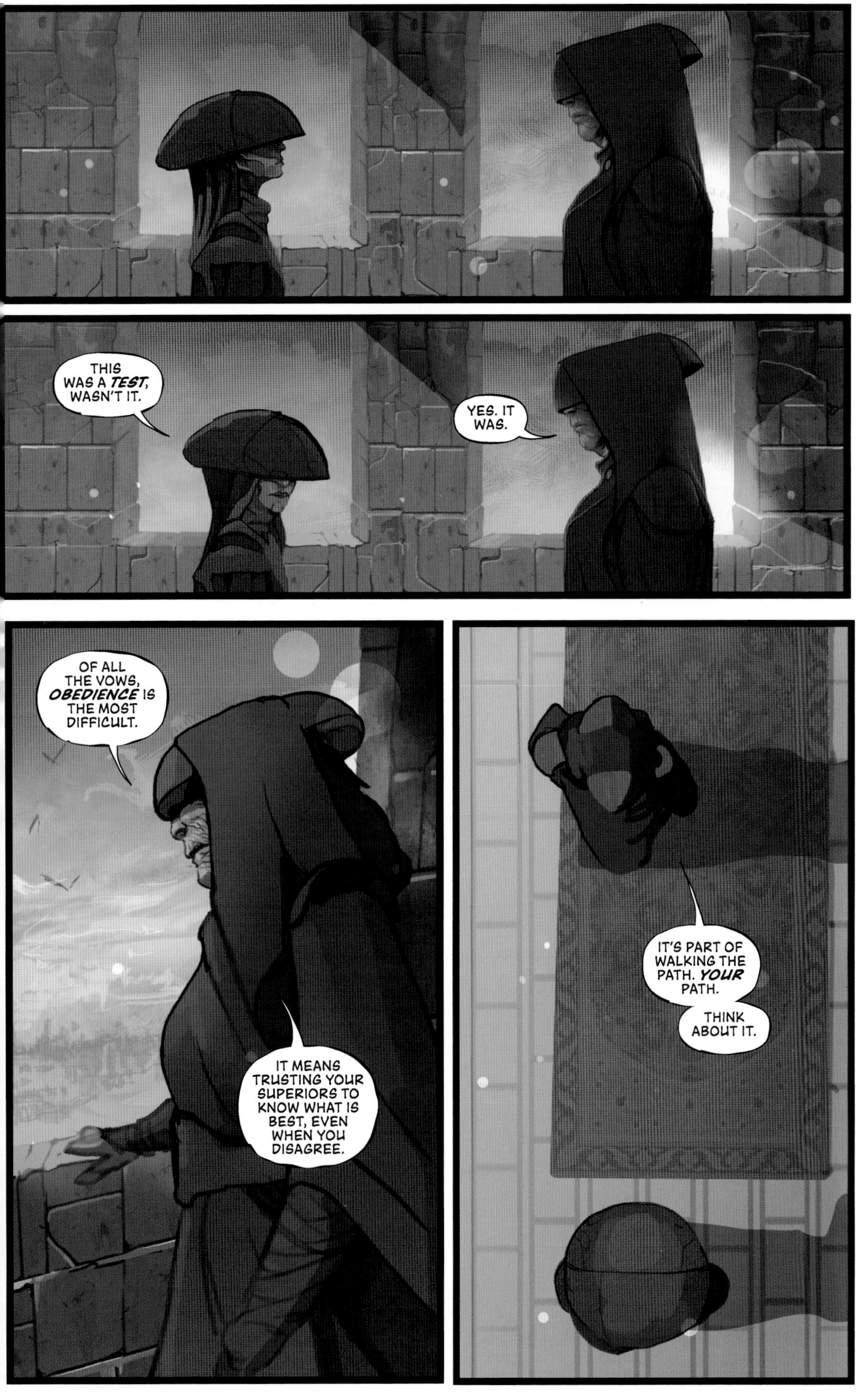
THIS WAS A *TEST*, WASN'T IT.
YES. IT WAS.
OF ALL THE VOWS, *OBEDIENCE* IS THE MOST DIFFICULT.
IT MEANS TRUSTING YOUR SUPERIORS TO KNOW WHAT IS BEST, EVEN WHEN YOU DISAGREE.
IT'S PART OF WALKING THE PATH. *YOUR* PATH.
THINK ABOUT IT.

THE PATH IS HIDDEN FROM ME.

IF I HAD A SIGN-- SOMETHING TO LIGHT THE WAY--BUT THERE'S *NOTHING*.

ONLY MY OWN *STUPIDITY*.

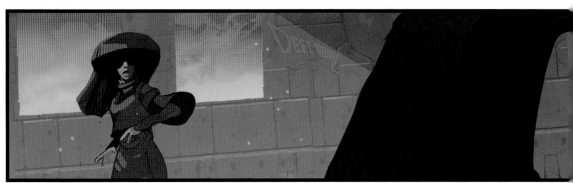

RUN... CHASED...

SEND HELP...

...BY THE LIGHTS. IT'S A *DISTRESS* SIGNAL.

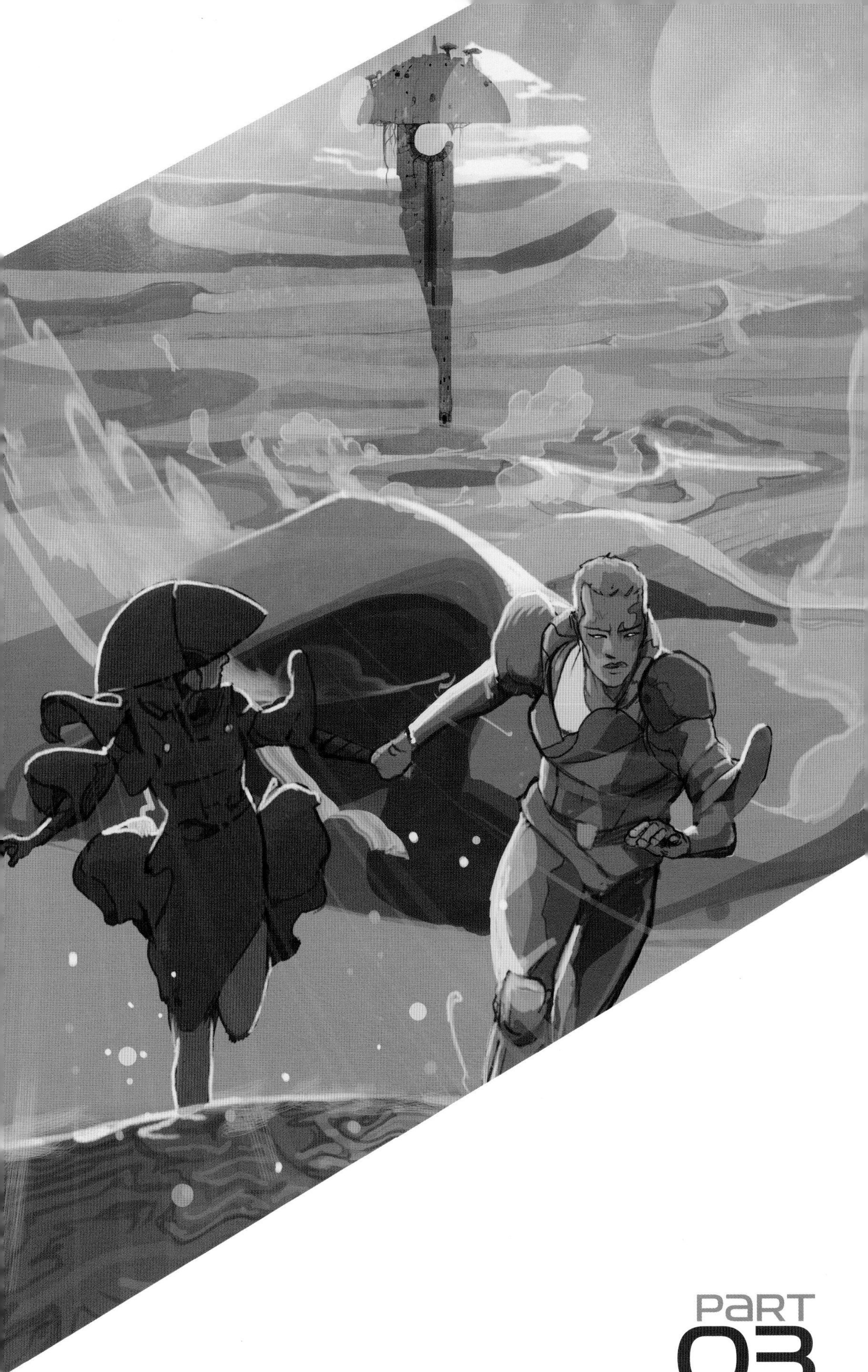

PART 03

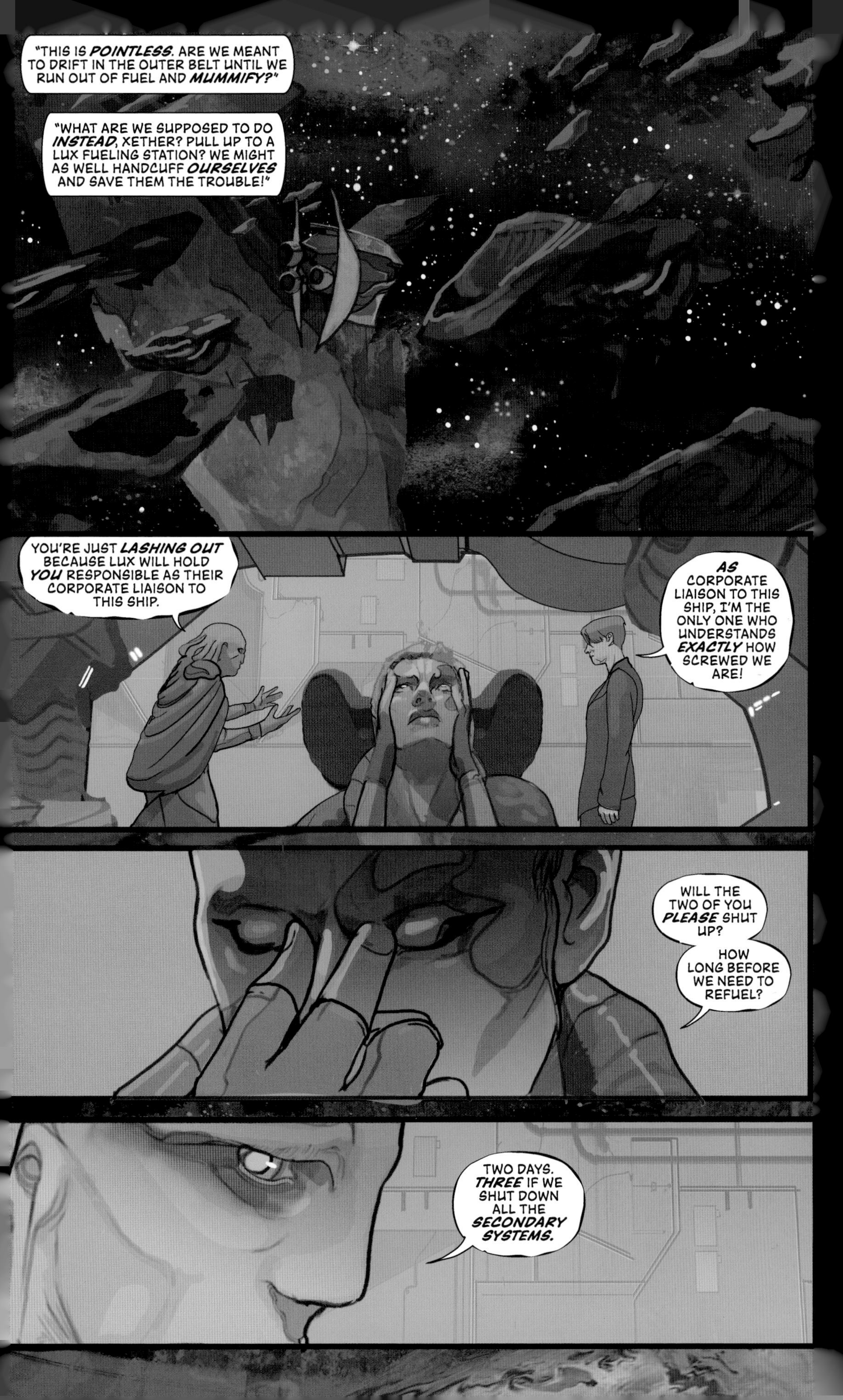
"THIS IS POINTLESS. ARE WE MEANT TO DRIFT IN THE OUTER BELT UNTIL WE RUN OUT OF FUEL AND MUMMIFY?"
"WHAT ARE WE SUPPOSED TO DO INSTEAD, XETHER? PULL UP TO A LUX FUELING STATION? WE MIGHT AS WELL HANDCUFF OURSELVES AND SAVE THEM THE TROUBLE!"
YOU'RE JUST LASHING OUT BECAUSE LUX WILL HOLD YOU RESPONSIBLE AS THEIR CORPORATE LIAISON TO THIS SHIP.
AS CORPORATE LIAISON TO THIS SHIP, I'M THE ONLY ONE WHO UNDERSTANDS EXACTLY HOW SCREWED WE ARE!
WILL THE TWO OF YOU PLEASE SHUT UP?
HOW LONG BEFORE WE NEED TO REFUEL?
TWO DAYS. THREE IF WE SHUT DOWN ALL THE SECONDARY SYSTEMS.

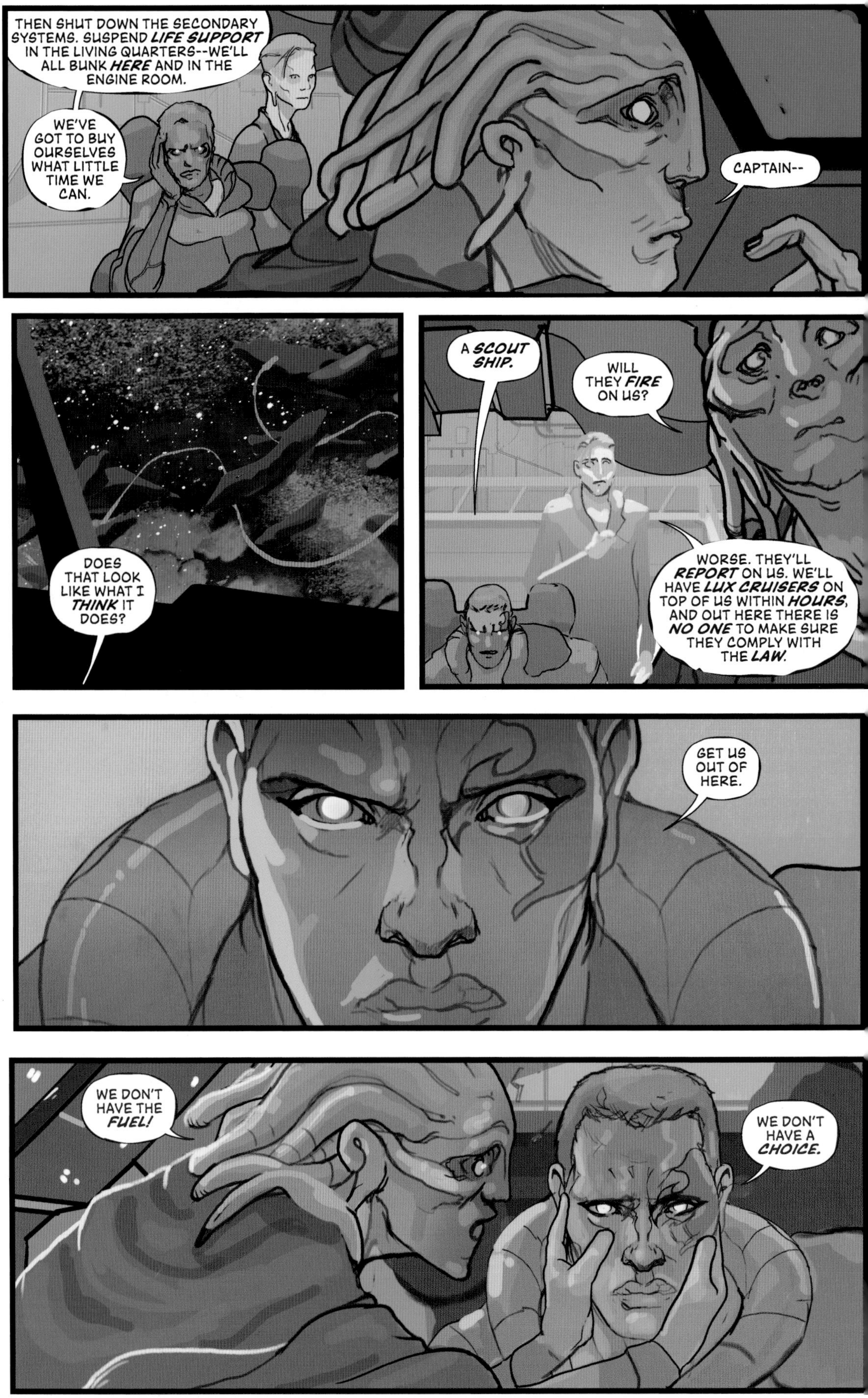
THEN SHUT DOWN THE SECONDARY SYSTEMS. SUSPEND LIFE SUPPORT IN THE LIVING QUARTERS--WE'LL ALL BUNK HERE AND IN THE ENGINE ROOM.
WE'VE GOT TO BUY OURSELVES WHAT LITTLE TIME WE CAN.
CAPTAIN--
DOES THAT LOOK LIKE WHAT I THINK IT DOES?
A SCOUT SHIP.
WILL THEY FIRE ON US?
WORSE. THEY'LL REPORT ON US. WE'LL HAVE LUX CRUISERS ON TOP OF US WITHIN HOURS, AND OUT HERE THERE IS NO ONE TO MAKE SURE THEY COMPLY WITH THE LAW.
GET US OUT OF HERE.
WE DON'T HAVE THE FUEL!
WE DON'T HAVE A CHOICE.

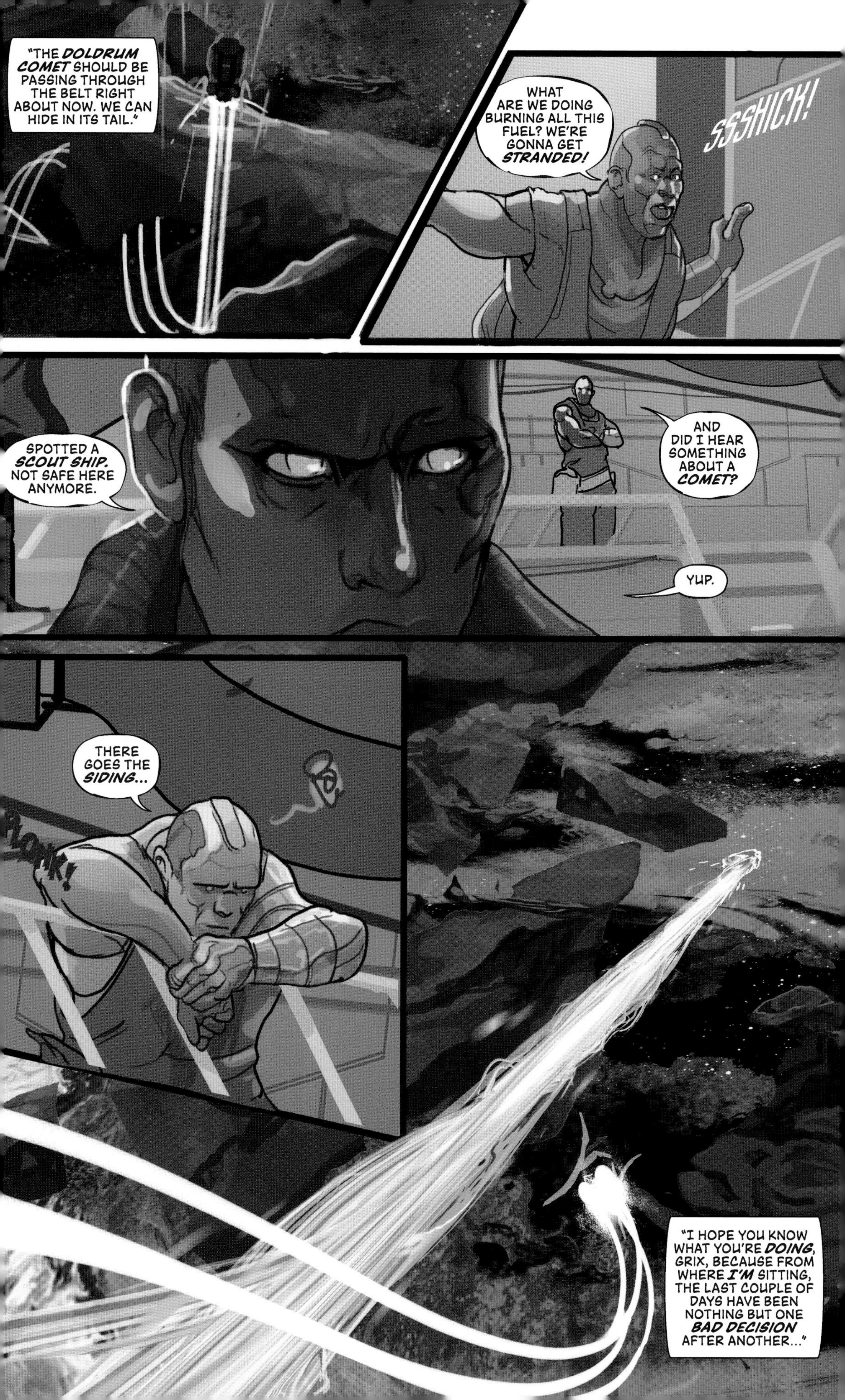
"THE DOLDRUM COMET SHOULD BE PASSING THROUGH THE BELT RIGHT ABOUT NOW. WE CAN HIDE IN ITS TAIL."
WHAT ARE WE DOING BURNING ALL THIS FUEL? WE'RE GONNA GET STRANDED!
SSSHICK!
SPOTTED A SCOUT SHIP. NOT SAFE HERE ANYMORE.
AND DID I HEAR SOMETHING ABOUT A COMET?
YUP.
THERE GOES THE SIDING...
PLONK!
"I HOPE YOU KNOW WHAT YOU'RE DOING, GRIX, BECAUSE FROM WHERE I'M SITTING, THE LAST COUPLE OF DAYS HAVE BEEN NOTHING BUT ONE BAD DECISION AFTER ANOTHER..."

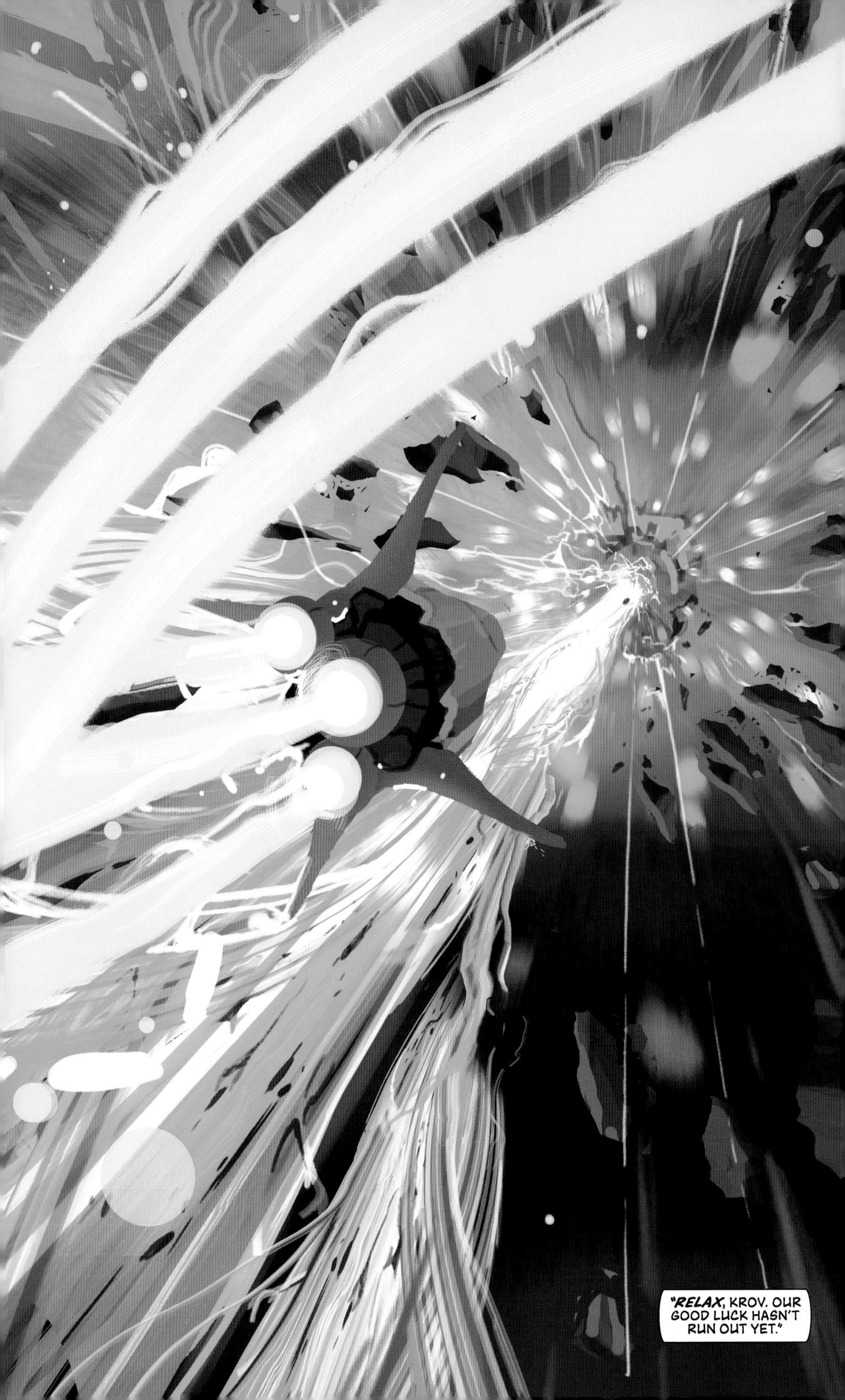
"RELAX, KROV. OUR GOOD LUCK HASN'T RUN OUT YET."

MEANWHILE ON DUNI.

IN THIS WORLD OF GREED AND DESIRE, WE ARE TAUGHT TO *FEAR* WHAT WE CANNOT *SEE*.

TO *DISTRUST* ANYTHING WE CANNOT *POSSESS*--AND WE POSSESS *FIRST* WITH OUR *EYES*.

THAT IS WHY A NONE GOES ABOUT THEIR DAYS *VEILED* FROM WORLDLY THINGS. SO THAT THEY ARE *PROTECTED* FROM GREED, FROM THE DESIRES OF THE *EYES*, FROM THE ALLURE OF WEALTH AND POWER.

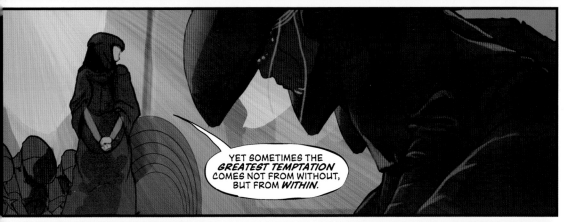

YET SOMETIMES THE *GREATEST TEMPTATION* COMES NOT FROM WITHOUT, BUT FROM *WITHIN*.

"DISOBEDIENCE. *PRIDE.* THINKING THAT *YOU* UNDERSTAND THE PATH IN WAYS YOUR *TEACHERS* DO NOT. THESE ARE FORMS OF *SPIRITUAL BLINDNESS.*"

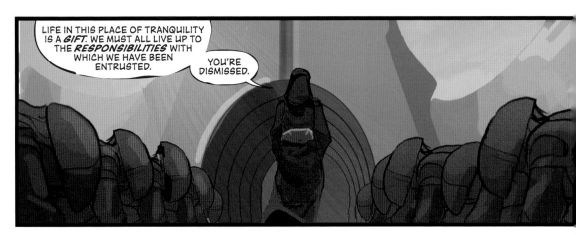

LIFE IN THIS PLACE OF TRANQUILITY IS A *GIFT*. WE MUST ALL LIVE UP TO THE *RESPONSIBILITIES* WITH WHICH WE HAVE BEEN ENTRUSTED.

YOU'RE DISMISSED.

IS IT JUST *ME*, OR WAS MOTHER PROXIMA PICKING ON YOU, VESS?

MAYBE.

WHY? EVERYONE SAYS YOU'RE THE *BEST* SCRIPTORIAN WE'VE HAD IN *YEARS*.

I SAID SOMETHING, KRIKKO.

SOMETHING I *SHOULDN'T* HAVE.

MOTHER PROXIMA IS *SO* PATIENT AND FORGIVING. I'M *SURE* IT'S NOT AS BAD AS YOU THINK.

I'M SURE IT'S *WORSE*.

I HAD A... A *SIGN*. A MESSAGE. AND I *RESPONDED*.

WHAT DO YOU *MEAN*? WHAT KIND OF SIGN?

I'VE BEEN HAVING...DOUBTS. FEARS THAT NOT EVERYTHING I BELIEVED ABOUT THIS PLACE IS *TRUE*. AND THE *SIGN*...

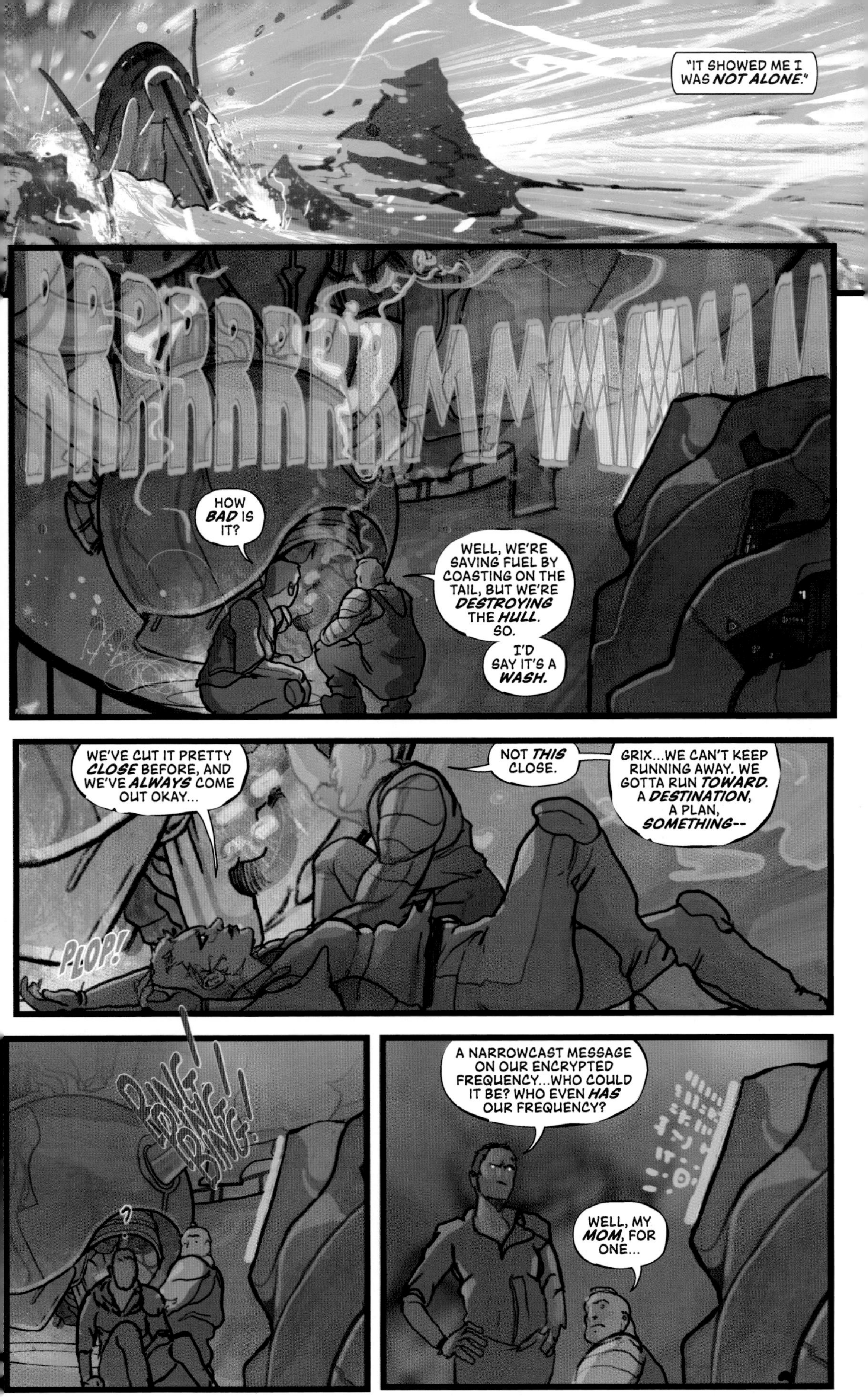
"IT SHOWED ME I WAS NOT ALONE."
RRRRRRRRRAMMMMMMM
HOW BAD IS IT?
WELL, WE'RE SAVING FUEL BY COASTING ON THE TAIL, BUT WE'RE DESTROYING THE HULL. SO.
I'D SAY IT'S A WASH.
WE'VE CUT IT PRETTY CLOSE BEFORE, AND WE'VE ALWAYS COME OUT OKAY...
NOT THIS CLOSE.
GRIX...WE CAN'T KEEP RUNNING AWAY. WE GOTTA RUN TOWARD. A DESTINATION, A PLAN, SOMETHING--
PLOP!
A NARROWCAST MESSAGE ON OUR ENCRYPTED FREQUENCY...WHO COULD IT BE? WHO EVEN HAS OUR FREQUENCY?
WELL, MY MOM, FOR ONE...

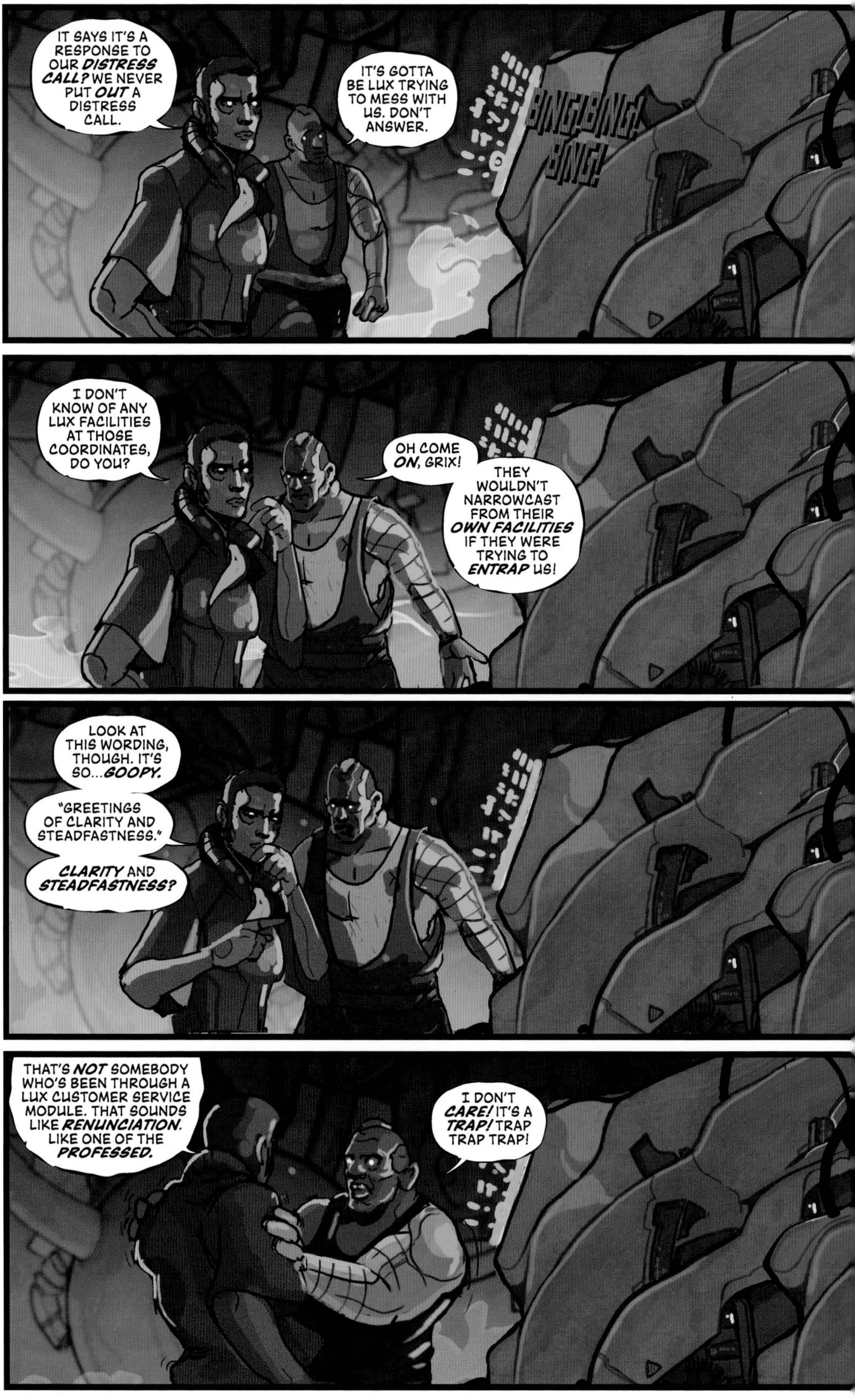

IT SAYS IT'S A RESPONSE TO OUR DISTRESS CALL? WE NEVER PUT OUT A DISTRESS CALL.
IT'S GOTTA BE LUX TRYING TO MESS WITH US. DON'T ANSWER.
BING! BING! BING!
I DON'T KNOW OF ANY LUX FACILITIES AT THOSE COORDINATES, DO YOU?
OH COME ON, GRIX!
THEY WOULDN'T NARROWCAST FROM THEIR OWN FACILITIES IF THEY WERE TRYING TO ENTRAP US!
LOOK AT THIS WORDING, THOUGH. IT'S SO...GOOPY.
"GREETINGS OF CLARITY AND STEADFASTNESS."
CLARITY AND STEADFASTNESS?
THAT'S NOT SOMEBODY WHO'S BEEN THROUGH A LUX CUSTOMER SERVICE MODULE. THAT SOUNDS LIKE RENUNCIATION. LIKE ONE OF THE PROFESSED.
I DON'T CARE! IT'S A TRAP! TRAP TRAP TRAP!

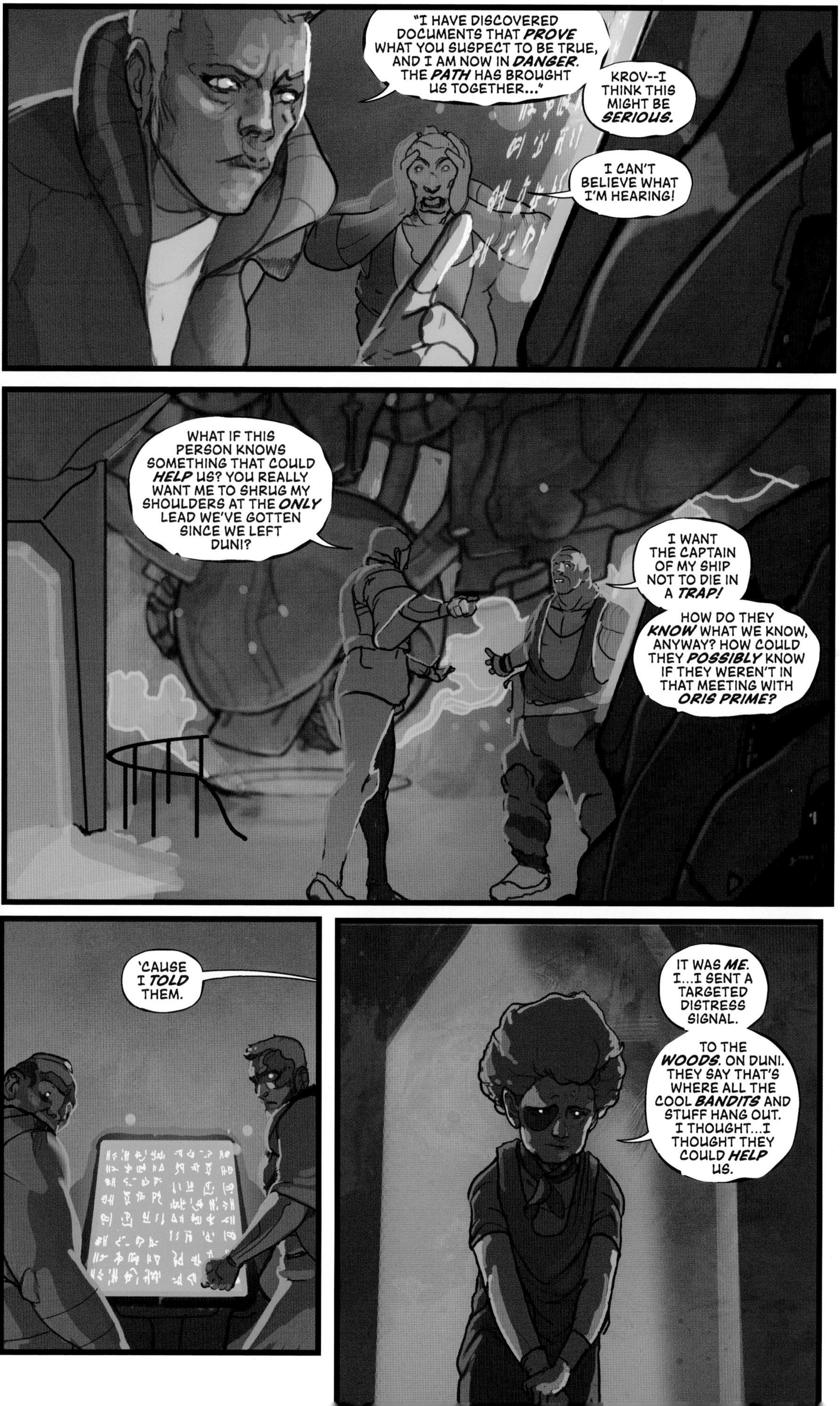
"I HAVE DISCOVERED DOCUMENTS THAT PROVE WHAT YOU SUSPECT TO BE TRUE, AND I AM NOW IN DANGER. THE PATH HAS BROUGHT US TOGETHER..."
KROV--I THINK THIS MIGHT BE SERIOUS.
I CAN'T BELIEVE WHAT I'M HEARING!
WHAT IF THIS PERSON KNOWS SOMETHING THAT COULD HELP US? YOU REALLY WANT ME TO SHRUG MY SHOULDERS AT THE ONLY LEAD WE'VE GOTTEN SINCE WE LEFT DUNI?
I WANT THE CAPTAIN OF MY SHIP NOT TO DIE IN A TRAP!
HOW DO THEY KNOW WHAT WE KNOW, ANYWAY? HOW COULD THEY POSSIBLY KNOW IF THEY WEREN'T IN THAT MEETING WITH ORIS PRIME?
'CAUSE I TOLD THEM.
IT WAS ME. I...I SENT A TARGETED DISTRESS SIGNAL.
TO THE WOODS. ON DUNI. THEY SAY THAT'S WHERE ALL THE COOL BANDITS AND STUFF HANG OUT. I THOUGHT...I THOUGHT THEY COULD HELP US.

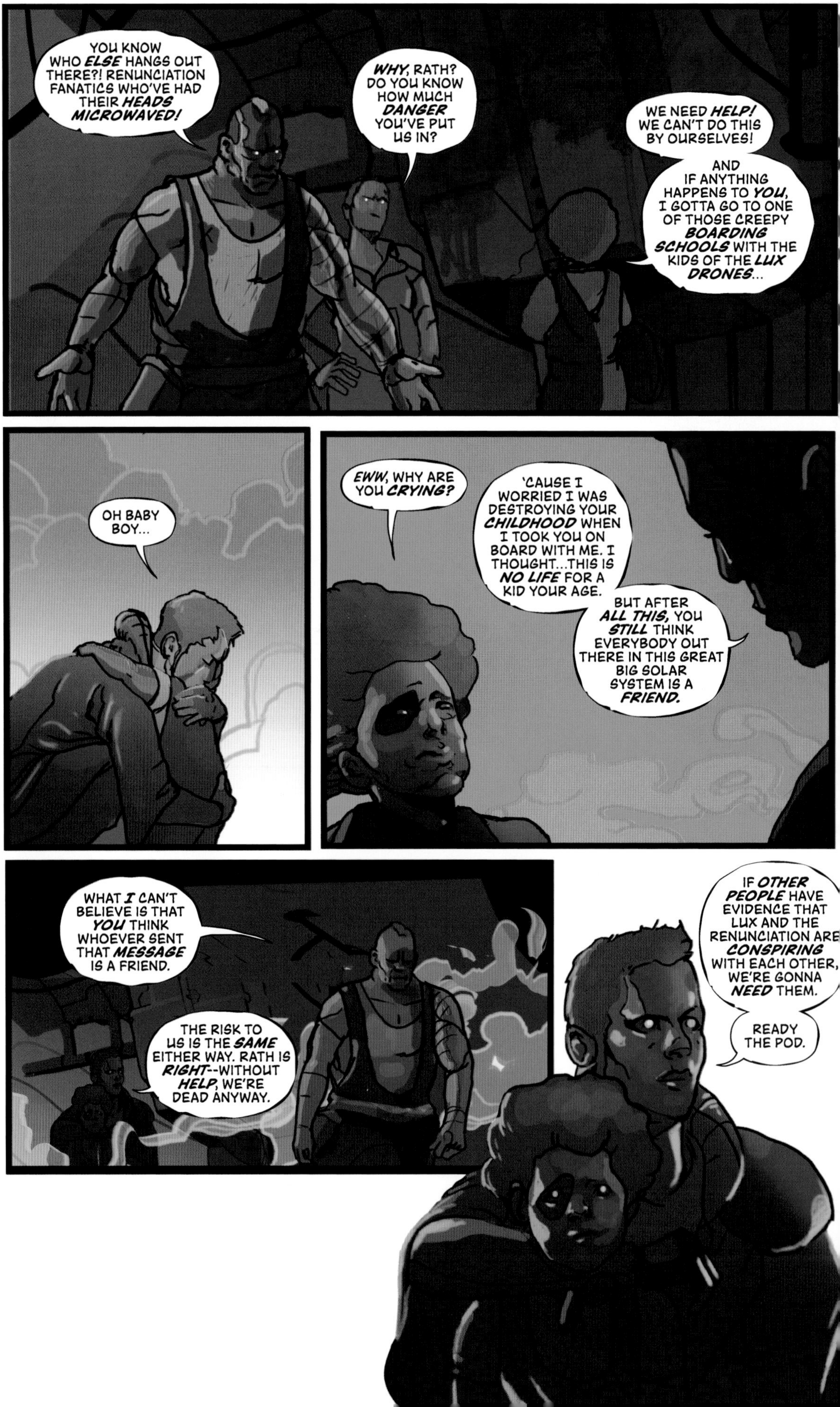
YOU KNOW WHO *ELSE* HANGS OUT THERE?! RENUNCIATION FANATICS WHO'VE HAD THEIR *HEADS MICROWAVED!*
WHY, RATH? DO YOU KNOW HOW MUCH *DANGER* YOU'VE PUT US IN?
WE NEED *HELP!* WE CAN'T DO THIS BY OURSELVES!
AND IF ANYTHING HAPPENS TO *YOU*, I GOTTA GO TO ONE OF THOSE CREEPY *BOARDING SCHOOLS* WITH THE KIDS OF THE *LUX DRONES*...
OH BABY BOY...
EWW, WHY ARE YOU *CRYING?*
'CAUSE I WORRIED I WAS DESTROYING YOUR *CHILDHOOD* WHEN I TOOK YOU ON BOARD WITH ME. I THOUGHT...THIS IS *NO LIFE* FOR A KID YOUR AGE.
BUT AFTER *ALL THIS,* YOU *STILL* THINK EVERYBODY OUT THERE IN THIS GREAT BIG SOLAR SYSTEM IS A *FRIEND.*
WHAT *I* CAN'T BELIEVE IS THAT *YOU* THINK WHOEVER SENT THAT *MESSAGE* IS A FRIEND.
THE RISK TO US IS THE *SAME* EITHER WAY. RATH IS *RIGHT*--WITHOUT *HELP*, WE'RE DEAD ANYWAY.
IF *OTHER PEOPLE* HAVE EVIDENCE THAT LUX AND THE RENUNCIATION ARE *CONSPIRING* WITH EACH OTHER, WE'RE GONNA *NEED* THEM.
READY THE POD.

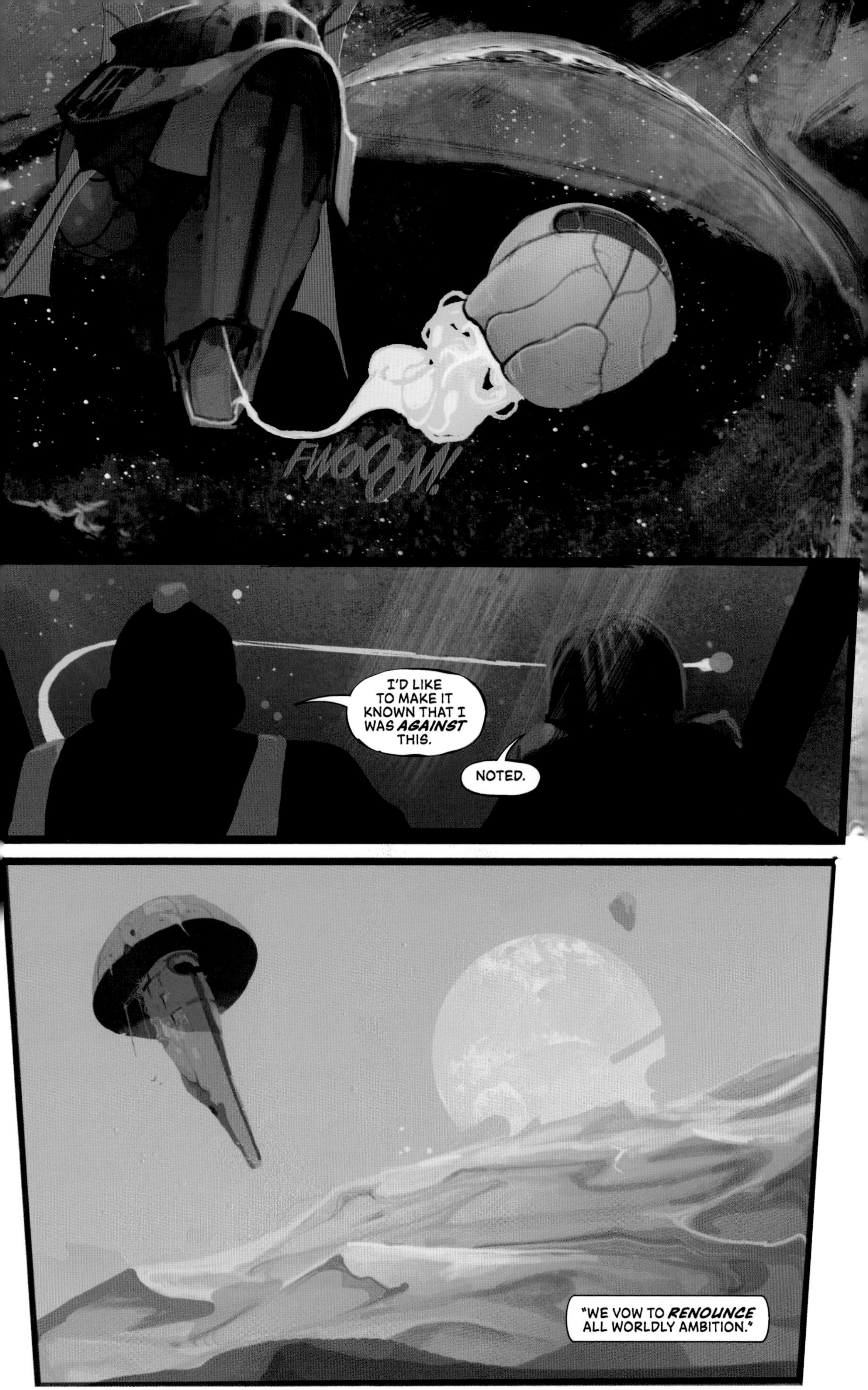
FWOOOM!
I'D LIKE TO MAKE IT KNOWN THAT I WAS AGAINST THIS.
NOTED.
"WE VOW TO RENOUNCE ALL WORLDLY AMBITION."

"AND TO WALK THE PATH TO THE *INVISIBLE KINGDOM*, THOUGH THE WAY BE LONG AND THE HARDSHIPS MANY...

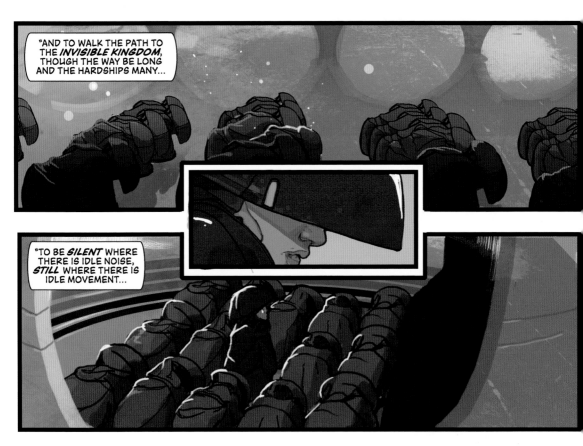

"TO BE *SILENT* WHERE THERE IS IDLE NOISE, *STILL* WHERE THERE IS IDLE MOVEMENT...

"TO *VEIL* OURSELVES FROM THE WORLD OF THINGS, AND OPEN OUR EYES TO THE WORLD BEYOND...

"...WE DAILY COMMIT OURSELVES, BODY AND MIND.

"FOR WE ARE THE NONES, AND THIS IS THE PATH."

...THIS IS *MADNESS.*

MOTHER IS *RIGHT*...I AM DISOBEDIENT, PRIDEFUL.

I *LACK* THE UNDERSTANDING TO DISCERN RIGHT FROM WRONG...

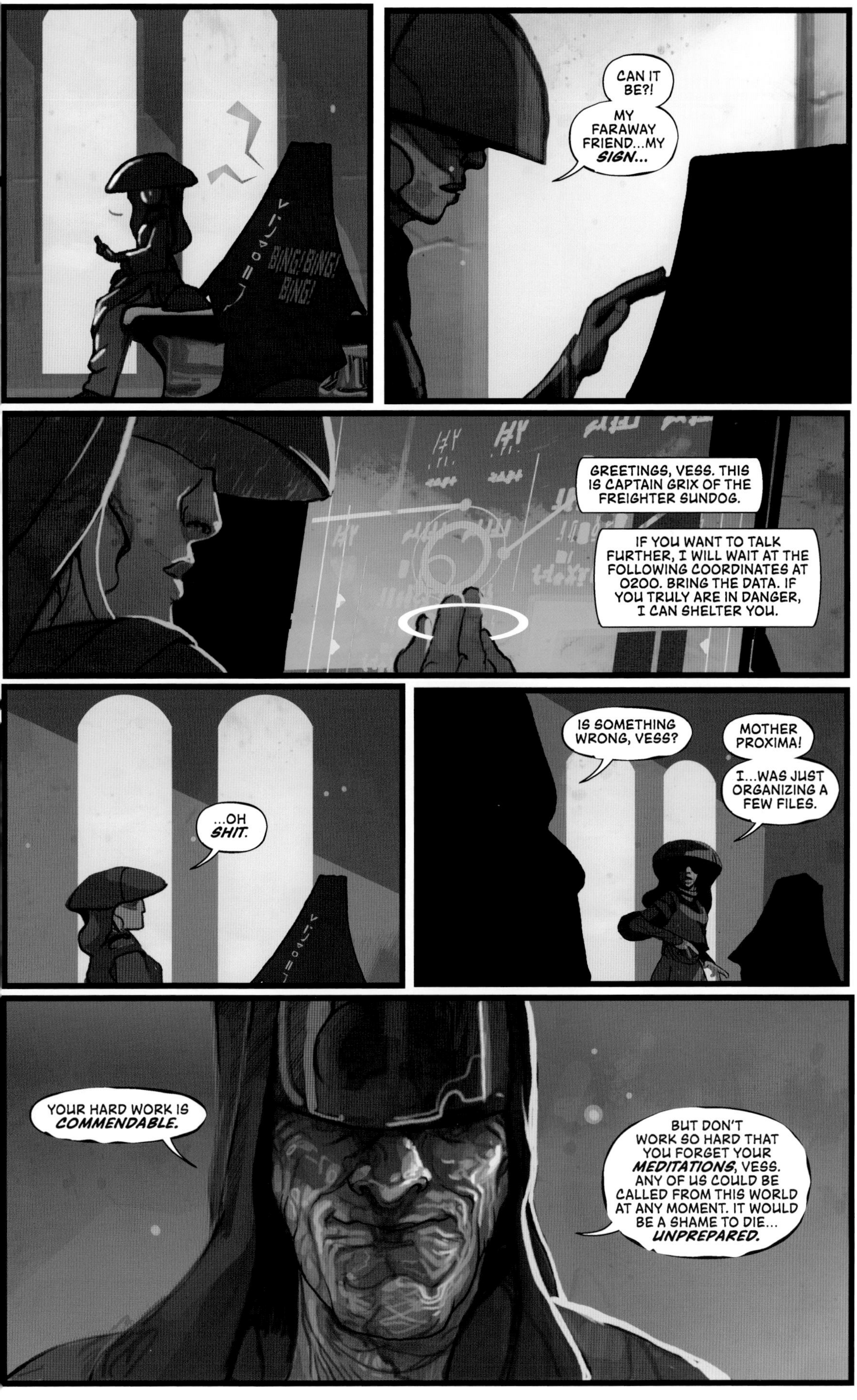
BING! BING! BING!
CAN IT BE?!
MY FARAWAY FRIEND...MY SIGN...
GREETINGS, VESS. THIS IS CAPTAIN GRIX OF THE FREIGHTER SUNDOG.
IF YOU WANT TO TALK FURTHER, I WILL WAIT AT THE FOLLOWING COORDINATES AT 0200. BRING THE DATA. IF YOU TRULY ARE IN DANGER, I CAN SHELTER YOU.
...OH SHIT.
IS SOMETHING WRONG, VESS?
MOTHER PROXIMA!
I...WAS JUST ORGANIZING A FEW FILES.
YOUR HARD WORK IS COMMENDABLE.
BUT DON'T WORK SO HARD THAT YOU FORGET YOUR MEDITATIONS, VESS. ANY OF US COULD BE CALLED FROM THIS WORLD AT ANY MOMENT. IT WOULD BE A SHAME TO DIE... UNPREPARED.

LATER.

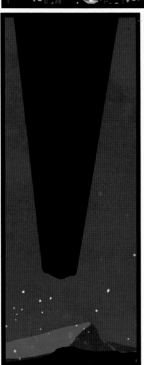

FSSH!

UGH!

NNGH...

I REALLY HOPE THIS ISN'T A *GIANT MISTAKE.*

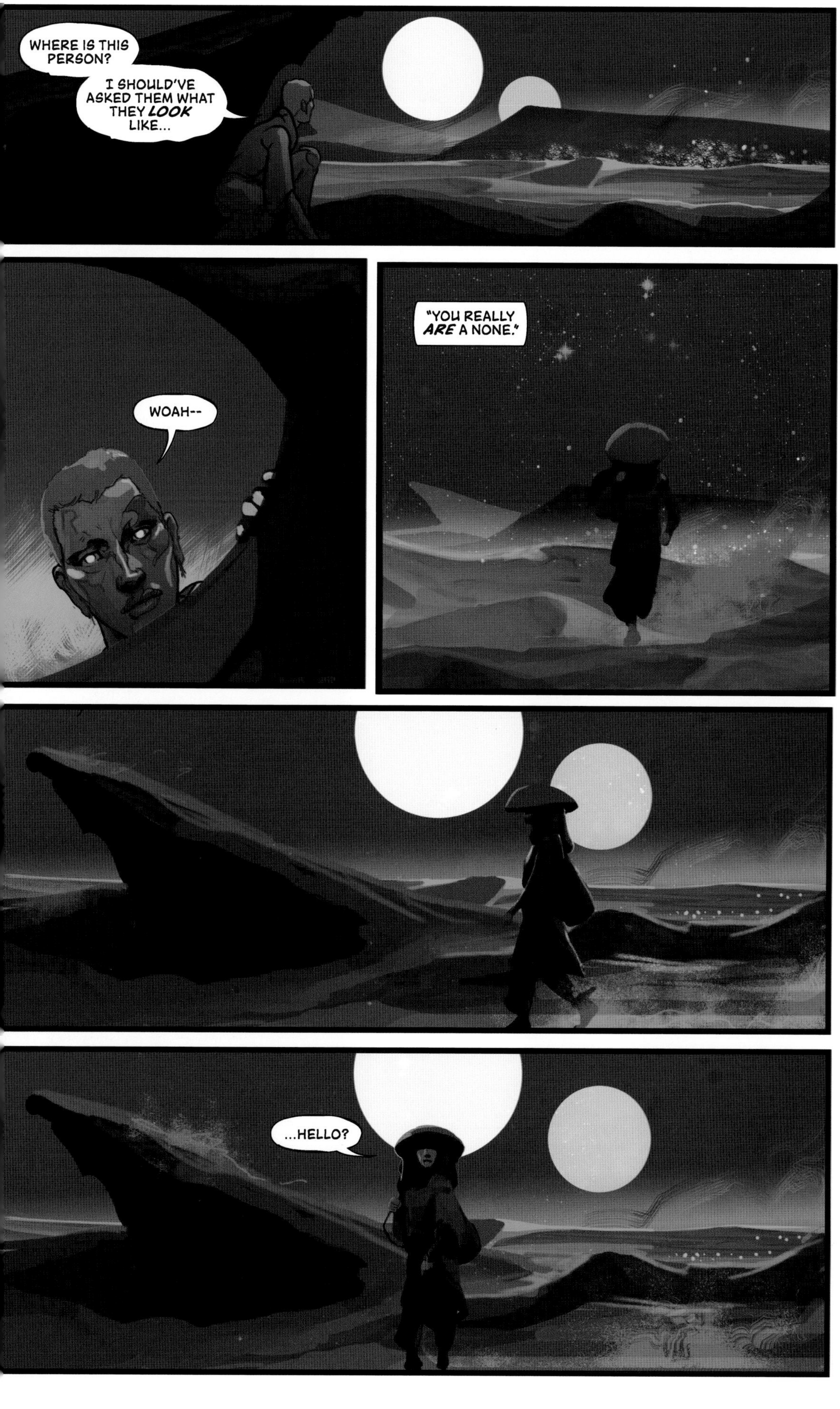
WHERE IS THIS PERSON?
I SHOULD'VE ASKED THEM WHAT THEY *LOOK* LIKE...
WOAH--
"YOU REALLY *ARE* A NONE."
...HELLO?

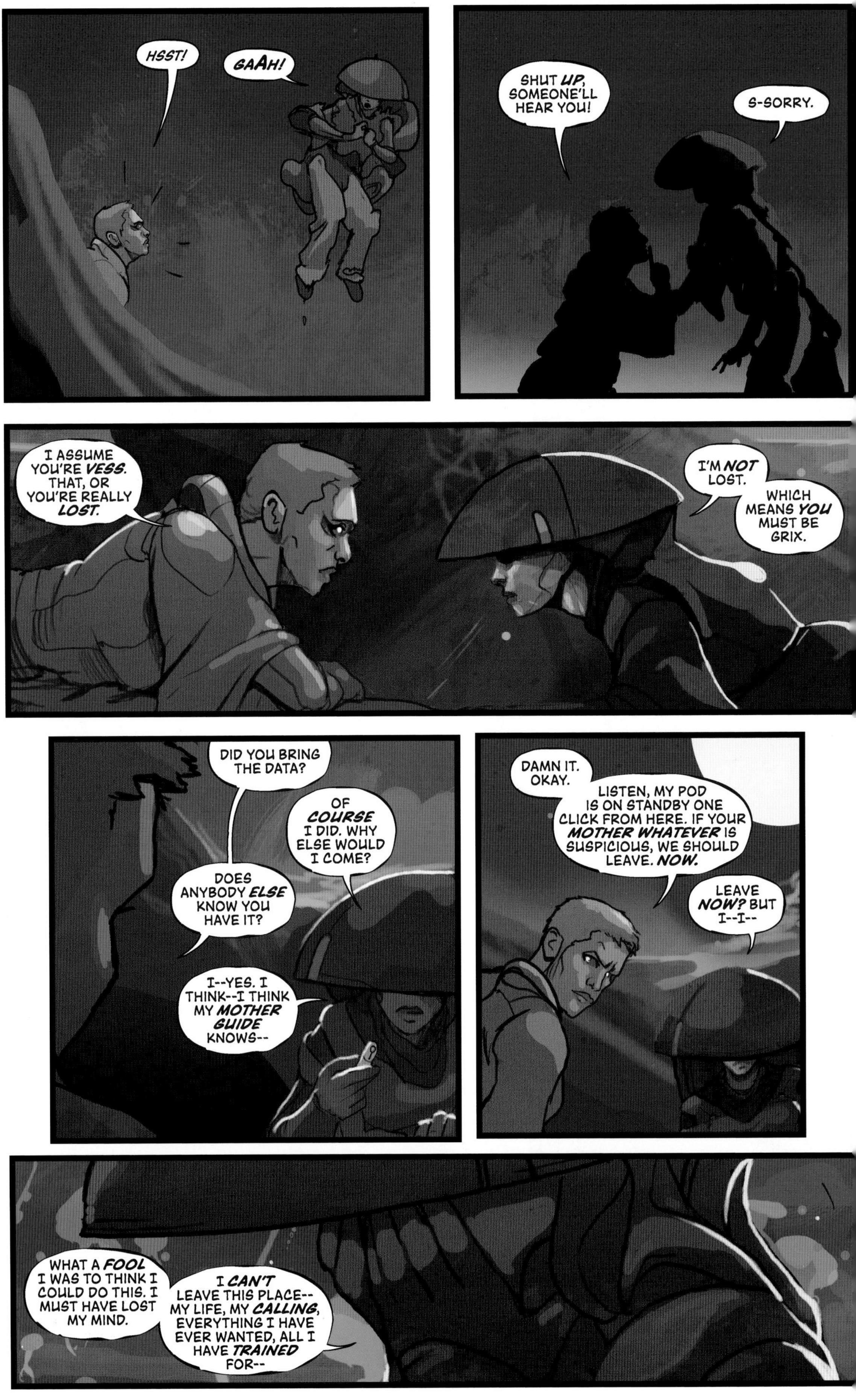
HSST!
GAAH!
SHUT UP, SOMEONE'LL HEAR YOU!
S-SORRY.
I ASSUME YOU'RE VESS. THAT, OR YOU'RE REALLY LOST.
I'M NOT LOST.
WHICH MEANS YOU MUST BE GRIX.
DID YOU BRING THE DATA?
OF COURSE I DID. WHY ELSE WOULD I COME?
DOES ANYBODY ELSE KNOW YOU HAVE IT?
I--YES. I THINK--I THINK MY MOTHER GUIDE KNOWS--
DAMN IT. OKAY.
LISTEN, MY POD IS ON STANDBY ONE CLICK FROM HERE. IF YOUR MOTHER WHATEVER IS SUSPICIOUS, WE SHOULD LEAVE. NOW.
LEAVE NOW? BUT I--I--
WHAT A FOOL I WAS TO THINK I COULD DO THIS. I MUST HAVE LOST MY MIND.
I CAN'T LEAVE THIS PLACE-- MY LIFE, MY CALLING, EVERYTHING I HAVE EVER WANTED, ALL I HAVE TRAINED FOR--

I'LL GIVE YOU THE DATA STICK AND GO *BACK*. PERHAPS NO ONE HAS NOTICED I'VE GONE. I'VE DONE MY DUTY TO THE *TRUTH*, IT'S ENOUGH--

WHAT? ARE YOU *DELUSIONAL?* IF THE RENUNCIATION KNOWS YOU HAVE *DIRT* ON THEM, DO YOU REALLY THINK THEY'LL LET YOU LIVE?

THIS IS MY *PATH*. IF I LEAVE, IT WAS ALL FOR *NOTHING*--

I'M *SORRY*, CAPTAIN GRIX. I WISH YOU LUCK.

HEY! WAIT! YOU CAN'T JUST WALK AWAY! THIS IS BIGGER THAN *EITHER* OF US!

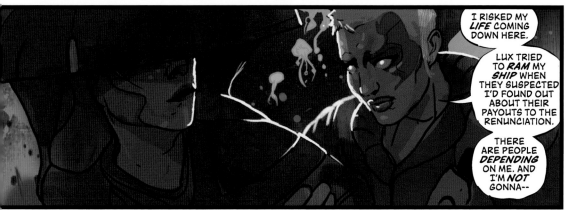

I RISKED MY *LIFE* COMING DOWN HERE.

LUX TRIED TO *RAM* MY *SHIP* WHEN THEY SUSPECTED I'D FOUND OUT ABOUT THEIR PAYOUTS TO THE RENUNCIATION.

THERE ARE PEOPLE *DEPENDING* ON ME. AND I'M *NOT* GONNA--

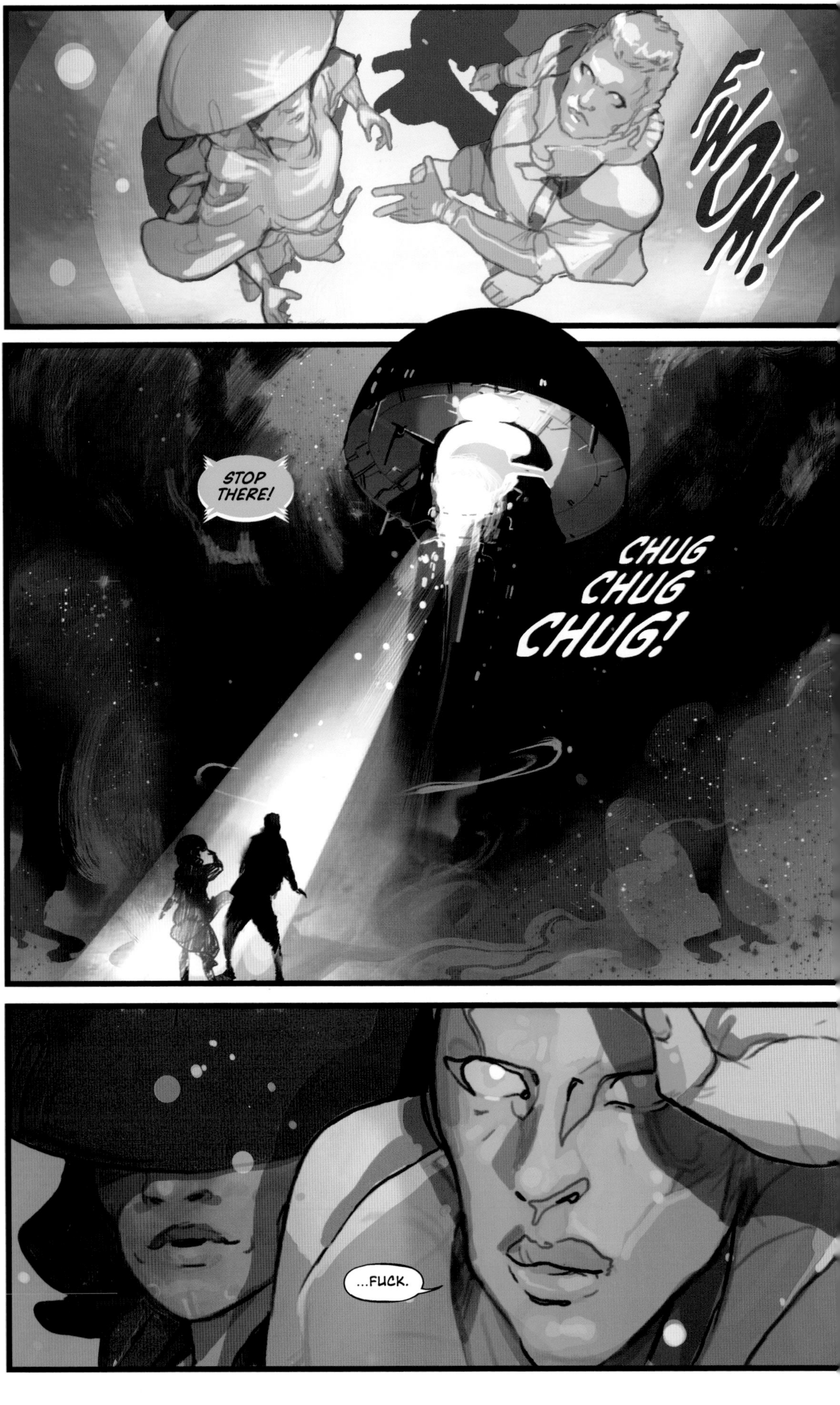
FWOM!
STOP THERE!
CHUG CHUG CHUG!
...FUCK.

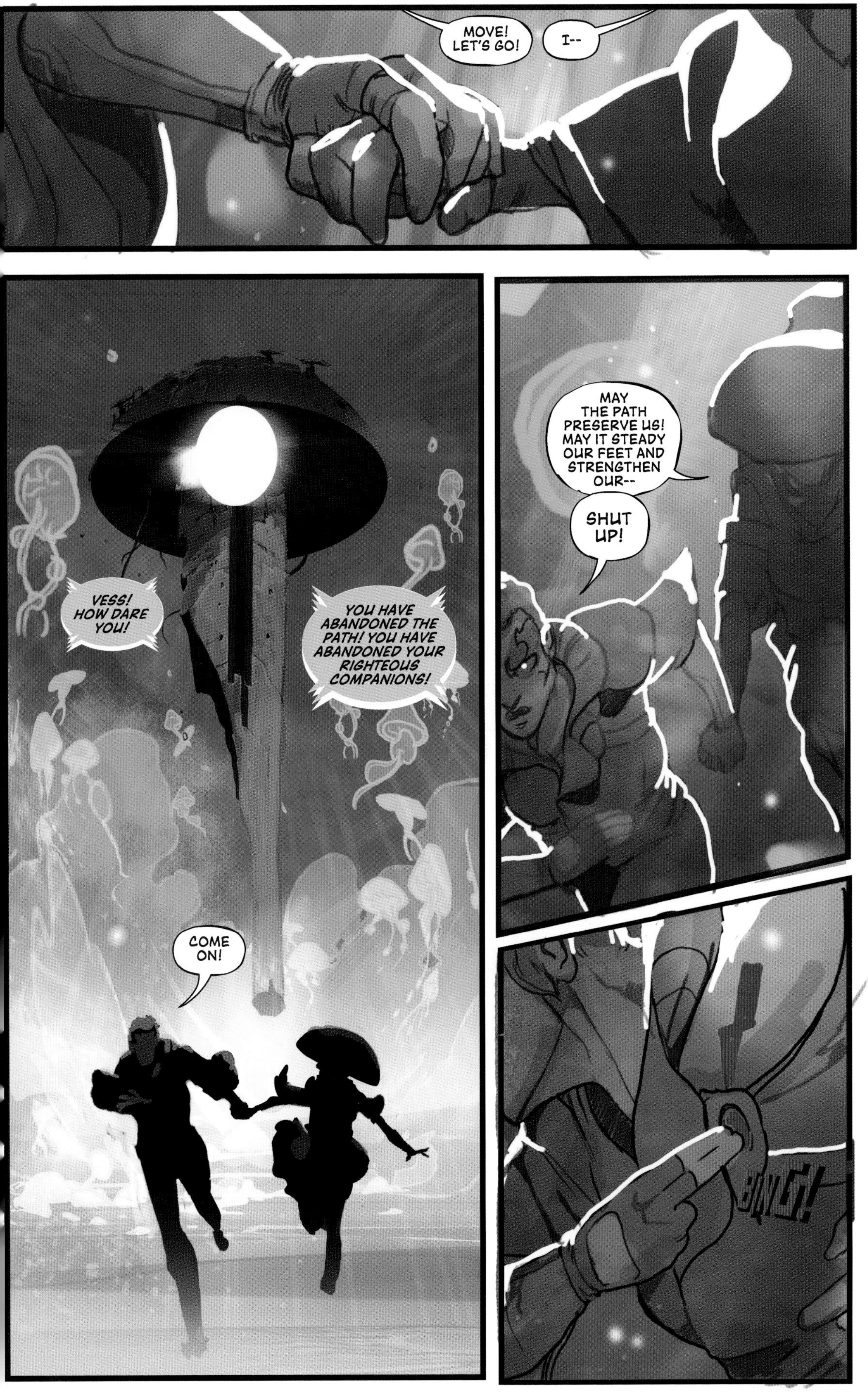
MOVE! LET'S GO!
I--
VESS! HOW DARE YOU!
YOU HAVE ABANDONED THE PATH! YOU HAVE ABANDONED YOUR RIGHTEOUS COMPANIONS!
COME ON!
MAY THE PATH PRESERVE US! MAY IT STEADY OUR FEET AND STRENGTHEN OUR--
SHUT UP!
BING!

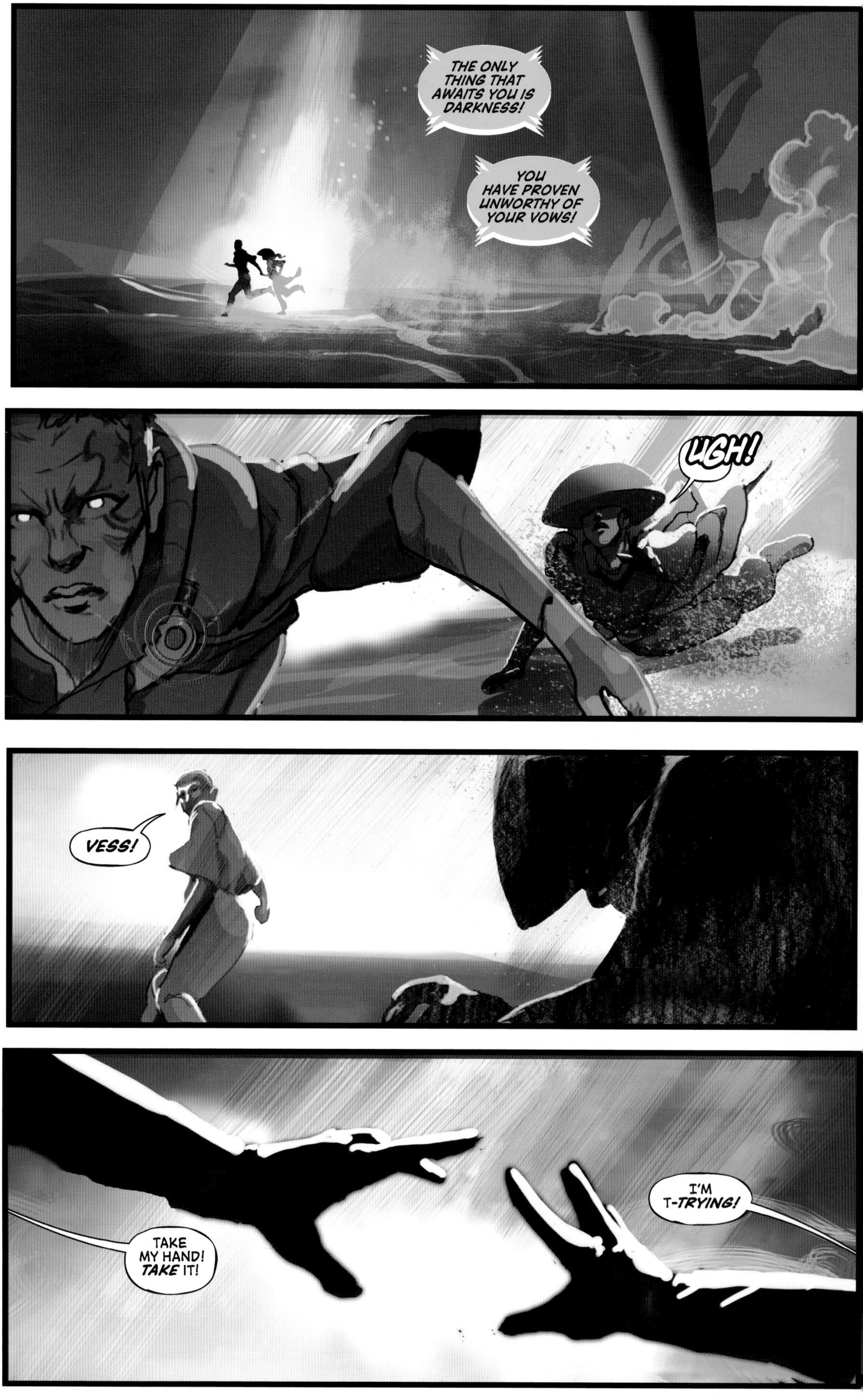
THE ONLY THING THAT AWAITS YOU IS DARKNESS!
YOU HAVE PROVEN UNWORTHY OF YOUR VOWS!
UGH!
VESS!
I'M T-TRYING!
TAKE MY HAND! TAKE IT!

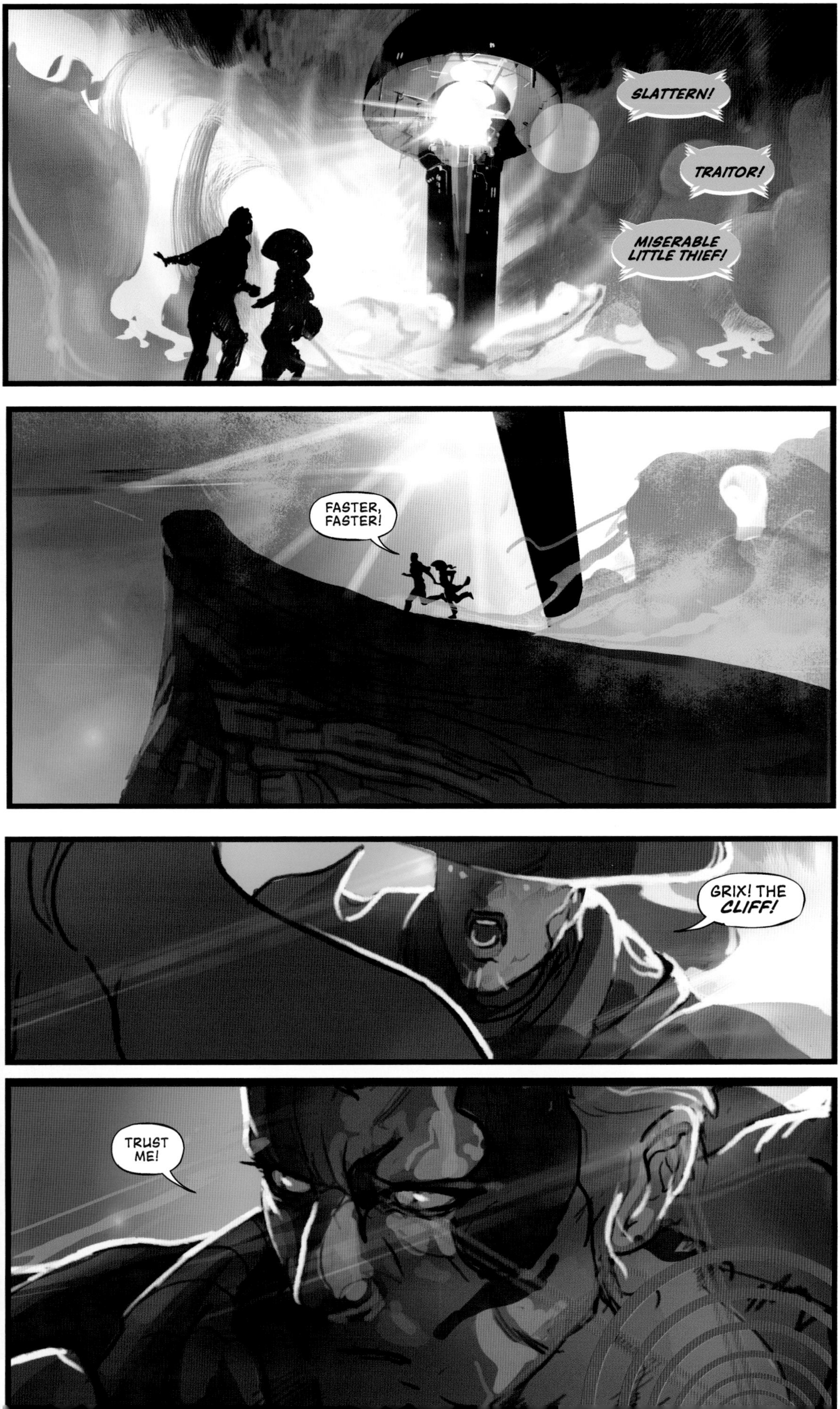
SLATTERN!
TRAITOR!
MISERABLE LITTLE THIEF!
FASTER, FASTER!
GRIX! THE CLIFF!
TRUST ME!

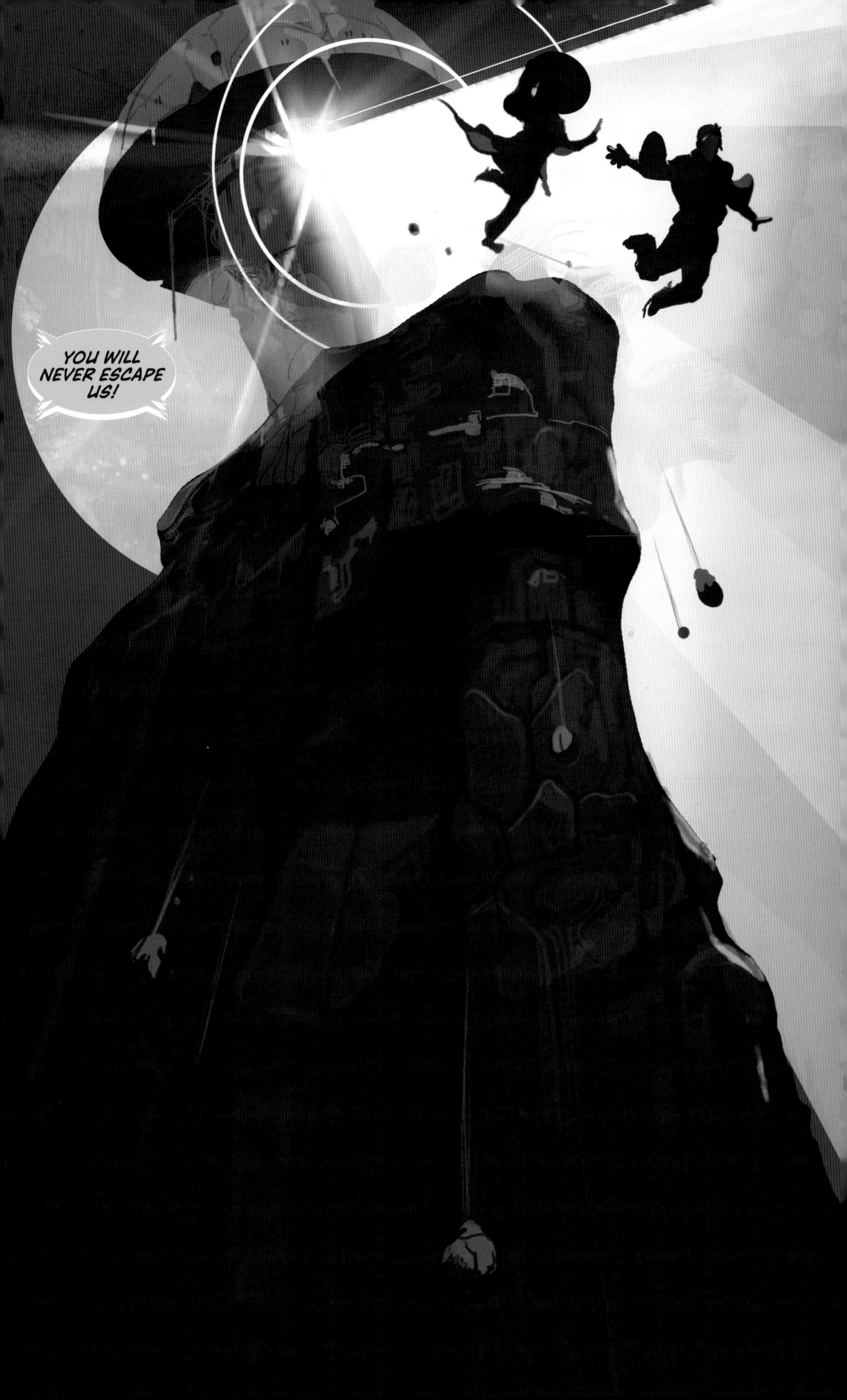
YOU WILL NEVER ESCAPE US!

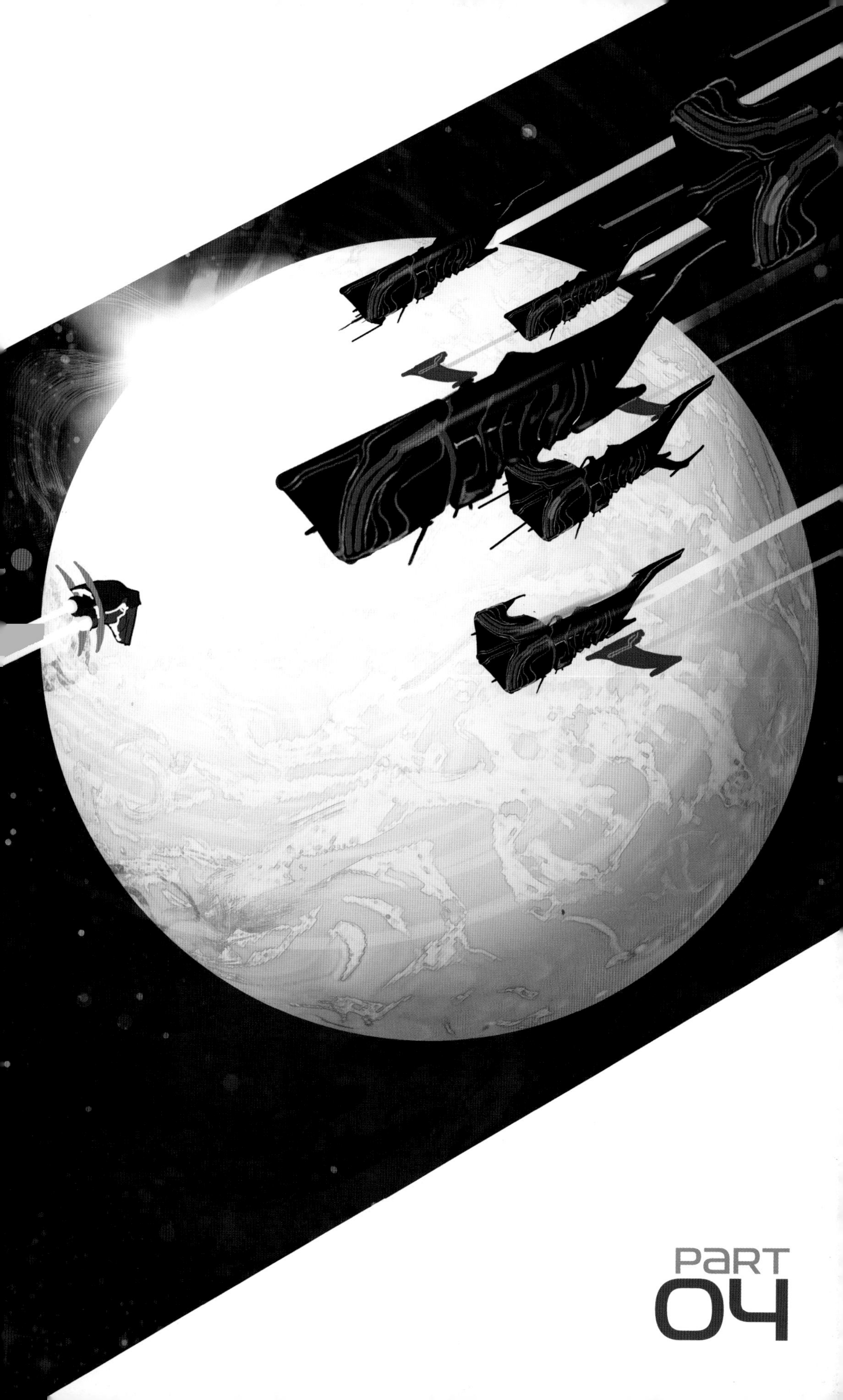

PART 04

"THE INVISIBLE KINGDOM IS AT HAND.

"IT CALLS TO YOU EVEN NOW, IN THE SPACES BETWEEN YOUR *BREATHS*.

"YOU WALK THE PATH WHETHER YOU SEE IT OR NOT...

UGH!

UNH!

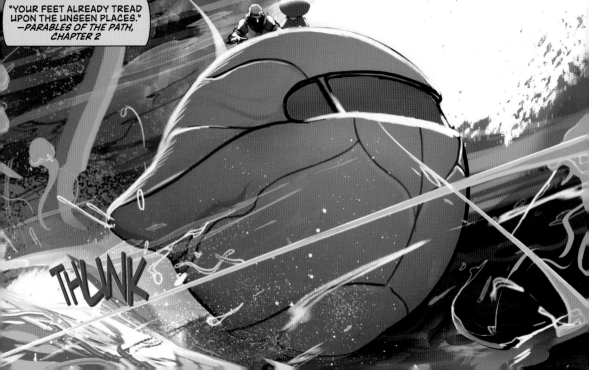

"YOUR FEET ALREADY TREAD UPON THE UNSEEN PLACES."
—*PARABLES OF THE PATH, CHAPTER 2*

THUNK

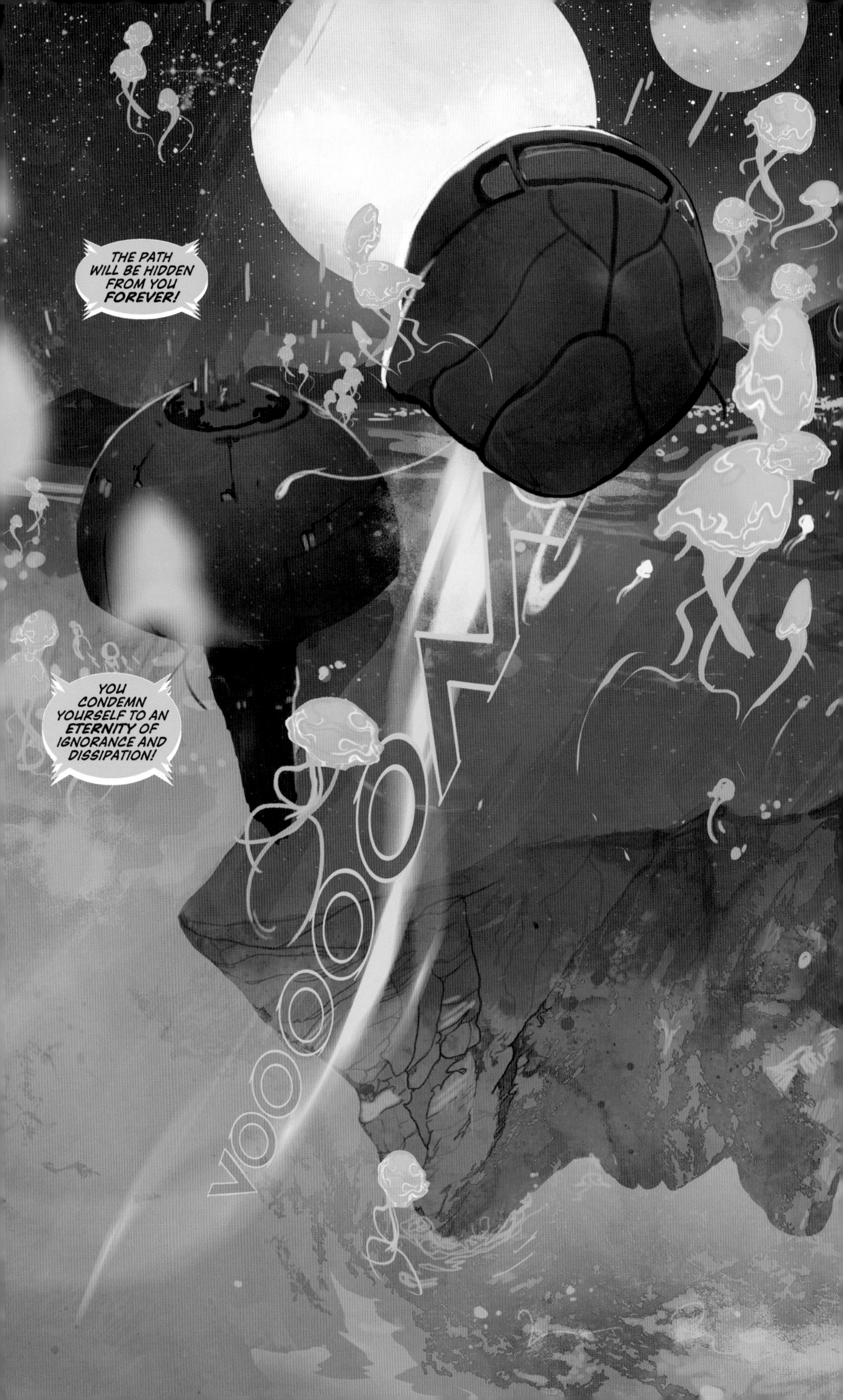
THE PATH WILL BE HIDDEN FROM YOU FOREVER!
YOU CONDEMN YOURSELF TO AN ETERNITY OF IGNORANCE AND DISSIPATION!
VOOOOOOM

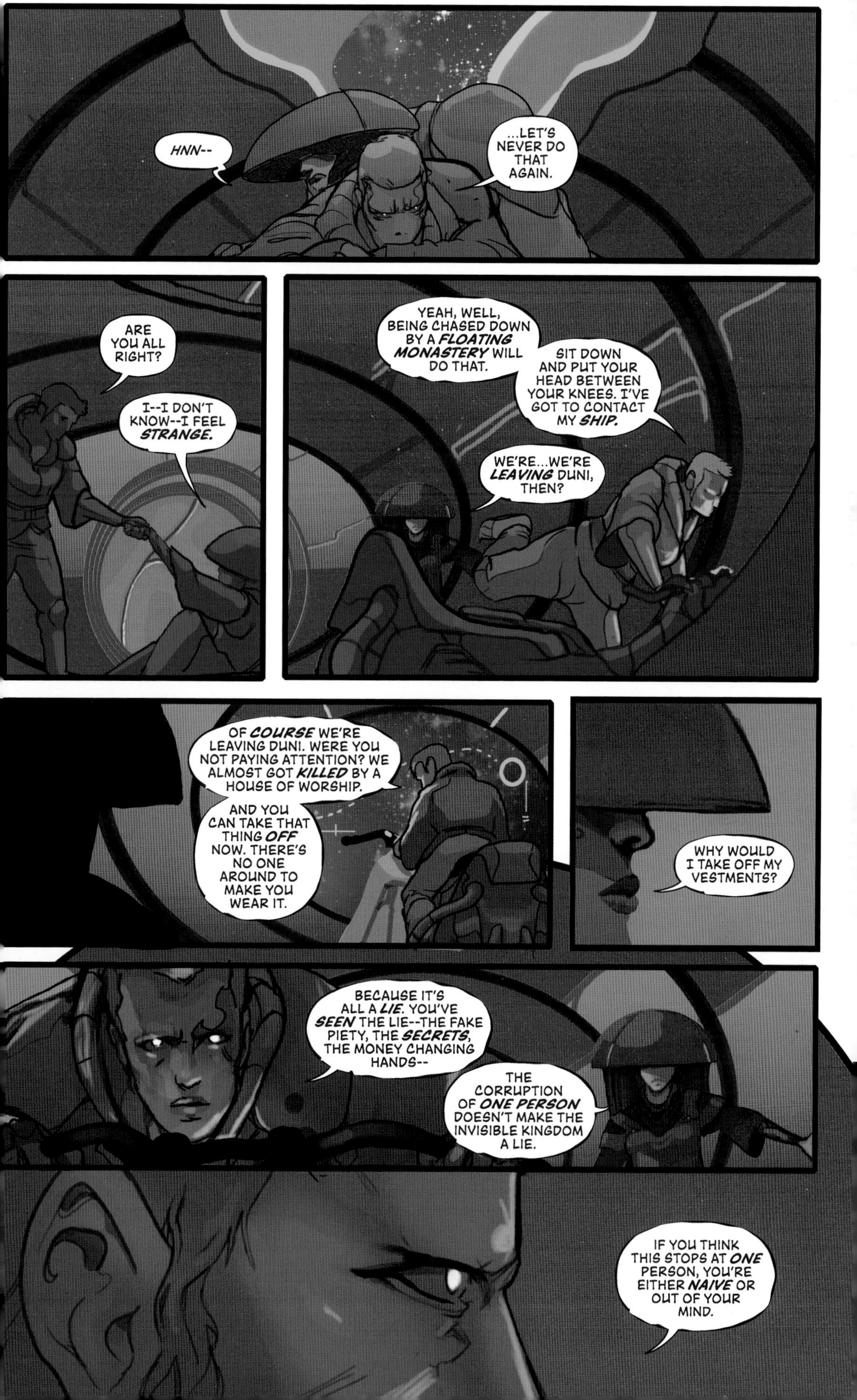
HNN--
...LET'S NEVER DO THAT AGAIN.
ARE YOU ALL RIGHT?
I--I DON'T KNOW--I FEEL STRANGE.
YEAH, WELL, BEING CHASED DOWN BY A FLOATING MONASTERY WILL DO THAT.
SIT DOWN AND PUT YOUR HEAD BETWEEN YOUR KNEES. I'VE GOT TO CONTACT MY SHIP.
WE'RE...WE'RE LEAVING DUNI, THEN?
OF COURSE WE'RE LEAVING DUNI. WERE YOU NOT PAYING ATTENTION? WE ALMOST GOT KILLED BY A HOUSE OF WORSHIP.
AND YOU CAN TAKE THAT THING OFF NOW. THERE'S NO ONE AROUND TO MAKE YOU WEAR IT.
WHY WOULD I TAKE OFF MY VESTMENTS?
BECAUSE IT'S ALL A LIE. YOU'VE SEEN THE LIE--THE FAKE PIETY, THE SECRETS, THE MONEY CHANGING HANDS--
THE CORRUPTION OF ONE PERSON DOESN'T MAKE THE INVISIBLE KINGDOM A LIE.
IF YOU THINK THIS STOPS AT ONE PERSON, YOU'RE EITHER NAIVE OR OUT OF YOUR MIND.

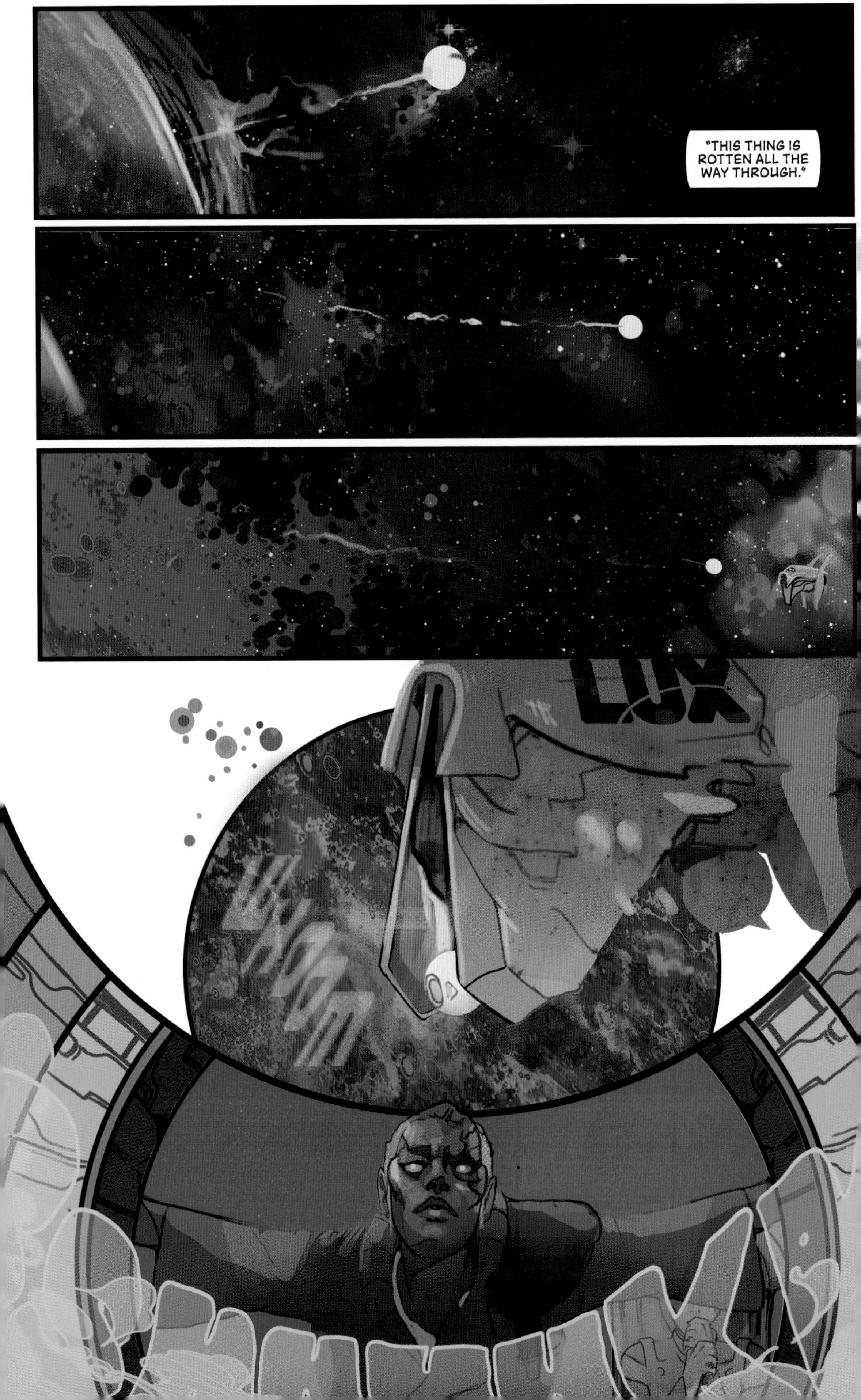
"THIS THING IS ROTTEN ALL THE WAY THROUGH."

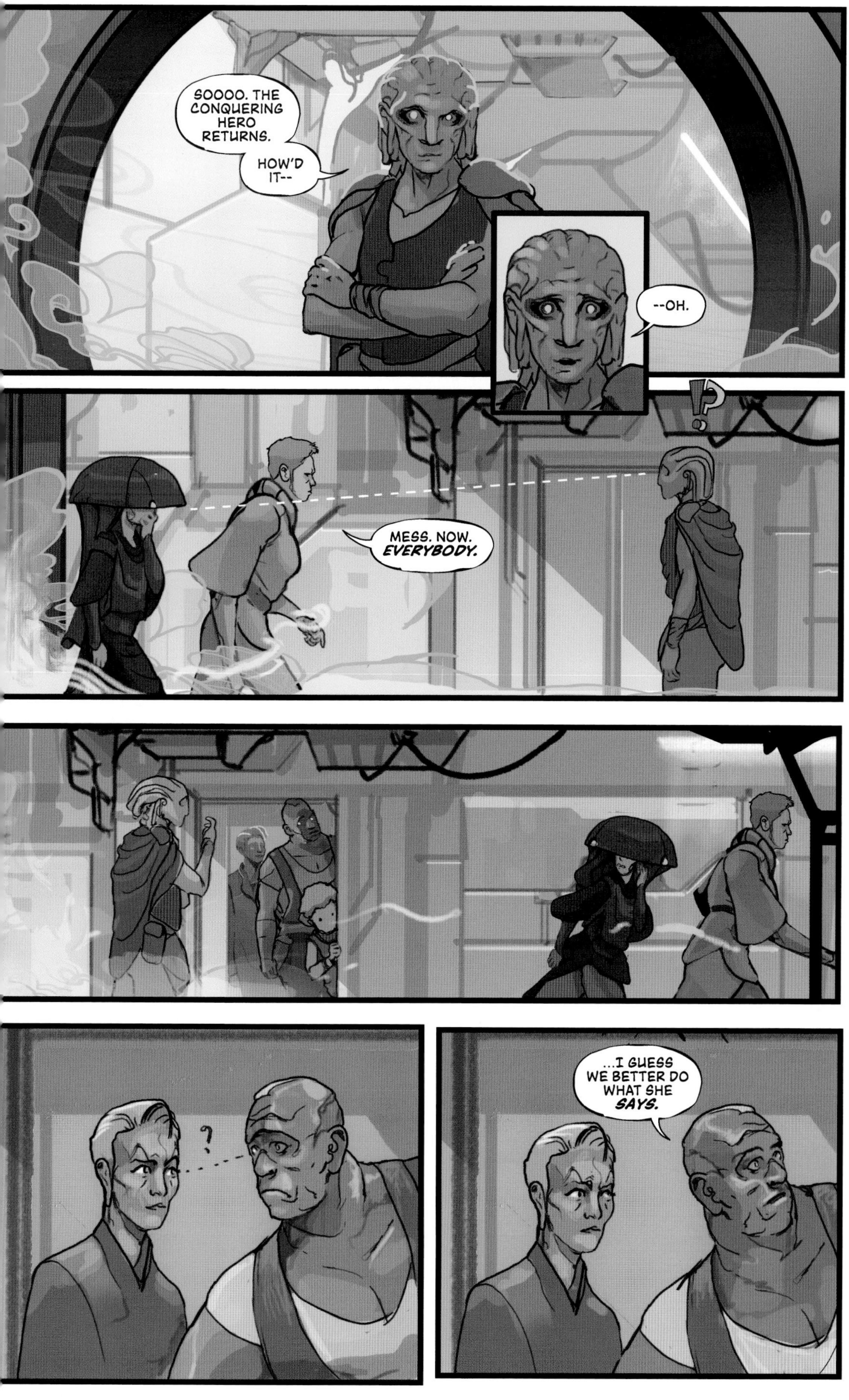
SOOOO. THE CONQUERING HERO RETURNS.
HOW'D IT--
--OH.
!?
MESS. NOW. *EVERYBODY.*
?
...I GUESS WE BETTER DO WHAT SHE *SAYS.*

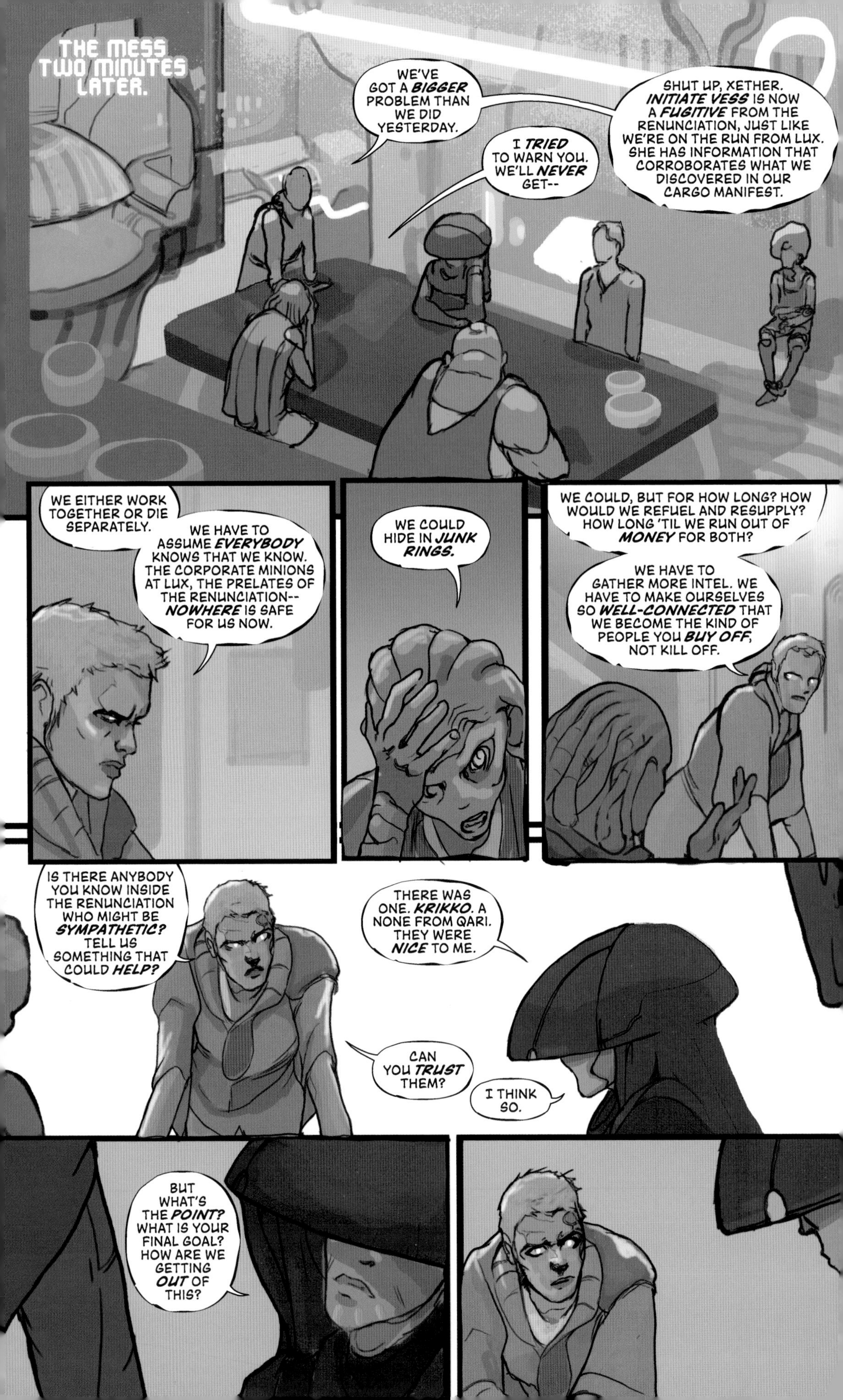
THE MESS TWO MINUTES LATER.
WE'VE GOT A BIGGER PROBLEM THAN WE DID YESTERDAY.
SHUT UP, XETHER. INITIATE VESS IS NOW A FUGITIVE FROM THE RENUNCIATION, JUST LIKE WE'RE ON THE RUN FROM LUX. SHE HAS INFORMATION THAT CORROBORATES WHAT WE DISCOVERED IN OUR CARGO MANIFEST.
I TRIED TO WARN YOU. WE'LL NEVER GET--
WE EITHER WORK TOGETHER OR DIE SEPARATELY.
WE HAVE TO ASSUME EVERYBODY KNOWS THAT WE KNOW. THE CORPORATE MINIONS AT LUX, THE PRELATES OF THE RENUNCIATION-- NOWHERE IS SAFE FOR US NOW.
WE COULD HIDE IN JUNK RINGS.
WE COULD, BUT FOR HOW LONG? HOW WOULD WE REFUEL AND RESUPPLY? HOW LONG 'TIL WE RUN OUT OF MONEY FOR BOTH?
WE HAVE TO GATHER MORE INTEL. WE HAVE TO MAKE OURSELVES SO WELL-CONNECTED THAT WE BECOME THE KIND OF PEOPLE YOU BUY OFF, NOT KILL OFF.
IS THERE ANYBODY YOU KNOW INSIDE THE RENUNCIATION WHO MIGHT BE SYMPATHETIC? TELL US SOMETHING THAT COULD HELP?
THERE WAS ONE. KRIKKO. A NONE FROM QARI. THEY WERE NICE TO ME.
CAN YOU TRUST THEM?
I THINK SO.
BUT WHAT'S THE POINT? WHAT IS YOUR FINAL GOAL? HOW ARE WE GETTING OUT OF THIS?

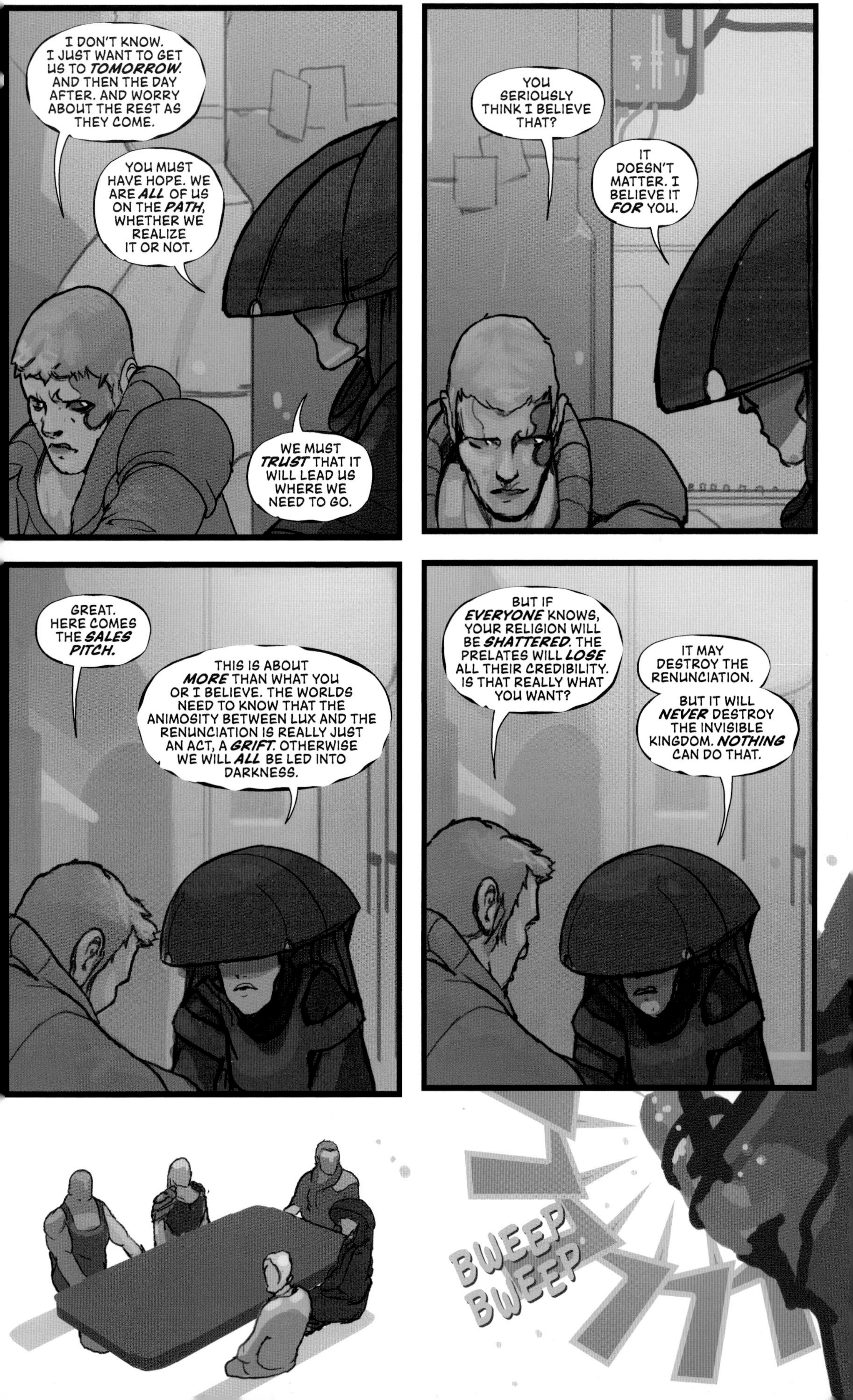

I DON'T KNOW. I JUST WANT TO GET US TO TOMORROW. AND THEN THE DAY AFTER. AND WORRY ABOUT THE REST AS THEY COME.
YOU MUST HAVE HOPE. WE ARE ALL OF US ON THE PATH, WHETHER WE REALIZE IT OR NOT.
WE MUST TRUST THAT IT WILL LEAD US WHERE WE NEED TO GO.
YOU SERIOUSLY THINK I BELIEVE THAT?
IT DOESN'T MATTER. I BELIEVE IT FOR YOU.
GREAT. HERE COMES THE SALES PITCH.
THIS IS ABOUT MORE THAN WHAT YOU OR I BELIEVE. THE WORLDS NEED TO KNOW THAT THE ANIMOSITY BETWEEN LUX AND THE RENUNCIATION IS REALLY JUST AN ACT, A GRIFT. OTHERWISE WE WILL ALL BE LED INTO DARKNESS.
BUT IF EVERYONE KNOWS, YOUR RELIGION WILL BE SHATTERED. THE PRELATES WILL LOSE ALL THEIR CREDIBILITY. IS THAT REALLY WHAT YOU WANT?
IT MAY DESTROY THE RENUNCIATION.
BUT IT WILL NEVER DESTROY THE INVISIBLE KINGDOM. NOTHING CAN DO THAT.
BWEEP BWEEP

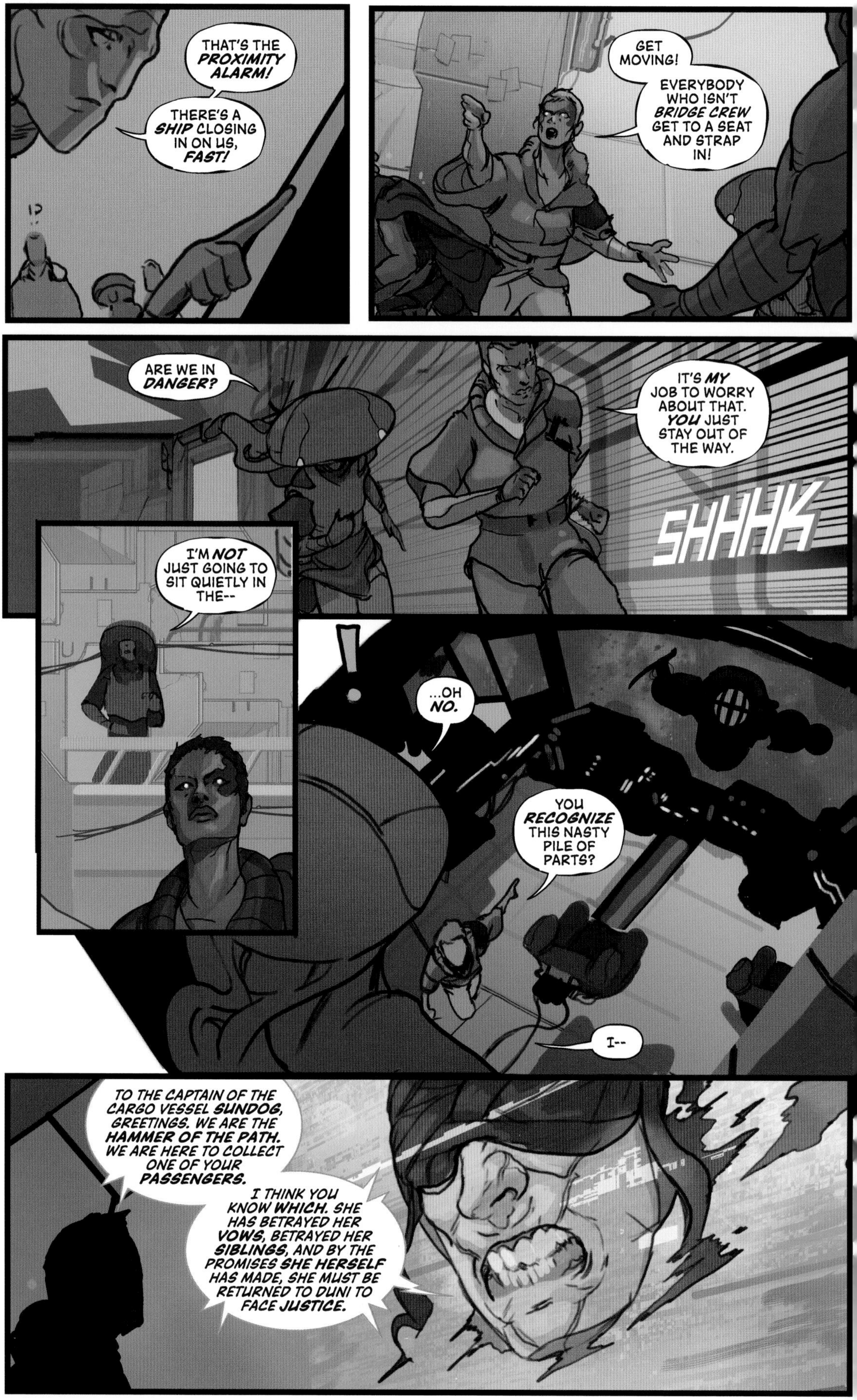
THAT'S THE PROXIMITY ALARM!
THERE'S A SHIP CLOSING IN ON US, FAST!
!?
GET MOVING!
EVERYBODY WHO ISN'T BRIDGE CREW GET TO A SEAT AND STRAP IN!
ARE WE IN DANGER?
IT'S MY JOB TO WORRY ABOUT THAT. YOU JUST STAY OUT OF THE WAY.
SHHHK
I'M NOT JUST GOING TO SIT QUIETLY IN THE--
!
...OH NO.
YOU RECOGNIZE THIS NASTY PILE OF PARTS?
I--
TO THE CAPTAIN OF THE CARGO VESSEL SUNDOG, GREETINGS. WE ARE THE HAMMER OF THE PATH. WE ARE HERE TO COLLECT ONE OF YOUR PASSENGERS.
I THINK YOU KNOW WHICH. SHE HAS BETRAYED HER VOWS, BETRAYED HER SIBLINGS, AND BY THE PROMISES SHE HERSELF HAS MADE, SHE MUST BE RETURNED TO DUNI TO FACE JUSTICE.

IT'S NOT MY PRACTICE TO HAND OVER PASSENGERS OF THIS SHIP TO *MILITANT GROUPS.*

IF SHE'S COMMITTED A *CRIME,* COME BACK HERE WITH AN *ARREST DECREE* FROM THE GOVERNMENT OF DUNI. *THEN* WE'LL TALK.

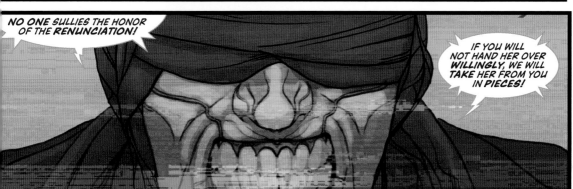

NO ONE SULLIES THE HONOR OF THE *RENUNCIATION!*

IF YOU WILL NOT HAND HER OVER WILLINGLY, WE WILL *TAKE HER FROM YOU IN PIECES!*

EVERYBODY HOLD ON TO SOMETHING THAT'S *BOLTED DOWN.*

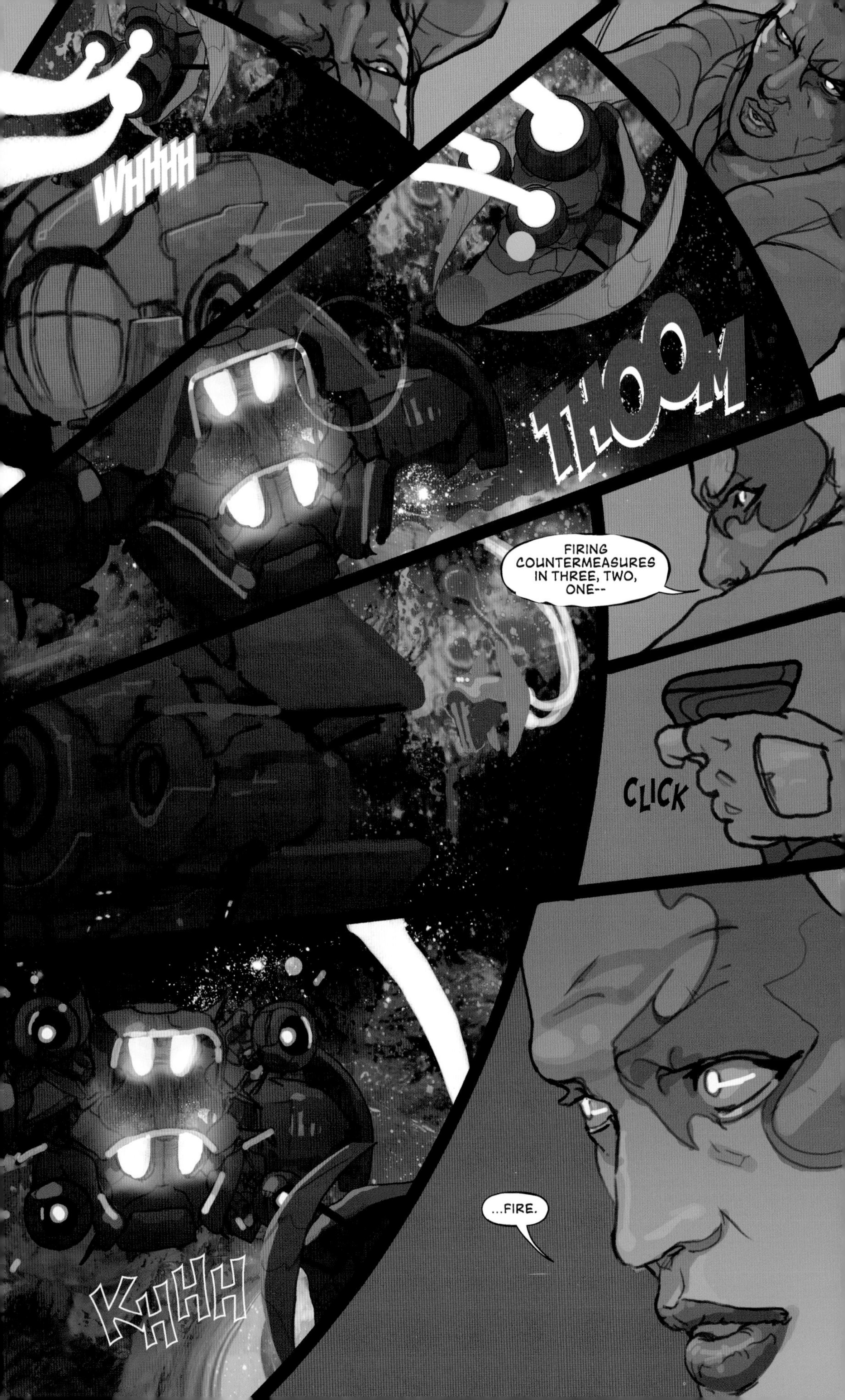
WHHHH
THOOM
FIRING COUNTERMEASURES IN THREE, TWO, ONE--
CLICK
...FIRE.
KHHH

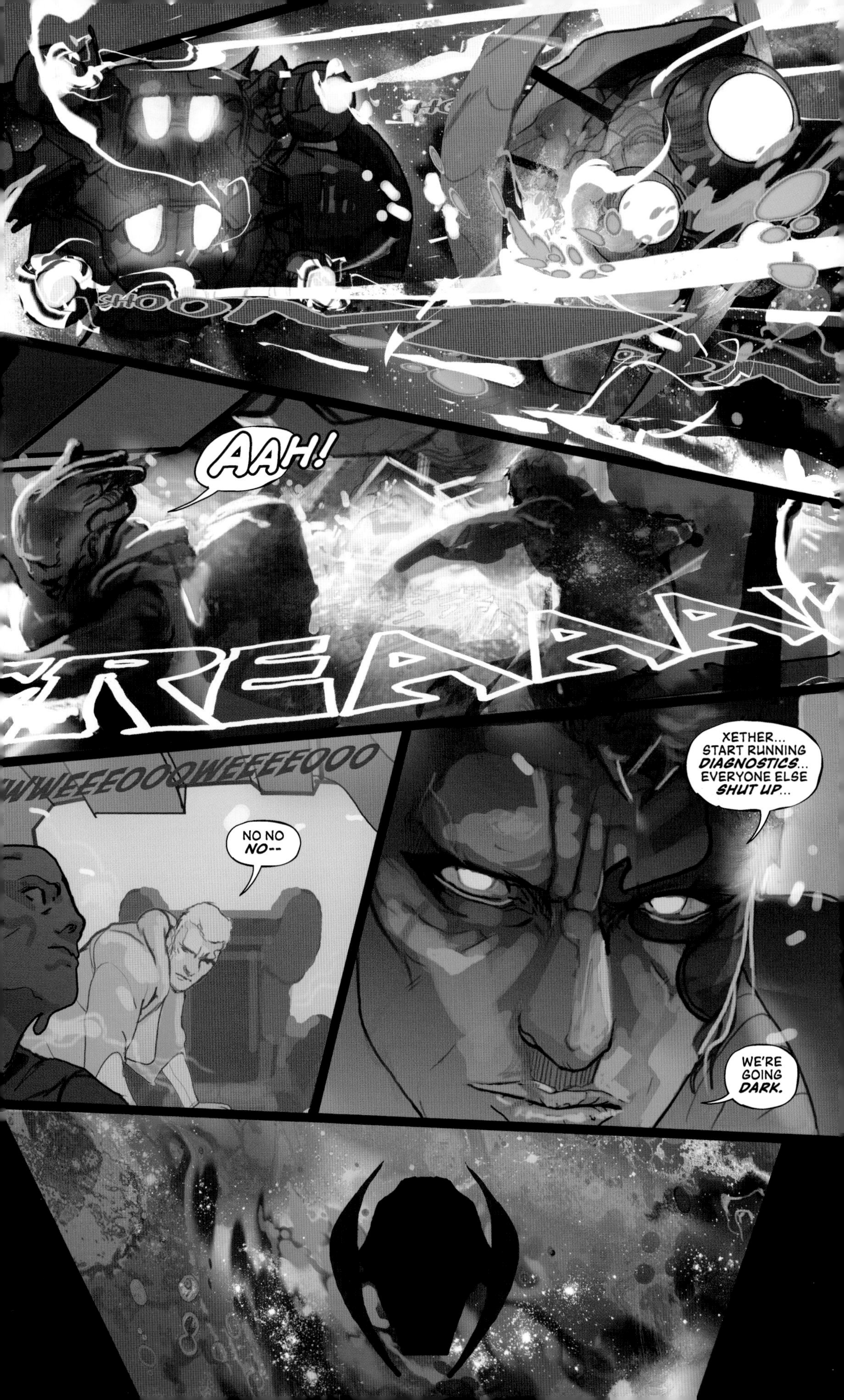
AAH!
WWEEEOOOWEEEEOOO
NO NO NO--
XETHER... START RUNNING DIAGNOSTICS... EVERYONE ELSE SHUT UP...
WE'RE GOING DARK.

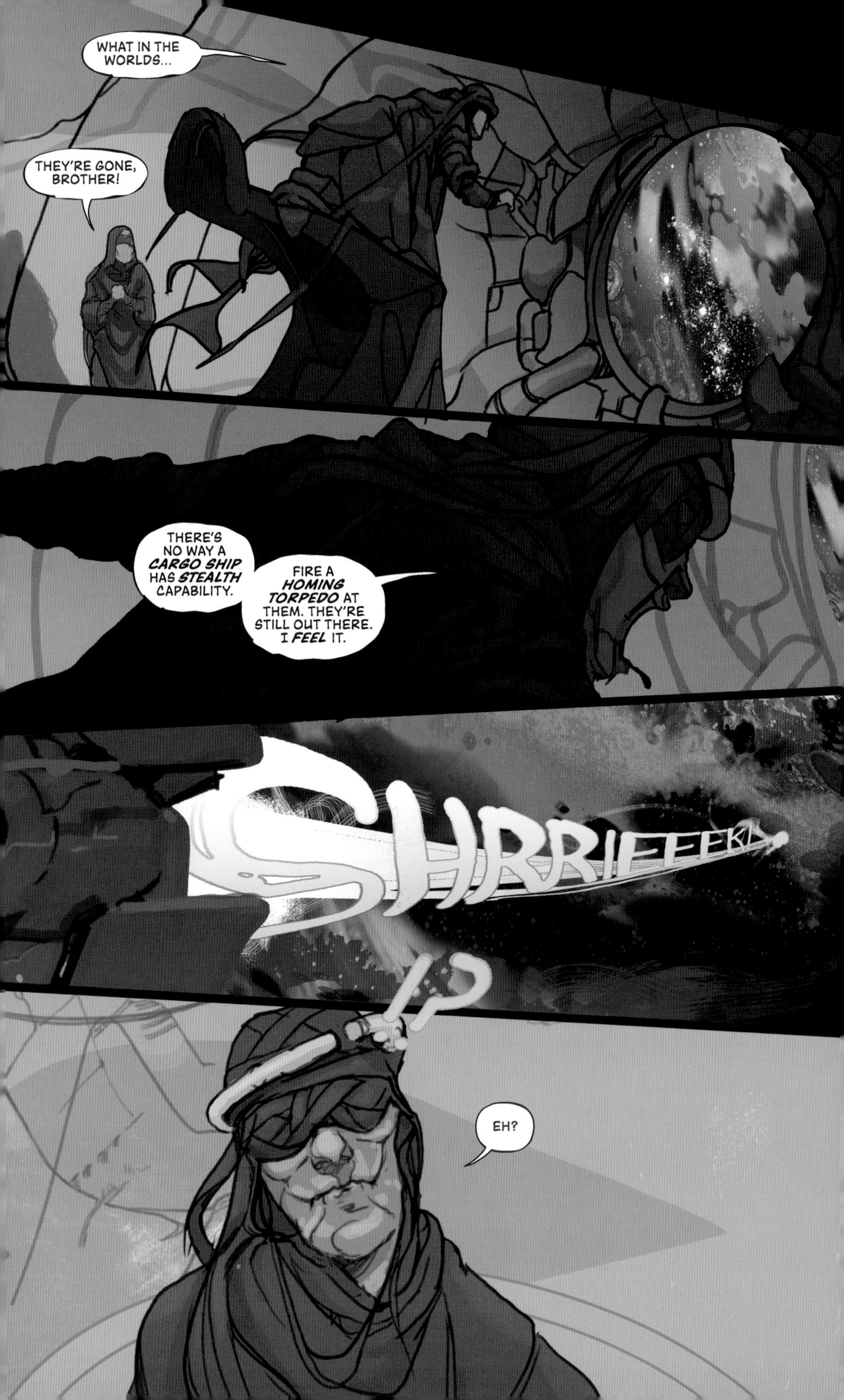
WHAT IN THE WORLDS...
THEY'RE GONE, BROTHER!
THERE'S NO WAY A CARGO SHIP HAS STEALTH CAPABILITY.
FIRE A HOMING TORPEDO AT THEM. THEY'RE STILL OUT THERE. I FEEL IT.
SHRRIEEEK!
!?
EH?

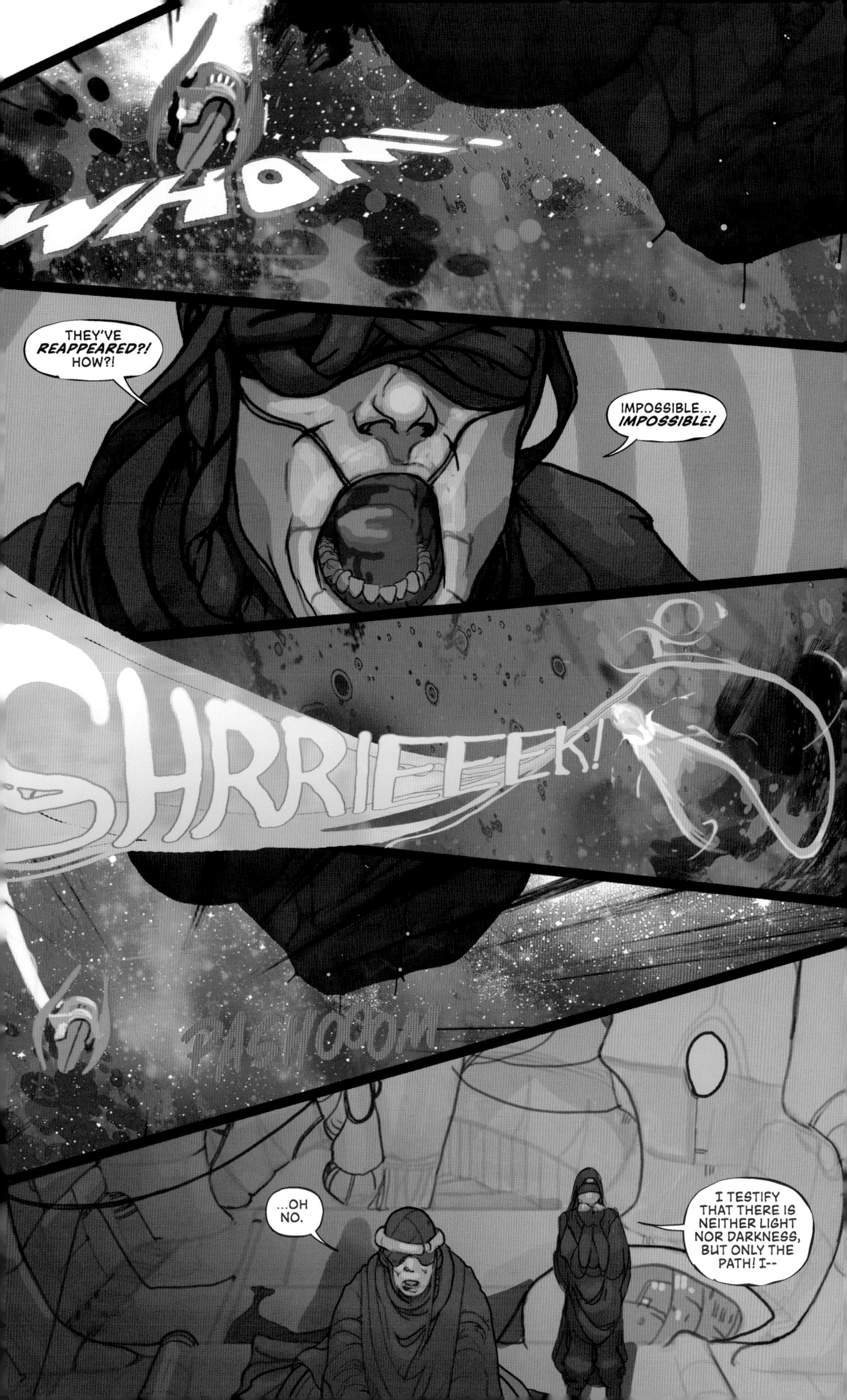
WHOM--
THEY'VE *REAPPEARED?!* HOW?!
IMPOSSIBLE... *IMPOSSIBLE!*
SHRRIEEEK!
...OH NO.
I TESTIFY THAT THERE IS NEITHER LIGHT NOR DARKNESS, BUT ONLY THE PATH! I--

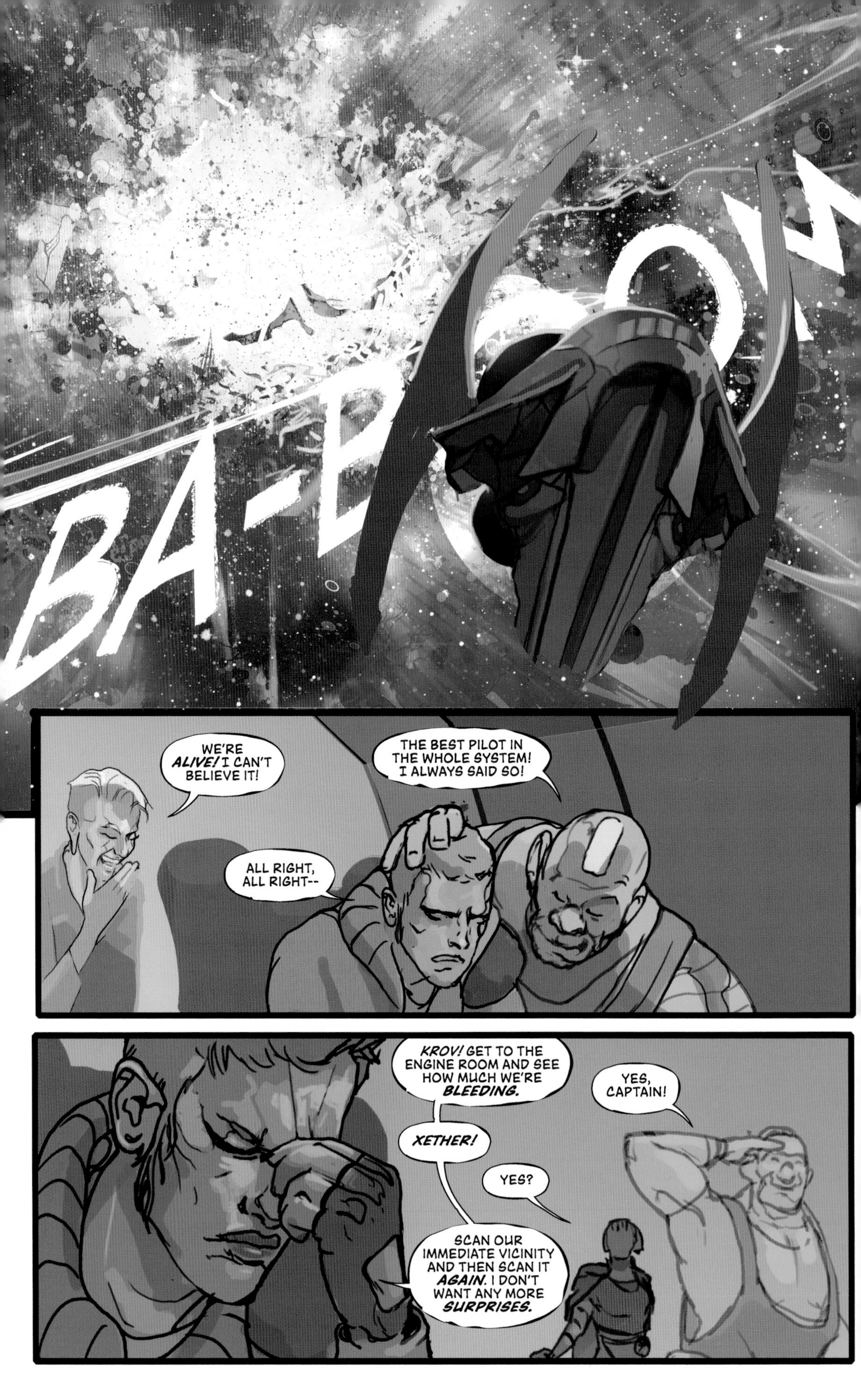
BA-B
WE'RE *ALIVE!* I CAN'T BELIEVE IT!
THE BEST PILOT IN THE WHOLE SYSTEM! I ALWAYS SAID SO!
ALL RIGHT, ALL RIGHT--
KROV! GET TO THE ENGINE ROOM AND SEE HOW MUCH WE'RE *BLEEDING.*
YES, CAPTAIN!
XETHER!
YES?
SCAN OUR IMMEDIATE VICINITY AND THEN SCAN IT *AGAIN.* I DON'T WANT ANY MORE *SURPRISES.*

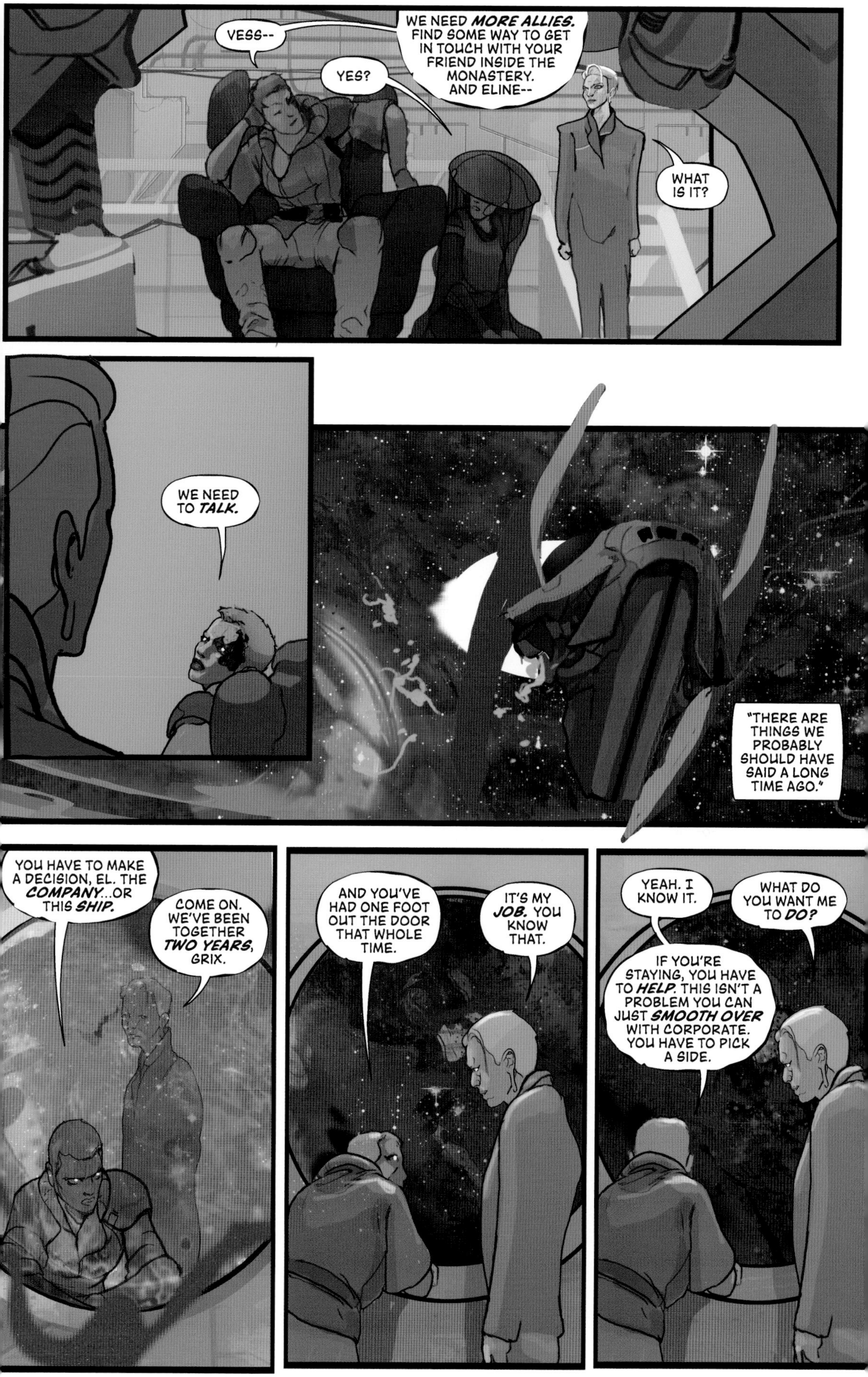
VESS--
WE NEED MORE ALLIES. FIND SOME WAY TO GET IN TOUCH WITH YOUR FRIEND INSIDE THE MONASTERY. AND ELINE--
YES?
WHAT IS IT?
WE NEED TO TALK.
"THERE ARE THINGS WE PROBABLY SHOULD HAVE SAID A LONG TIME AGO."
YOU HAVE TO MAKE A DECISION, EL. THE COMPANY...OR THIS SHIP.
COME ON. WE'VE BEEN TOGETHER TWO YEARS, GRIX.
AND YOU'VE HAD ONE FOOT OUT THE DOOR THAT WHOLE TIME.
IT'S MY JOB. YOU KNOW THAT.
YEAH. I KNOW IT.
WHAT DO YOU WANT ME TO DO?
IF YOU'RE STAYING, YOU HAVE TO HELP. THIS ISN'T A PROBLEM YOU CAN JUST SMOOTH OVER WITH CORPORATE. YOU HAVE TO PICK A SIDE.

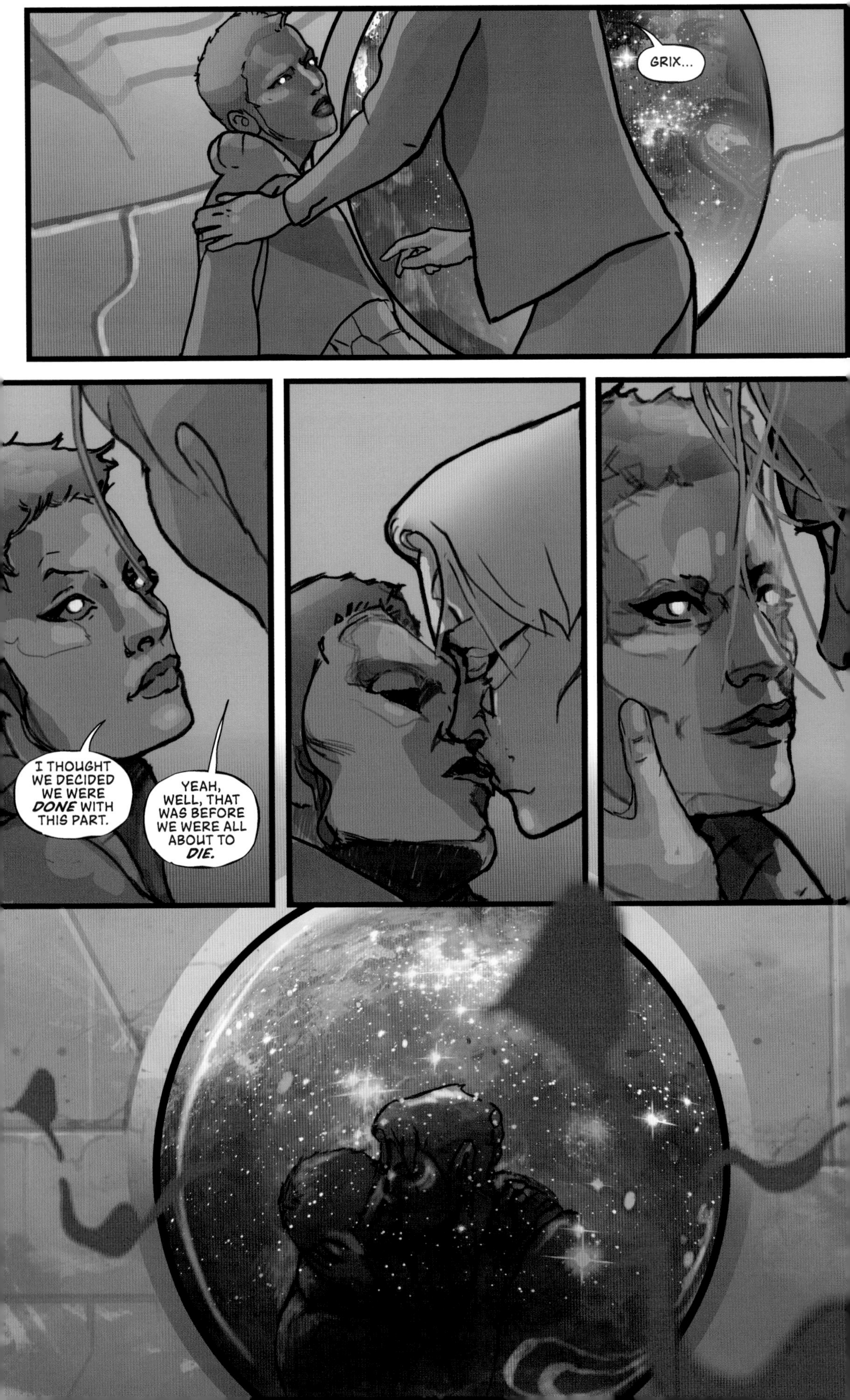
GRIX...
I THOUGHT WE DECIDED WE WERE *DONE* WITH THIS PART.
YEAH, WELL, THAT WAS BEFORE WE WERE ALL ABOUT TO *DIE.*

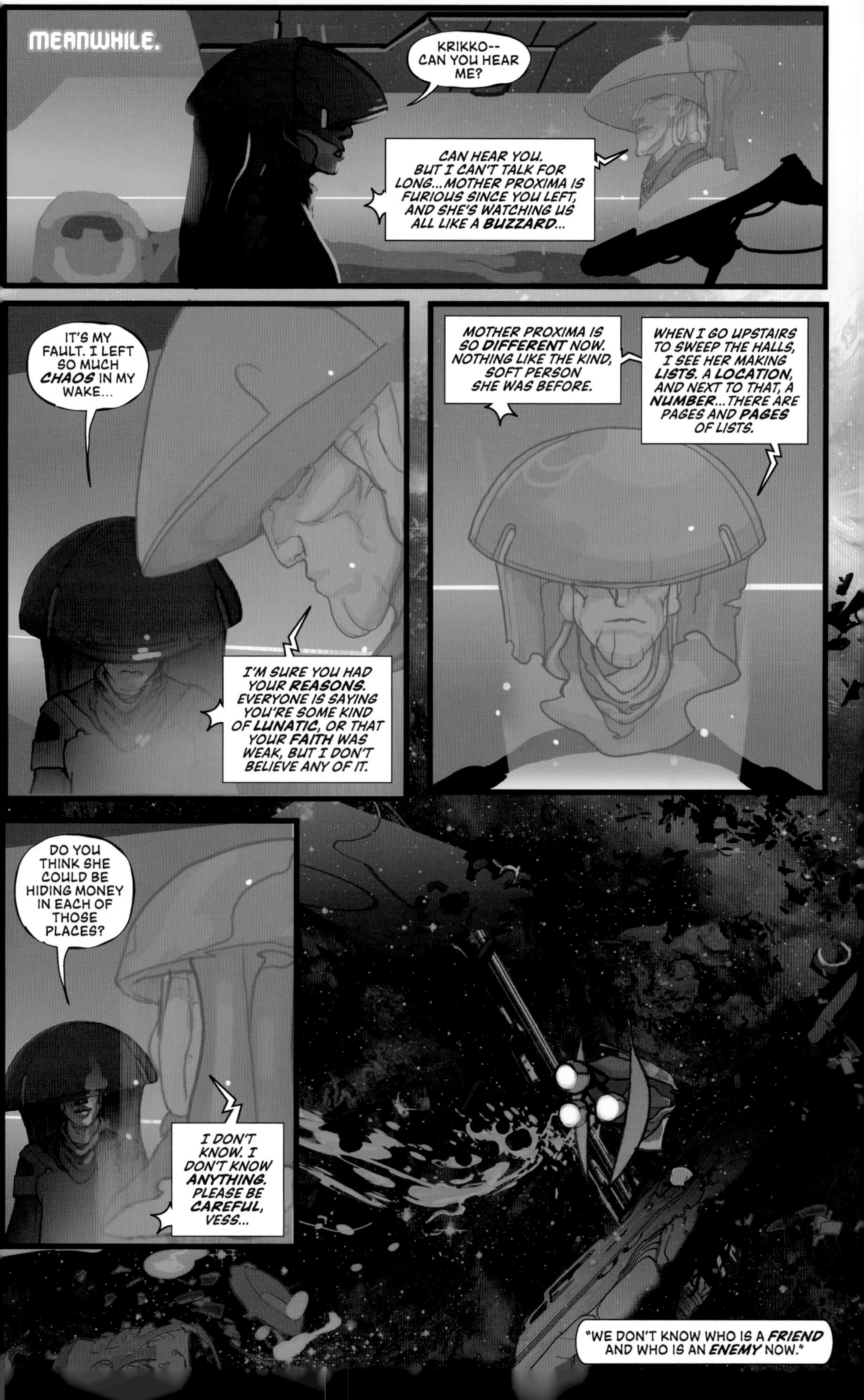
MEANWHILE.
KRIKKO-- CAN YOU HEAR ME?
CAN HEAR YOU. BUT I CAN'T TALK FOR LONG...MOTHER PROXIMA IS FURIOUS SINCE YOU LEFT, AND SHE'S WATCHING US ALL LIKE A BUZZARD...
IT'S MY FAULT. I LEFT SO MUCH CHAOS IN MY WAKE...
I'M SURE YOU HAD YOUR REASONS. EVERYONE IS SAYING YOU'RE SOME KIND OF LUNATIC, OR THAT YOUR FAITH WAS WEAK, BUT I DON'T BELIEVE ANY OF IT.
MOTHER PROXIMA IS SO DIFFERENT NOW. NOTHING LIKE THE KIND, SOFT PERSON SHE WAS BEFORE.
WHEN I GO UPSTAIRS TO SWEEP THE HALLS, I SEE HER MAKING LISTS. A LOCATION, AND NEXT TO THAT, A NUMBER...THERE ARE PAGES AND PAGES OF LISTS.
DO YOU THINK SHE COULD BE HIDING MONEY IN EACH OF THOSE PLACES?
I DON'T KNOW. I DON'T KNOW ANYTHING. PLEASE BE CAREFUL, VESS...
"WE DON'T KNOW WHO IS A FRIEND AND WHO IS AN ENEMY NOW."

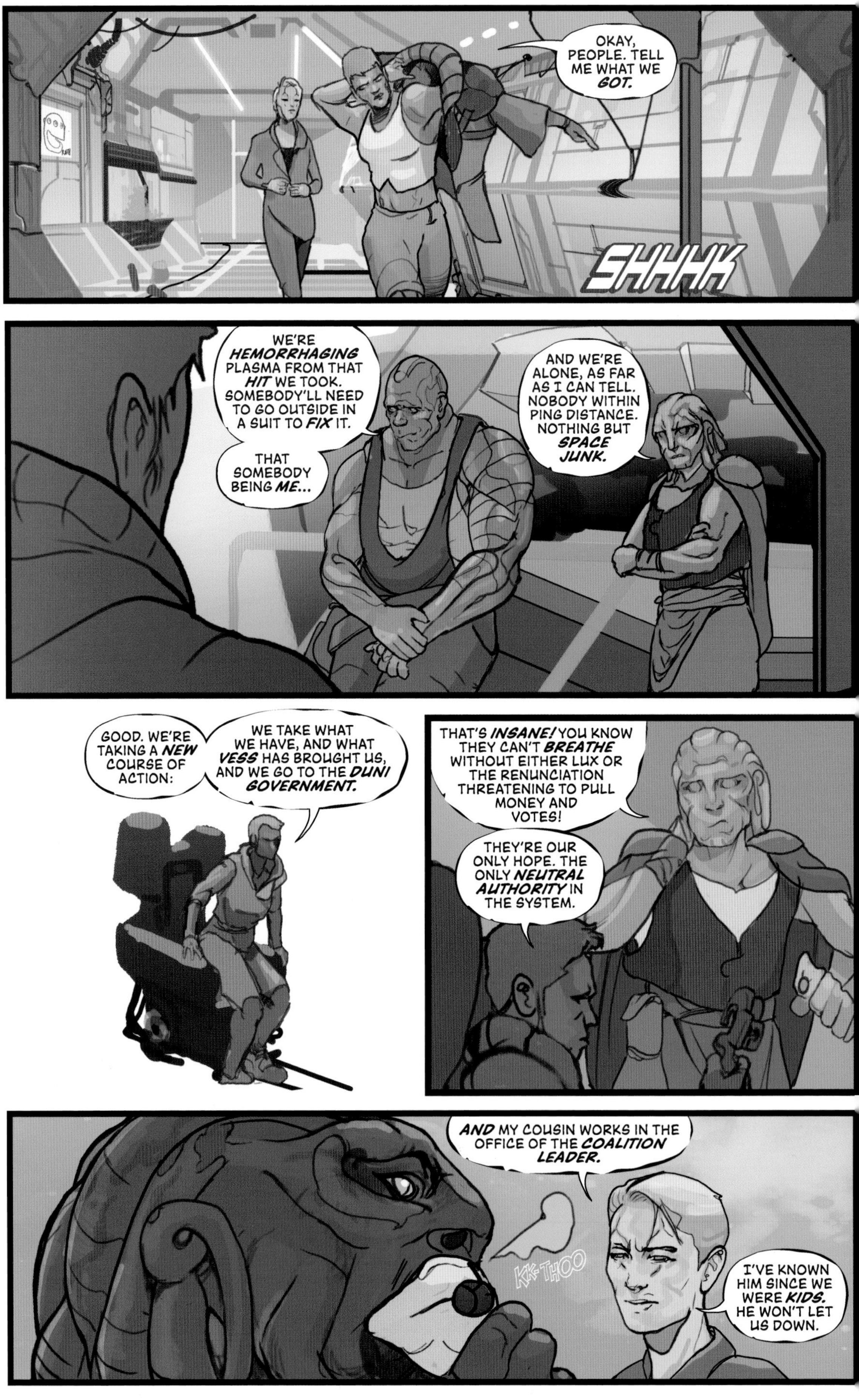

OKAY, PEOPLE. TELL ME WHAT WE *GOT.*
SHHHK
WE'RE *HEMORRHAGING* PLASMA FROM THAT *HIT* WE TOOK. SOMEBODY'LL NEED TO GO OUTSIDE IN A SUIT TO *FIX* IT.
THAT SOMEBODY BEING *ME...*
AND WE'RE ALONE, AS FAR AS I CAN TELL. NOBODY WITHIN PING DISTANCE. NOTHING BUT *SPACE JUNK.*
GOOD. WE'RE TAKING A *NEW* COURSE OF ACTION:
WE TAKE WHAT WE HAVE, AND WHAT *VESS* HAS BROUGHT US, AND WE GO TO THE *DUNI GOVERNMENT.*
THAT'S *INSANE!* YOU KNOW THEY CAN'T *BREATHE* WITHOUT EITHER LUX OR THE RENUNCIATION THREATENING TO PULL MONEY AND VOTES!
THEY'RE OUR ONLY HOPE. THE ONLY *NEUTRAL AUTHORITY* IN THE SYSTEM.
AND MY COUSIN WORKS IN THE OFFICE OF THE *COALITION LEADER.*
KK-THOO
I'VE KNOWN HIM SINCE WE WERE *KIDS.* HE WON'T LET US DOWN.

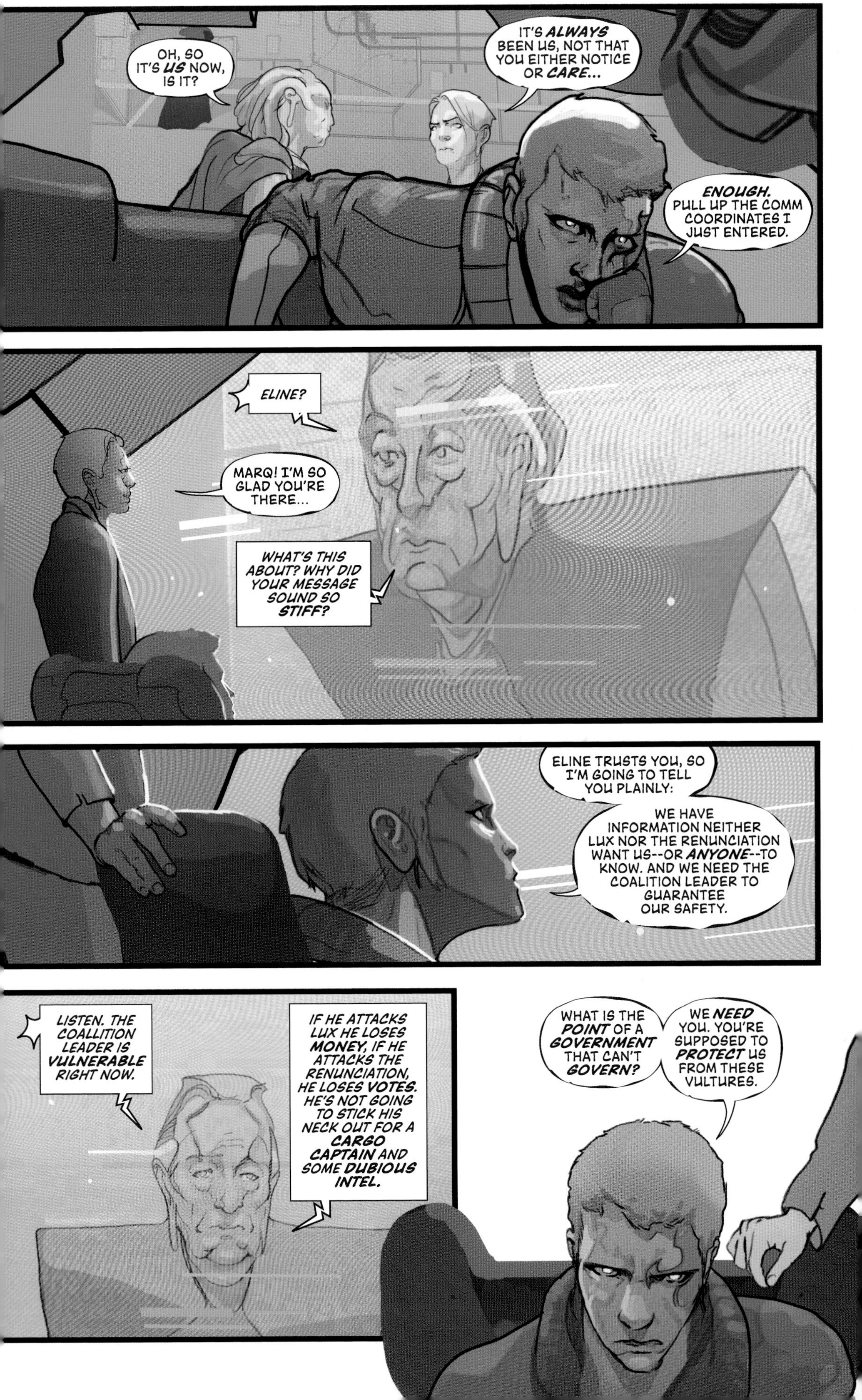
OH, SO IT'S US NOW, IS IT?
IT'S ALWAYS BEEN US, NOT THAT YOU EITHER NOTICE OR CARE...
ENOUGH. PULL UP THE COMM COORDINATES I JUST ENTERED.
ELINE?
MARQ! I'M SO GLAD YOU'RE THERE...
WHAT'S THIS ABOUT? WHY DID YOUR MESSAGE SOUND SO STIFF?
ELINE TRUSTS YOU, SO I'M GOING TO TELL YOU PLAINLY:
WE HAVE INFORMATION NEITHER LUX NOR THE RENUNCIATION WANT US--OR ANYONE--TO KNOW. AND WE NEED THE COALITION LEADER TO GUARANTEE OUR SAFETY.
LISTEN. THE COALLITION LEADER IS VULNERABLE RIGHT NOW.
IF HE ATTACKS LUX HE LOSES MONEY, IF HE ATTACKS THE RENUNCIATION, HE LOSES VOTES. HE'S NOT GOING TO STICK HIS NECK OUT FOR A CARGO CAPTAIN AND SOME DUBIOUS INTEL.
WHAT IS THE POINT OF A GOVERNMENT THAT CAN'T GOVERN?
WE NEED YOU. YOU'RE SUPPOSED TO PROTECT US FROM THESE VULTURES.

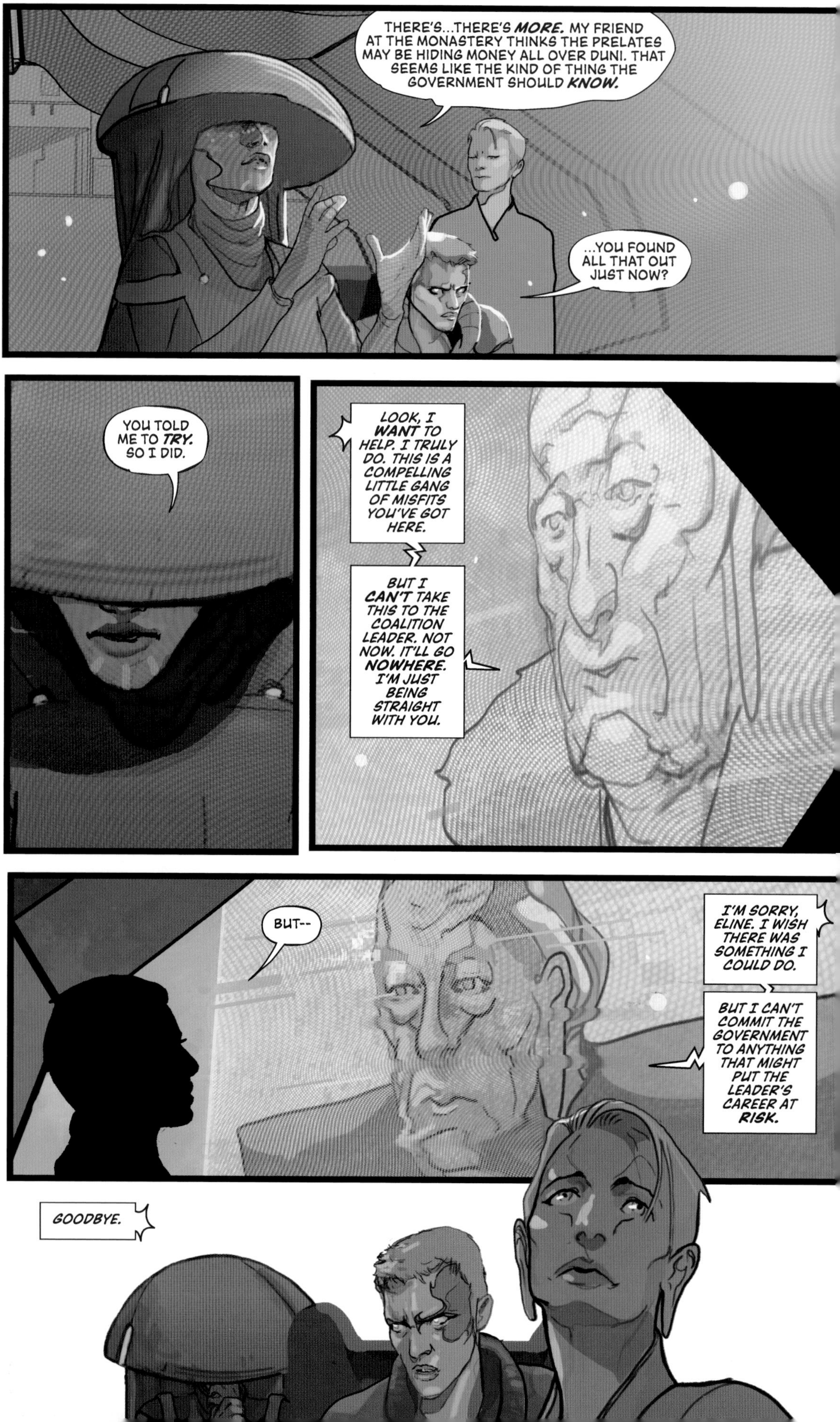
THERE'S...THERE'S MORE. MY FRIEND AT THE MONASTERY THINKS THE PRELATES MAY BE HIDING MONEY ALL OVER DUNI. THAT SEEMS LIKE THE KIND OF THING THE GOVERNMENT SHOULD KNOW.
...YOU FOUND ALL THAT OUT JUST NOW?
YOU TOLD ME TO TRY. SO I DID.
LOOK, I WANT TO HELP. I TRULY DO. THIS IS A COMPELLING LITTLE GANG OF MISFITS YOU'VE GOT HERE.
BUT I CAN'T TAKE THIS TO THE COALITION LEADER. NOT NOW. IT'LL GO NOWHERE. I'M JUST BEING STRAIGHT WITH YOU.
BUT--
I'M SORRY, ELINE. I WISH THERE WAS SOMETHING I COULD DO.
BUT I CAN'T COMMIT THE GOVERNMENT TO ANYTHING THAT MIGHT PUT THE LEADER'S CAREER AT RISK.
GOODBYE.

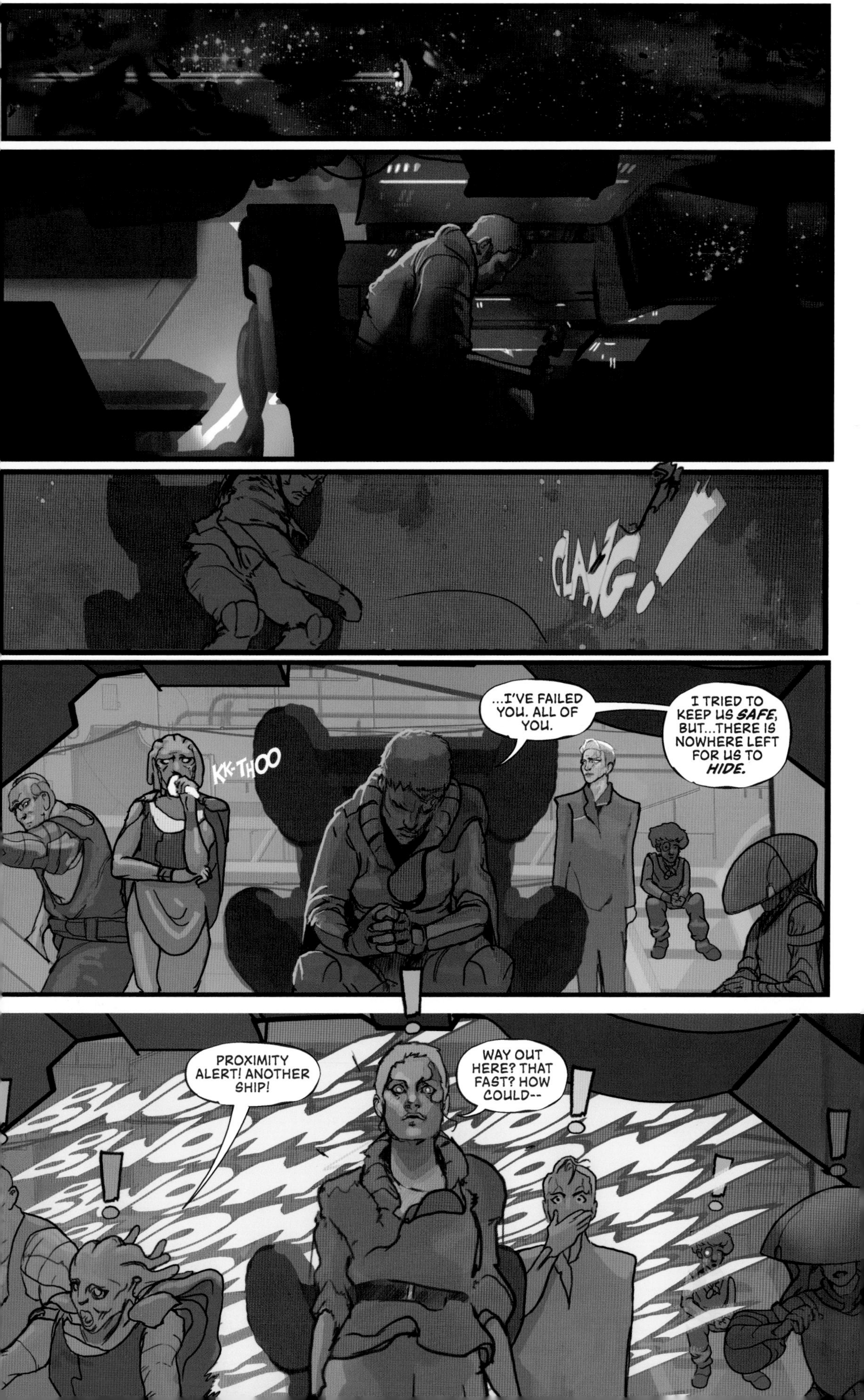
CLANG!
KK-THOO
...I'VE FAILED YOU. ALL OF YOU.
I TRIED TO KEEP US SAFE, BUT...THERE IS NOWHERE LEFT FOR US TO HIDE.
PROXIMITY ALERT! ANOTHER SHIP!
WAY OUT HERE? THAT FAST? HOW COULD--

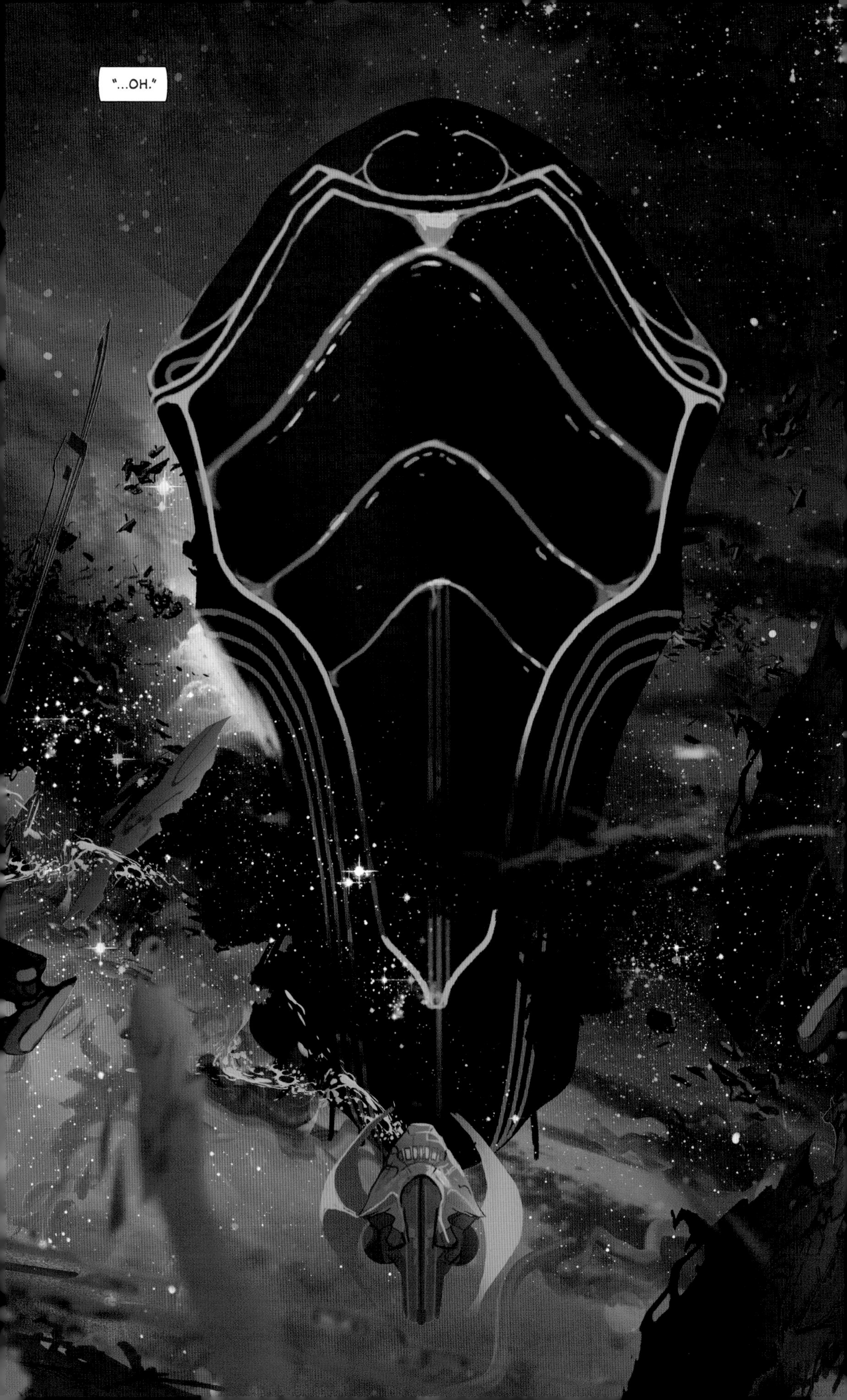
"...OH."

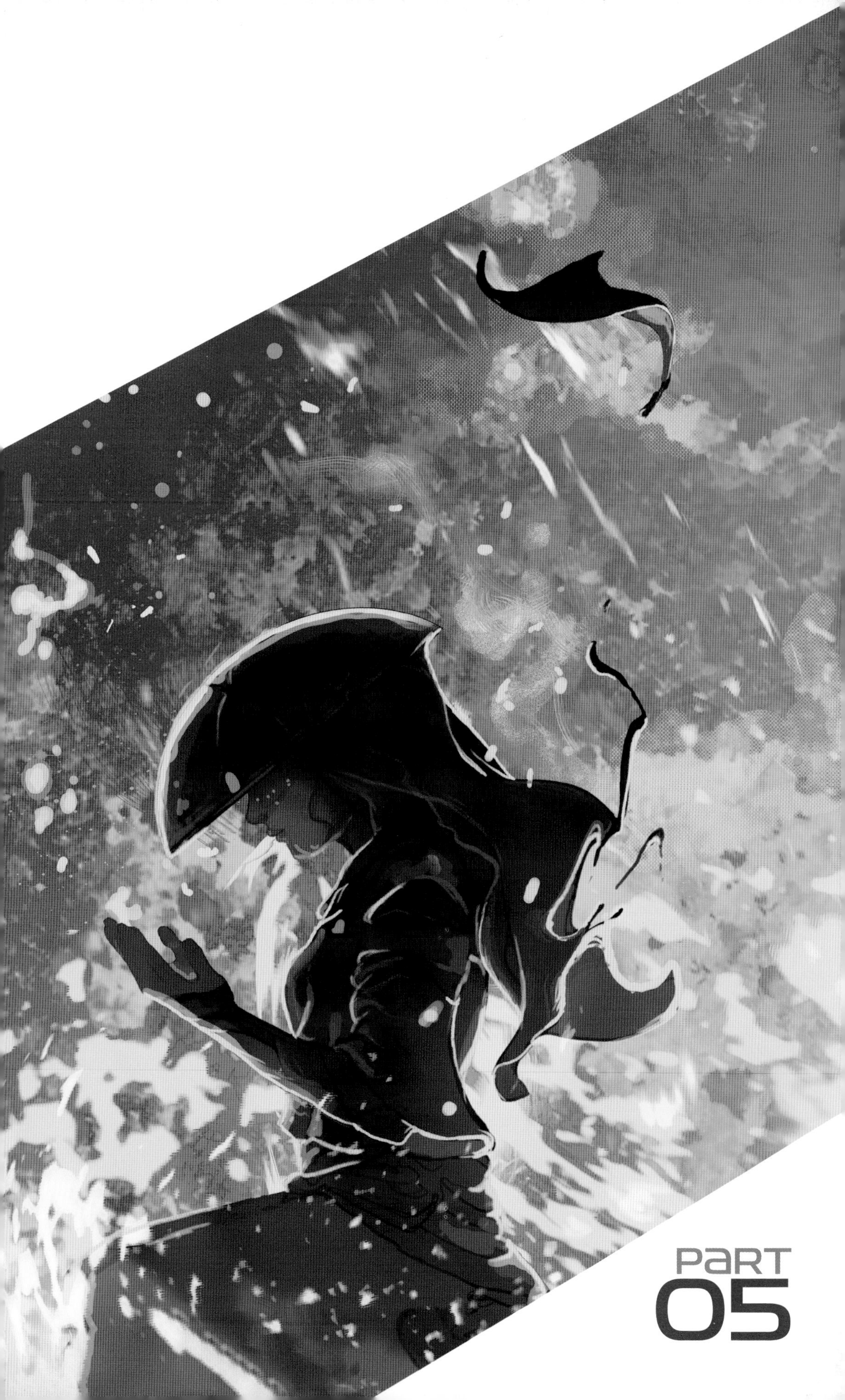

PART 05

JCPL

JESSAMINE COUNTY
PUBLIC LIBRARY

(859) 885-3523

Customer ID: ...6826

Items that you checked out

Title:
Invisible kingdom. Volume 1, Walking the path
ID 32530609969262
Due: Thursday, January 16, 2020

Title:
She could fly. Volume two, The lost pilot
ID 32530609972753
Due: Thursday, January 16, 2020

Total items: 2
Account balance: $6.90
12/26/2019 4:34 PM
Checked out: 26
Ready for pickup: 0

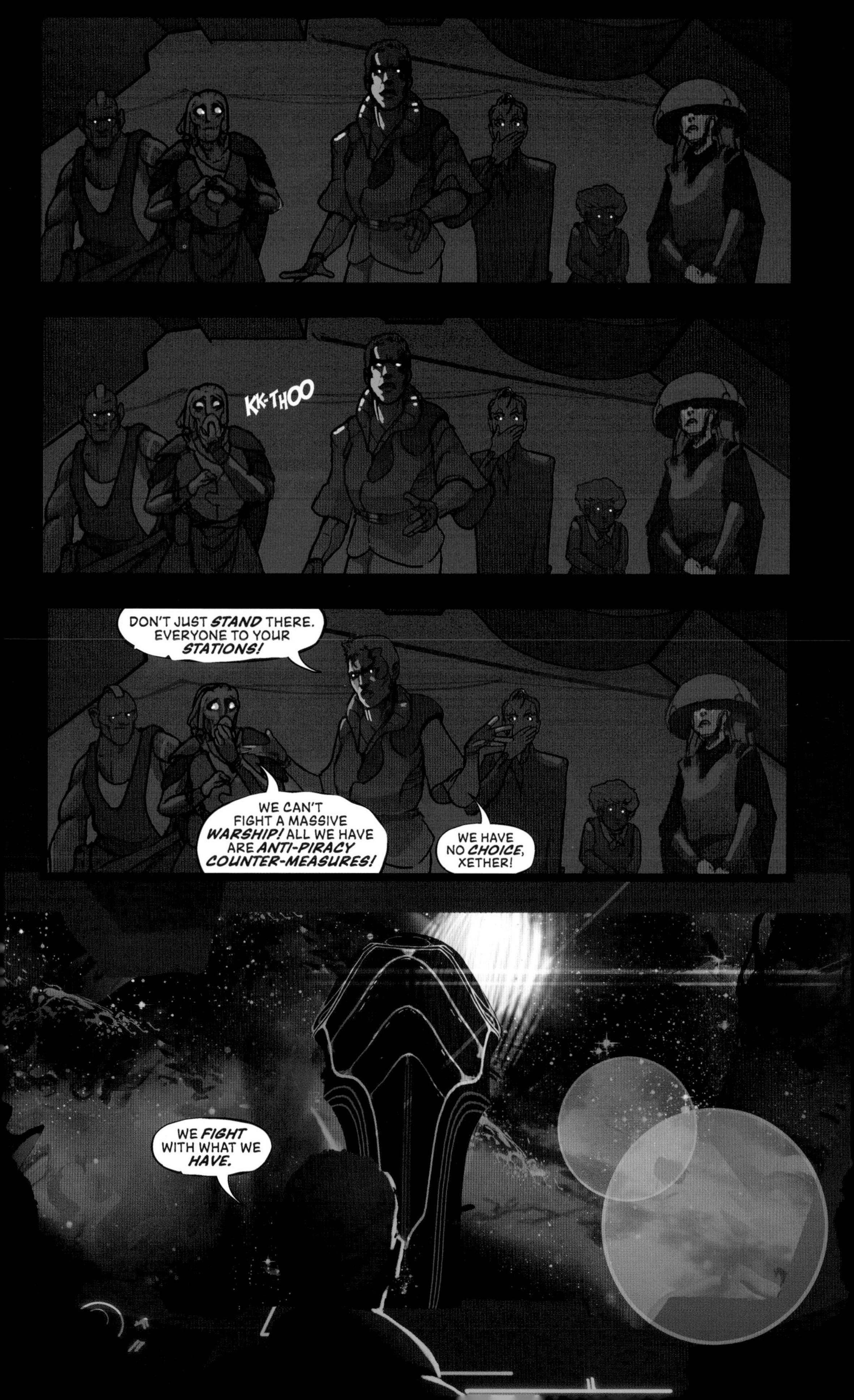
KK-THOO
DON'T JUST STAND THERE. EVERYONE TO YOUR STATIONS!
WE CAN'T FIGHT A MASSIVE WARSHIP! ALL WE HAVE ARE ANTI-PIRACY COUNTER-MEASURES!
WE HAVE NO CHOICE, XETHER!
WE FIGHT WITH WHAT WE HAVE.

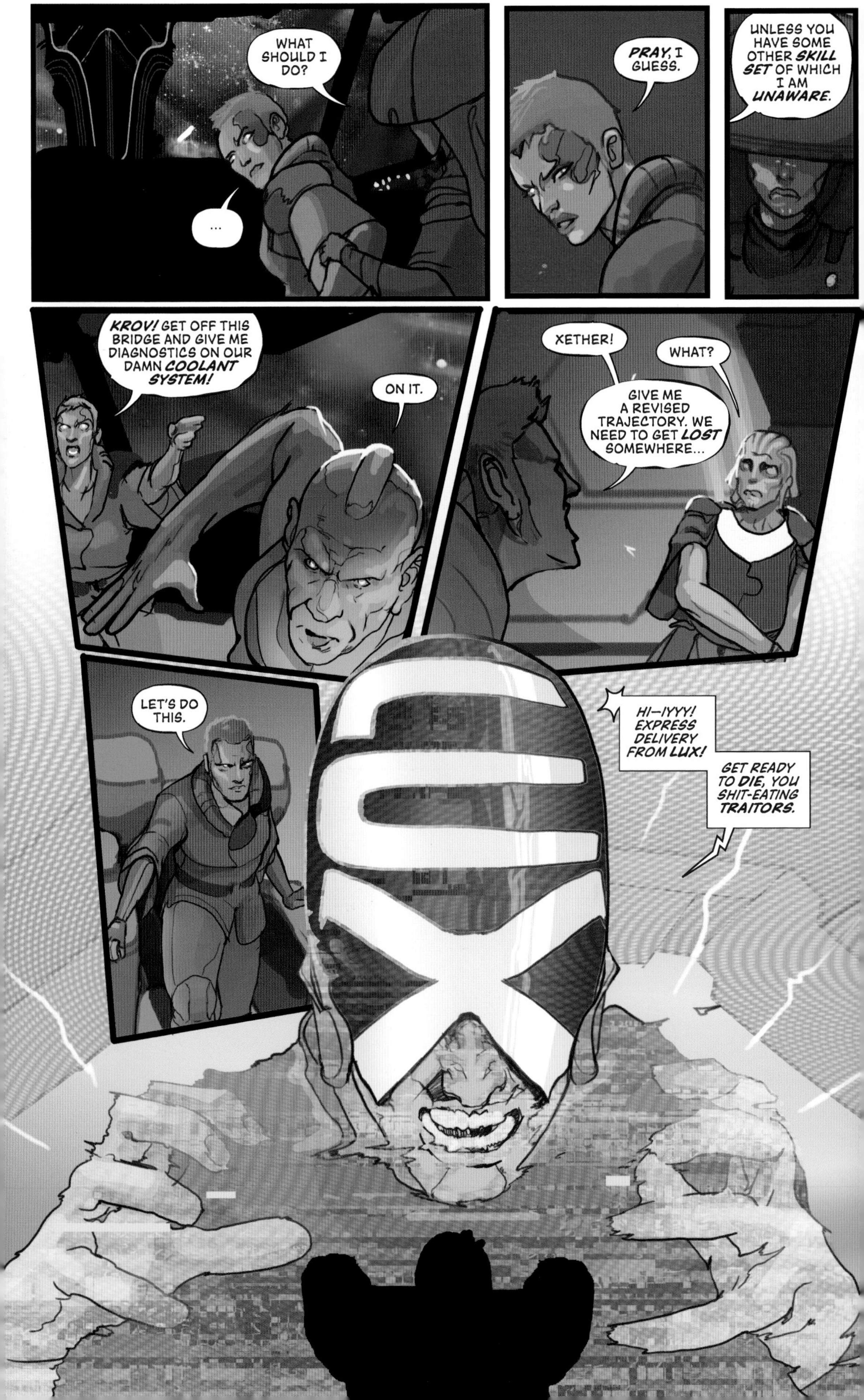
WHAT SHOULD I DO?
...
PRAY, I GUESS.
UNLESS YOU HAVE SOME OTHER SKILL SET OF WHICH I AM UNAWARE.
KROV! GET OFF THIS BRIDGE AND GIVE ME DIAGNOSTICS ON OUR DAMN COOLANT SYSTEM!
ON IT.
XETHER!
WHAT?
GIVE ME A REVISED TRAJECTORY. WE NEED TO GET LOST SOMEWHERE...
LET'S DO THIS.
HI—IYYY! EXPRESS DELIVERY FROM LUX!
GET READY TO DIE, YOU SHIT-EATING TRAITORS.

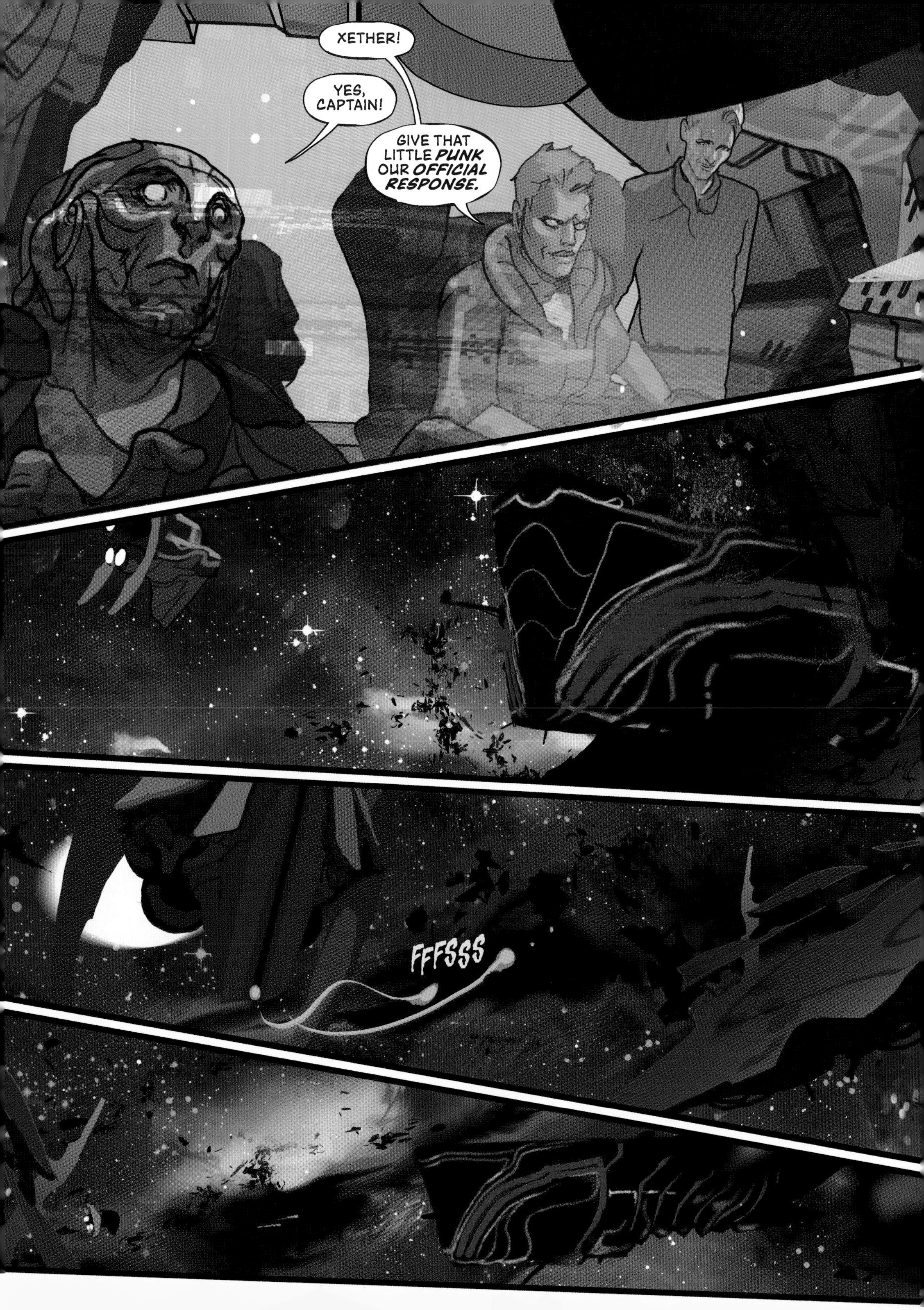
XETHER!
YES, CAPTAIN!
GIVE THAT LITTLE PUNK OUR OFFICIAL RESPONSE.
FFFSSS

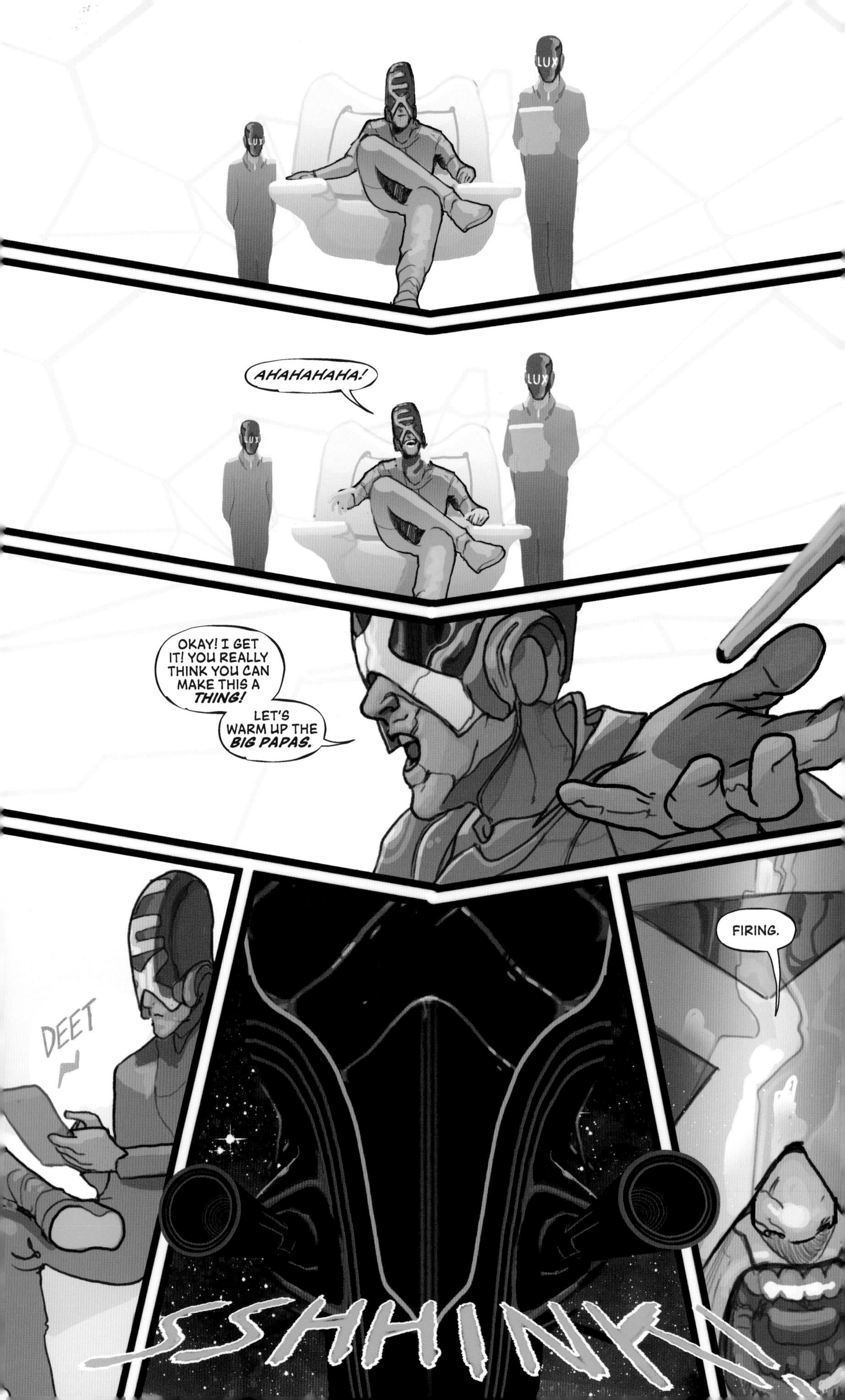
AHAHAHAHA!
OKAY! I GET IT! YOU REALLY THINK YOU CAN MAKE THIS A THING!
LET'S WARM UP THE BIG PAPAS.
DEET
FIRING.
SSHINK!!

"WE ARE ALL *DUST.*

"FLECKS OF MATTER IN A UNIVERSE WITH *NO CENTER.*

"BUT THAT DUST IS THE DUST FROM WHICH ALL THINGS WERE MADE.

"OUR SIBLINGS ARE THE *STARS.*

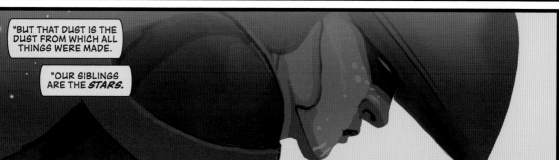

"AND IN A UNIVERSE WITHOUT A CENTER...

"*EACH* OF US IS THE MIDDLE.

"WE MATTER. *THIS* MATTERS. THIS MOMENT, AND THE NEXT, AND THE NEXT...

"SO *SAVE* US..."

PLEASE.

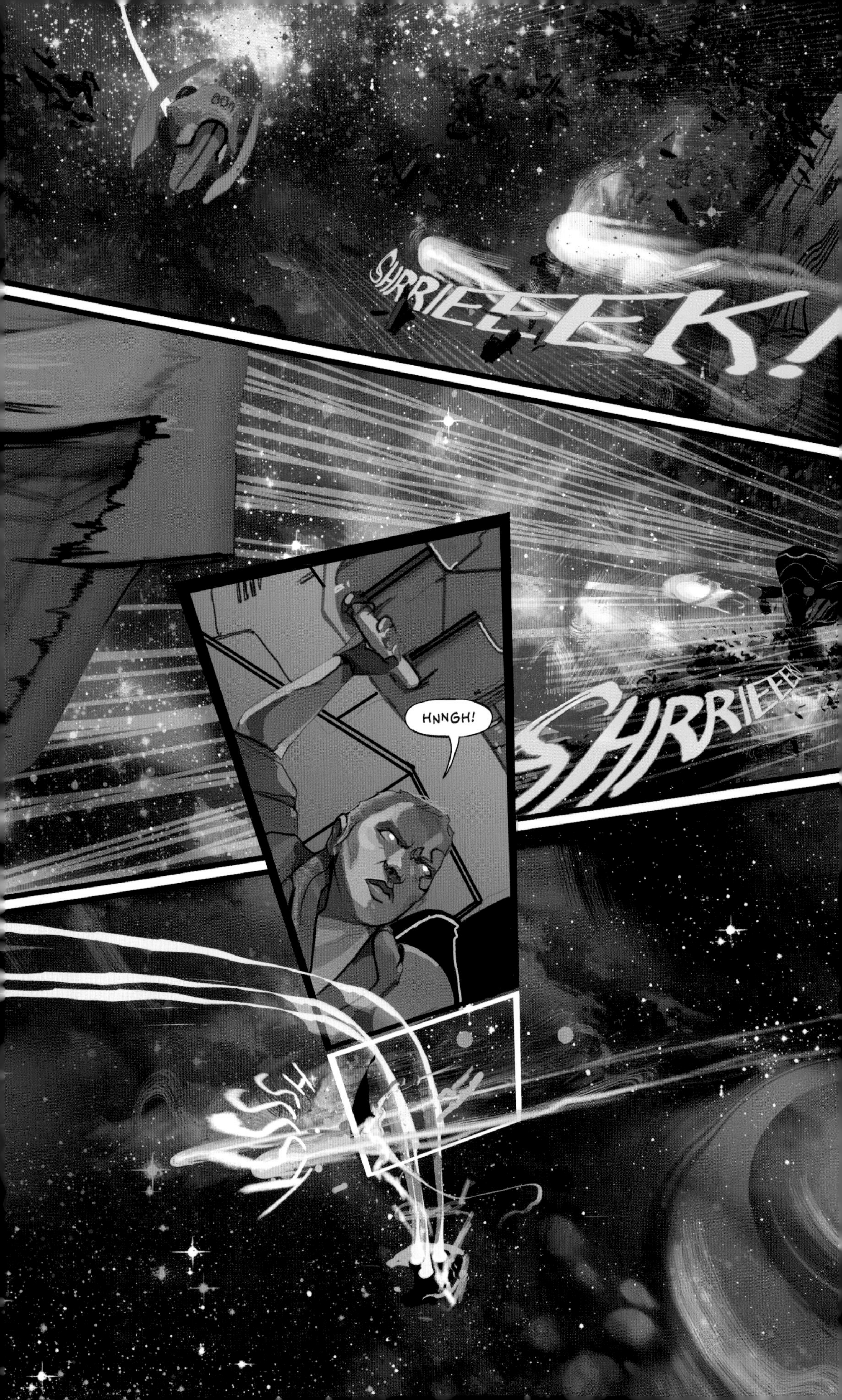
SHRRIEEEEK!
HNNGH!
SHRRIEEEE
SSH

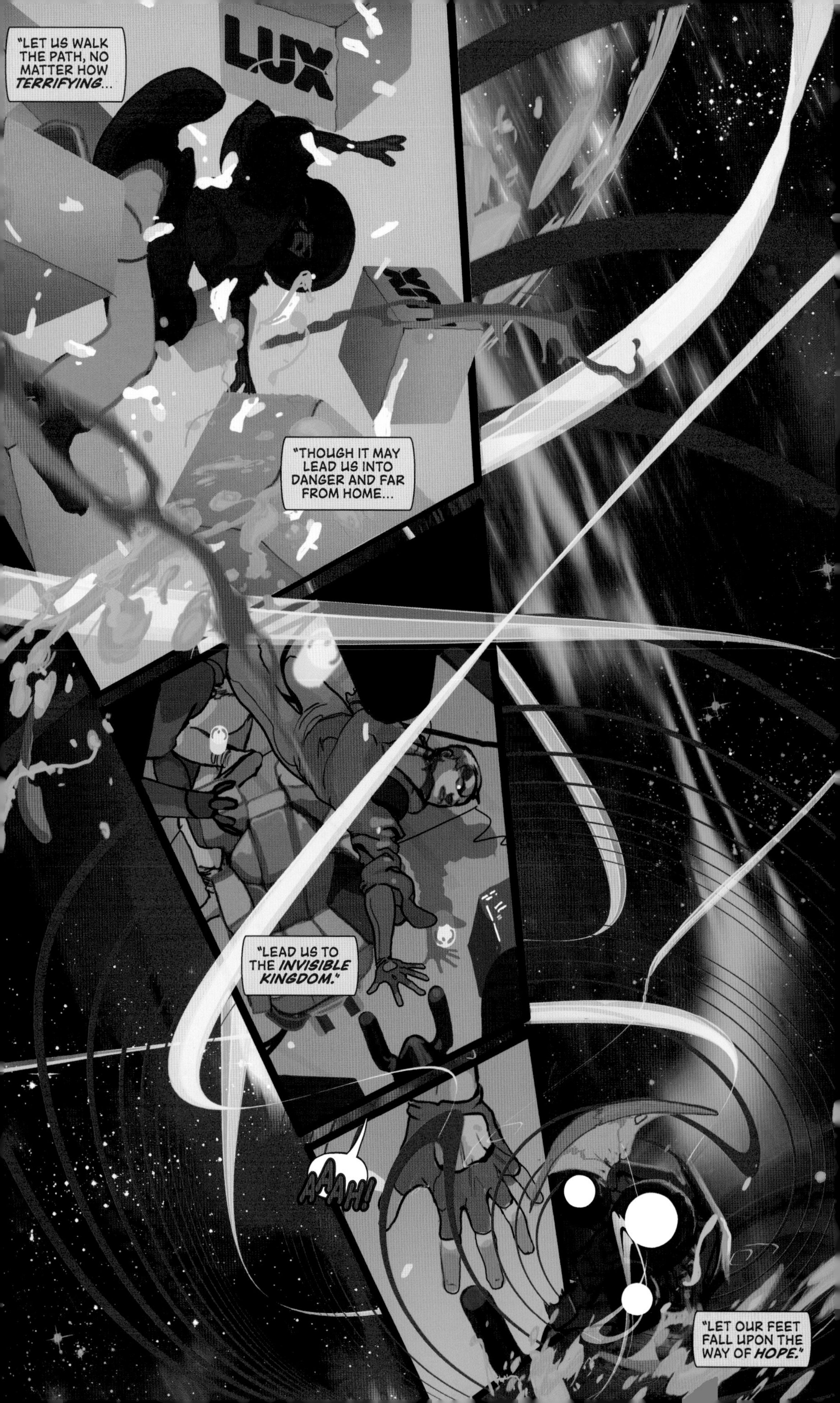
"LET US WALK THE PATH, NO MATTER HOW *TERRIFYING*...
LUX
"THOUGH IT MAY LEAD US INTO DANGER AND FAR FROM HOME...
"LEAD US TO THE *INVISIBLE KINGDOM.*"
AAAH!
"LET OUR FEET FALL UPON THE WAY OF *HOPE.*"

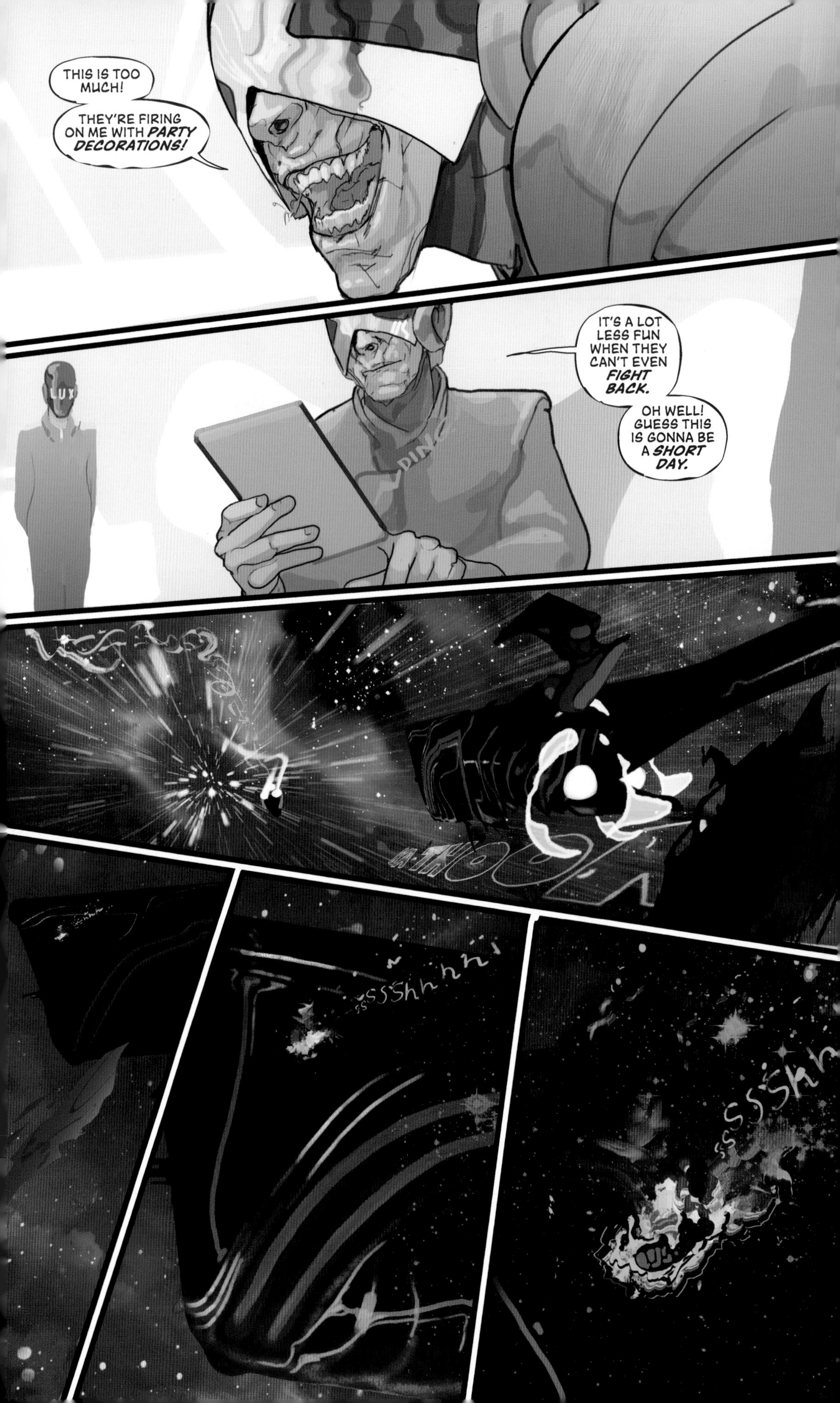
THIS IS TOO MUCH!
THEY'RE FIRING ON ME WITH *PARTY DECORATIONS!*
IT'S A LOT LESS FUN WHEN THEY CAN'T EVEN *FIGHT BACK.*
OH WELL! GUESS THIS IS GONNA BE A *SHORT DAY.*

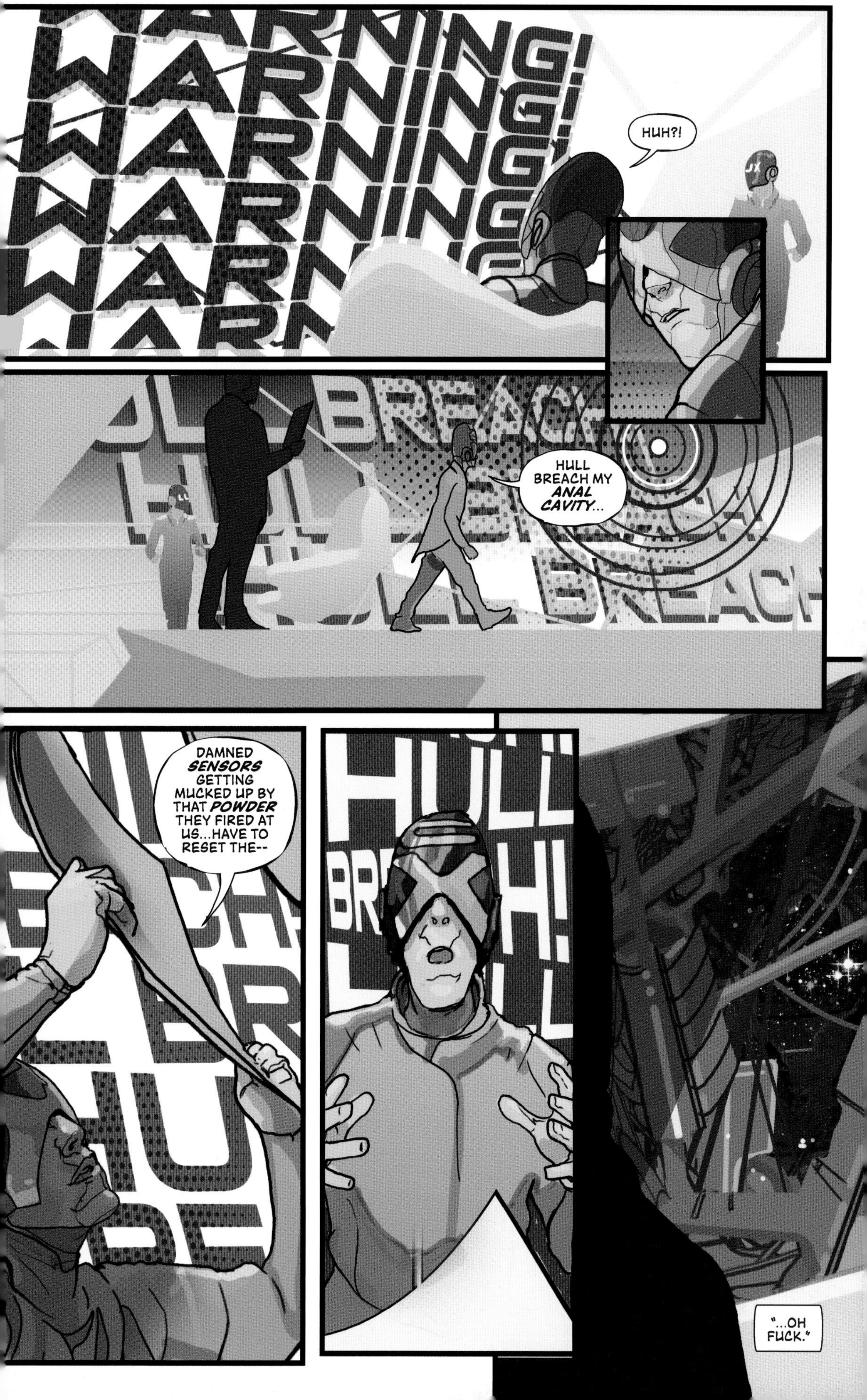
WARNING! WARNING! WARNING! WARNING!
HUH?!
HULL BREACH MY ANAL CAVITY...
DAMNED SENSORS GETTING MUCKED UP BY THAT POWDER THEY FIRED AT US...HAVE TO RESET THE--
HULL BREACH!
"...OH FUCK."

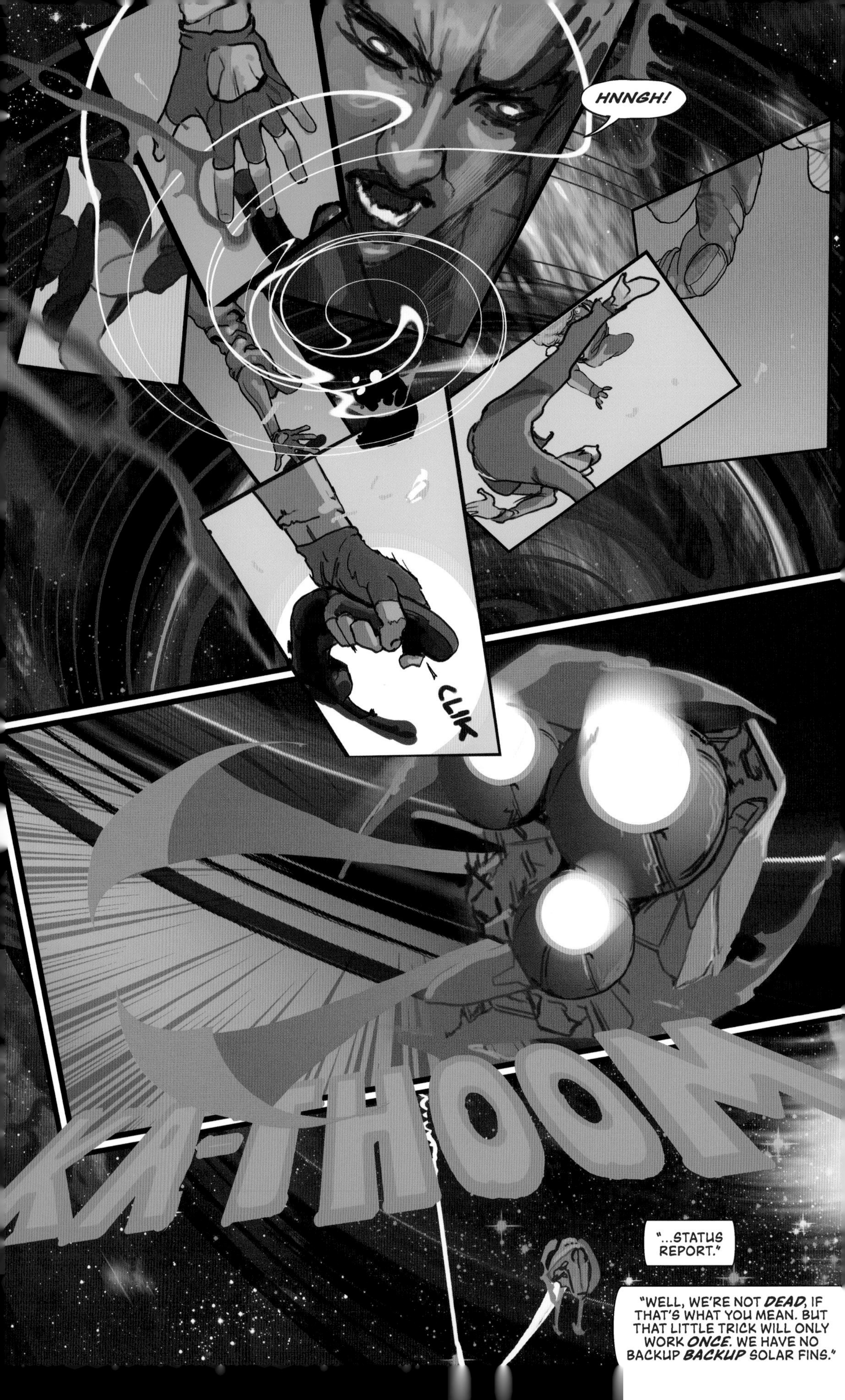
HNNGH!
CLIK
KA-THOOM
"...STATUS REPORT."
"WELL, WE'RE NOT *DEAD*, IF THAT'S WHAT YOU MEAN. BUT THAT LITTLE TRICK WILL ONLY WORK *ONCE*. WE HAVE NO BACKUP *BACKUP* SOLAR FINS."

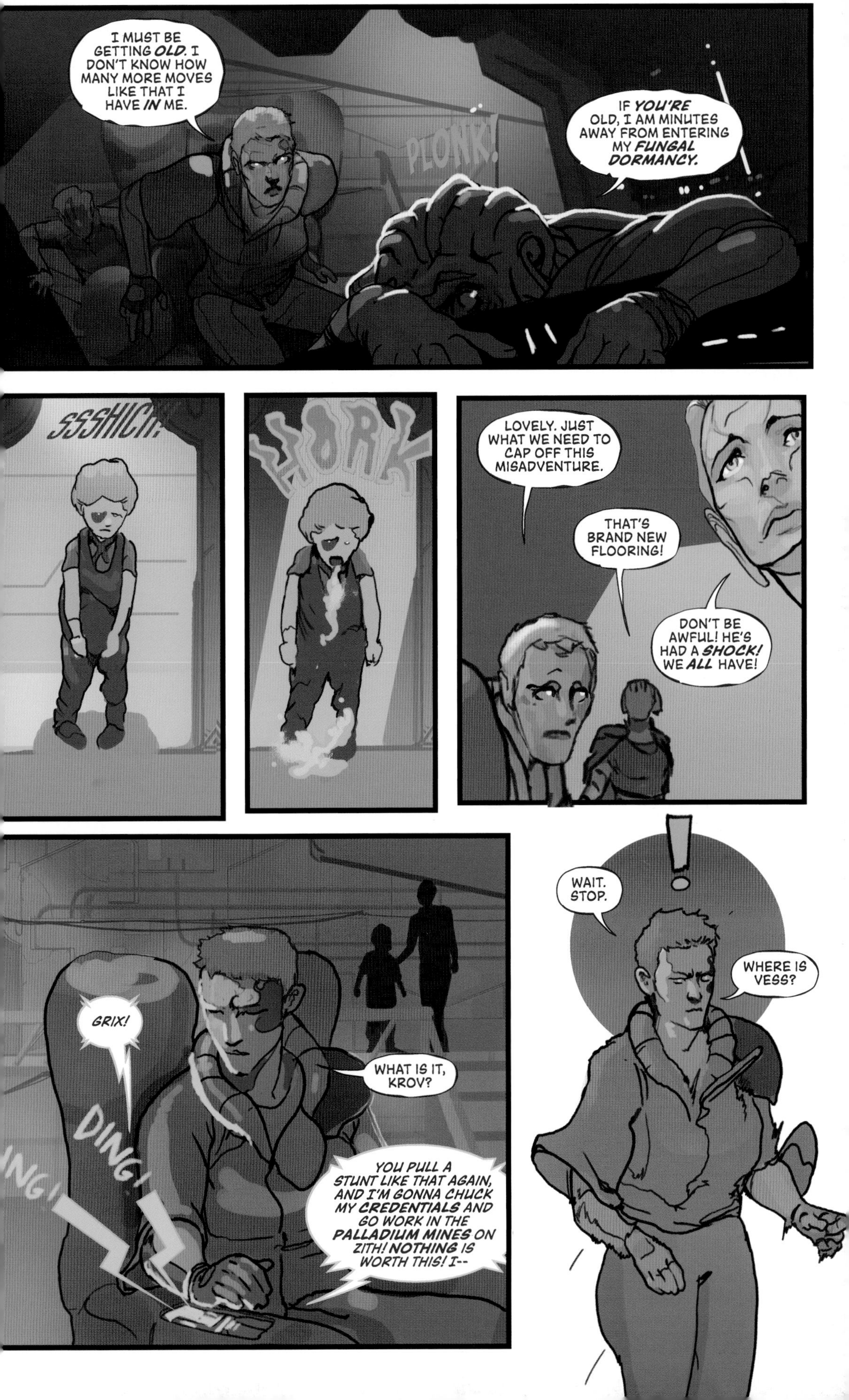

I MUST BE GETTING *OLD*. I DON'T KNOW HOW MANY MORE MOVES LIKE THAT I HAVE *IN* ME.
PLONK!
IF *YOU'RE* OLD, I AM MINUTES AWAY FROM ENTERING MY ***FUNGAL DORMANCY.***
SSSHICK!
HORK
LOVELY. JUST WHAT WE NEED TO CAP OFF THIS MISADVENTURE.
THAT'S BRAND NEW FLOORING!
DON'T BE AWFUL! HE'S HAD A ***SHOCK!*** WE ***ALL*** HAVE!
GRIX!
WHAT IS IT, KROV?
YOU PULL A STUNT LIKE THAT AGAIN, AND I'M GONNA CHUCK MY ***CREDENTIALS*** *AND GO WORK IN THE* ***PALLADIUM MINES*** *ON ZITH!* ***NOTHING*** *IS WORTH THIS! I--*
DING!
ING!
!
WAIT. STOP.
WHERE IS VESS?

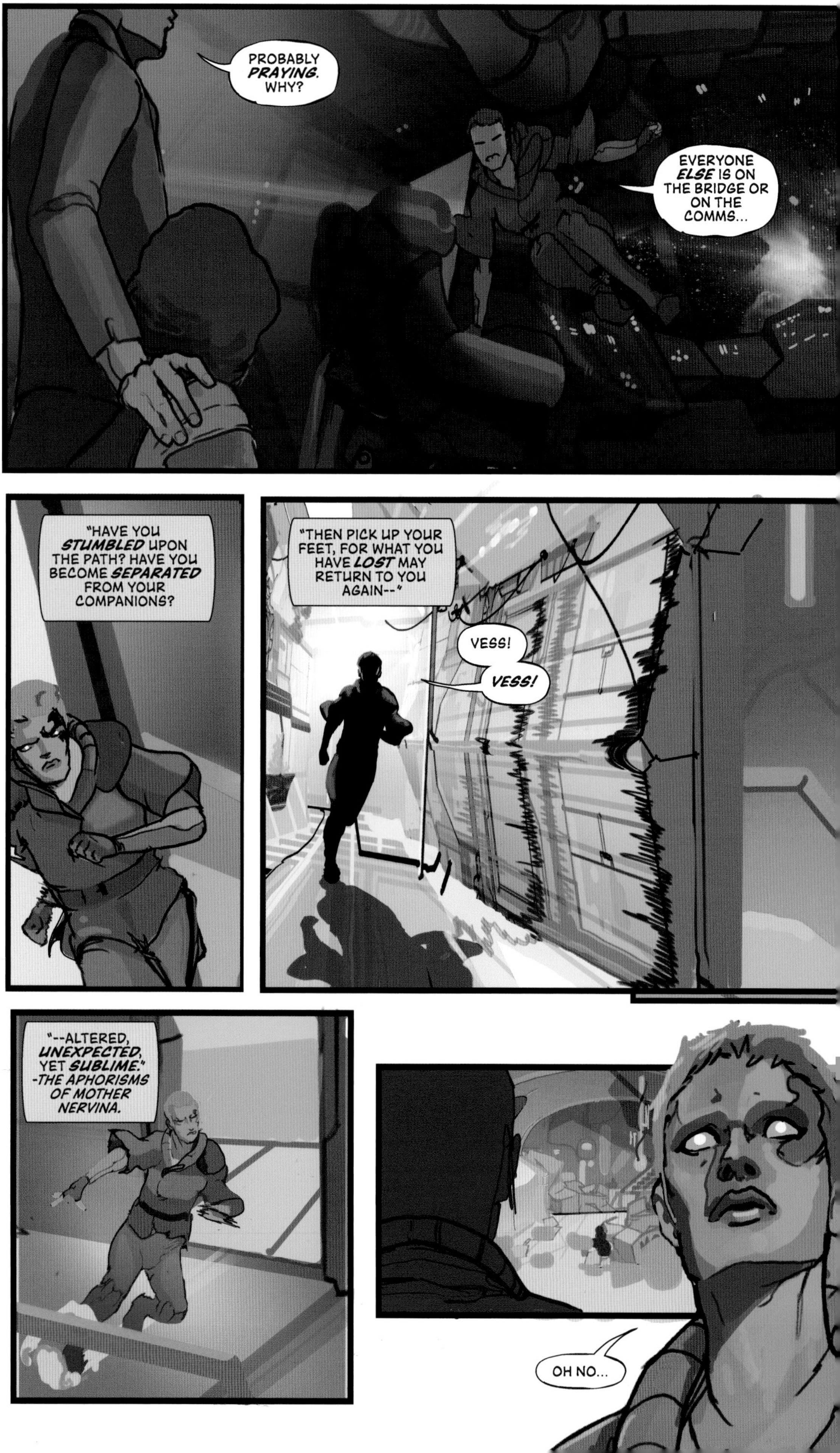

PROBABLY *PRAYING*. WHY?
EVERYONE *ELSE* IS ON THE BRIDGE OR ON THE COMMS...
"HAVE YOU *STUMBLED* UPON THE PATH? HAVE YOU BECOME *SEPARATED* FROM YOUR COMPANIONS?
"THEN PICK UP YOUR FEET, FOR WHAT YOU HAVE *LOST* MAY RETURN TO YOU AGAIN--"
VESS!
VESS!
"--ALTERED, *UNEXPECTED*, YET *SUBLIME*." *-THE APHORISMS OF MOTHER NERVINA.*
OH NO...

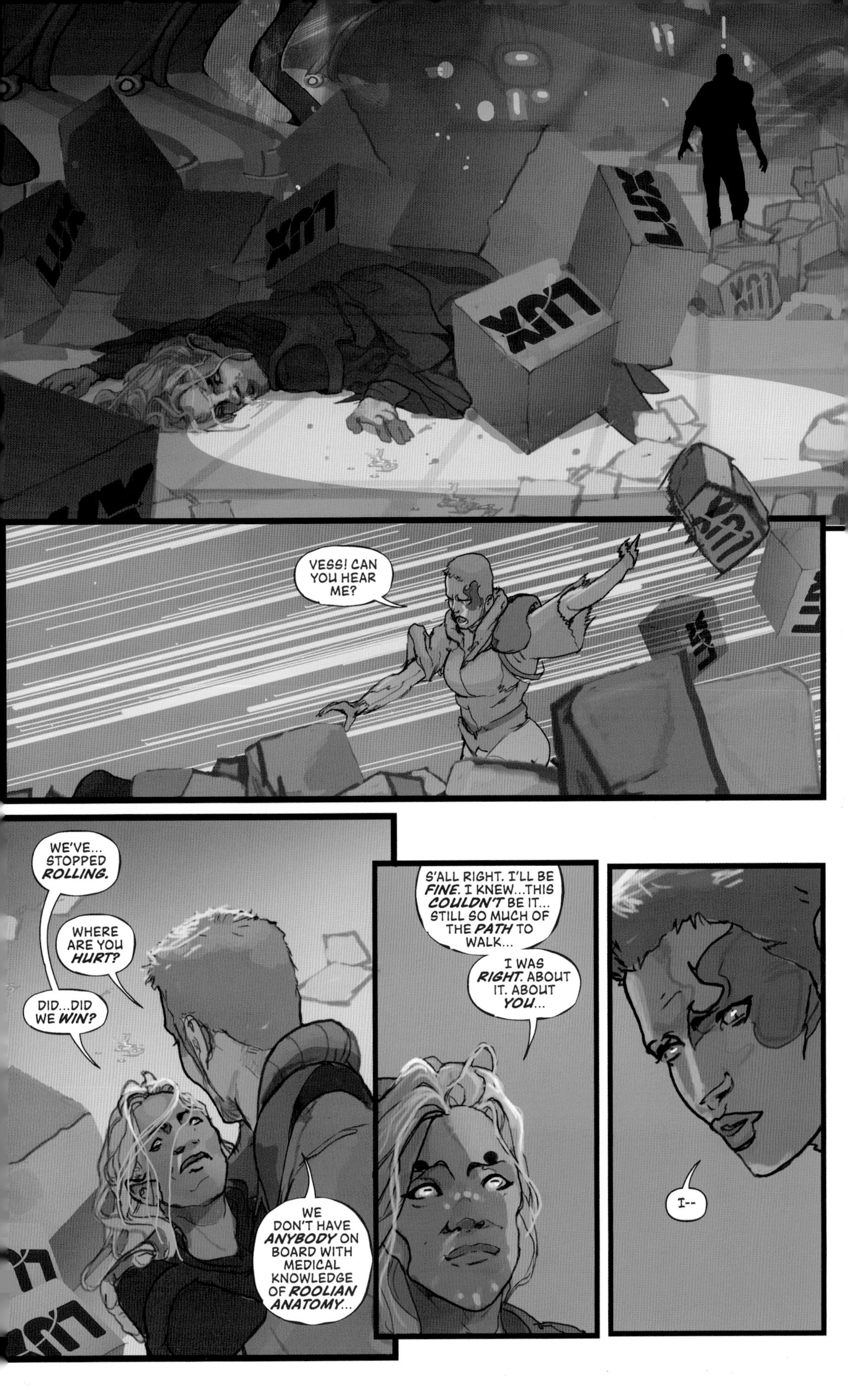

VESS! CAN YOU HEAR ME?
WE'VE... STOPPED ROLLING.
WHERE ARE YOU HURT?
DID...DID WE WIN?
WE DON'T HAVE ANYBODY ON BOARD WITH MEDICAL KNOWLEDGE OF ROOLIAN ANATOMY...
S'ALL RIGHT. I'LL BE FINE. I KNEW...THIS COULDN'T BE IT... STILL SO MUCH OF THE PATH TO WALK...
I WAS RIGHT. ABOUT IT. ABOUT YOU...
I--

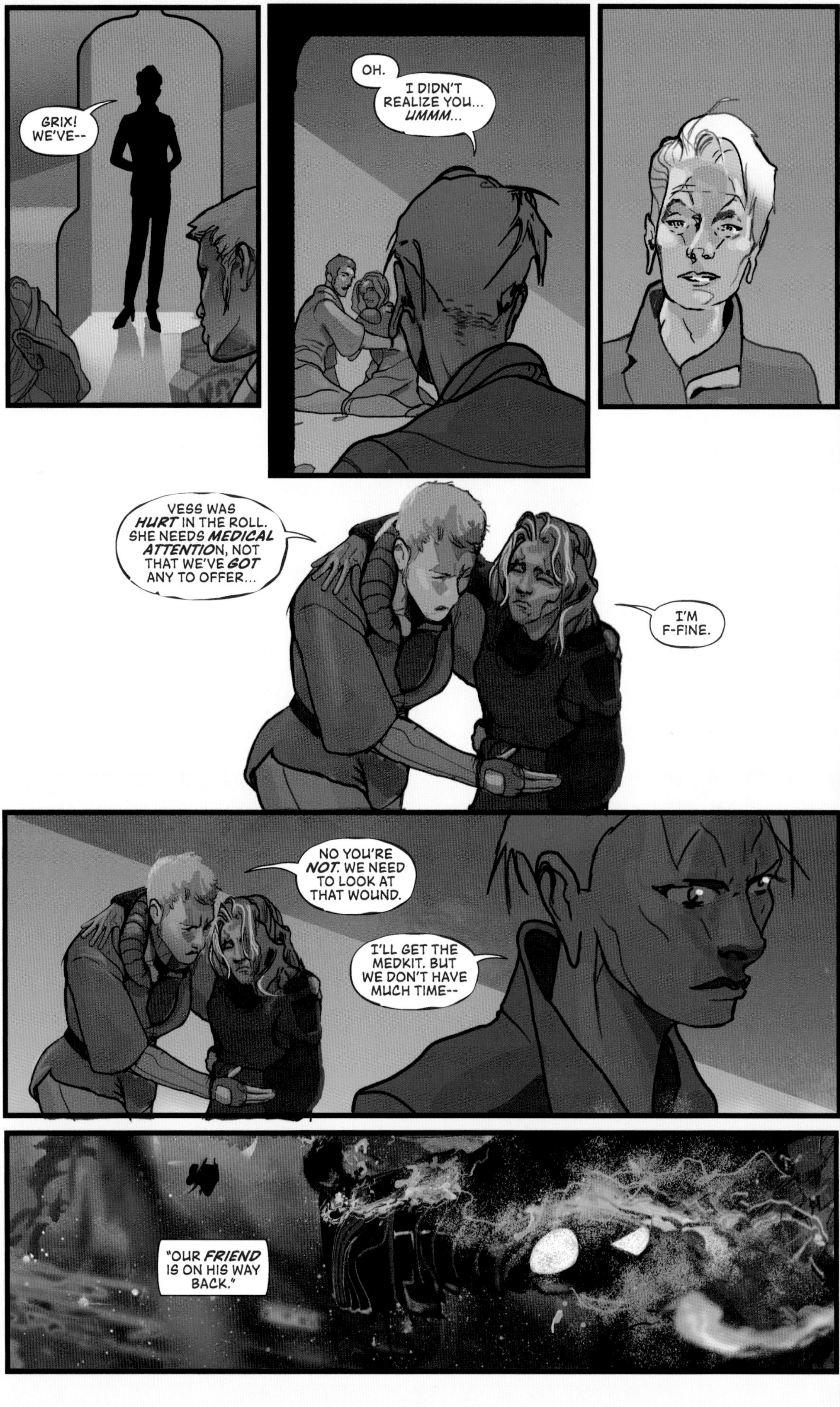
GRIX! WE'VE--
OH.
I DIDN'T REALIZE YOU... UMMM...
VESS WAS HURT IN THE ROLL. SHE NEEDS MEDICAL ATTENTION, NOT THAT WE'VE GOT ANY TO OFFER...
I'M F-FINE.
NO YOU'RE NOT. WE NEED TO LOOK AT THAT WOUND.
I'LL GET THE MEDKIT. BUT WE DON'T HAVE MUCH TIME--
"OUR FRIEND IS ON HIS WAY BACK."

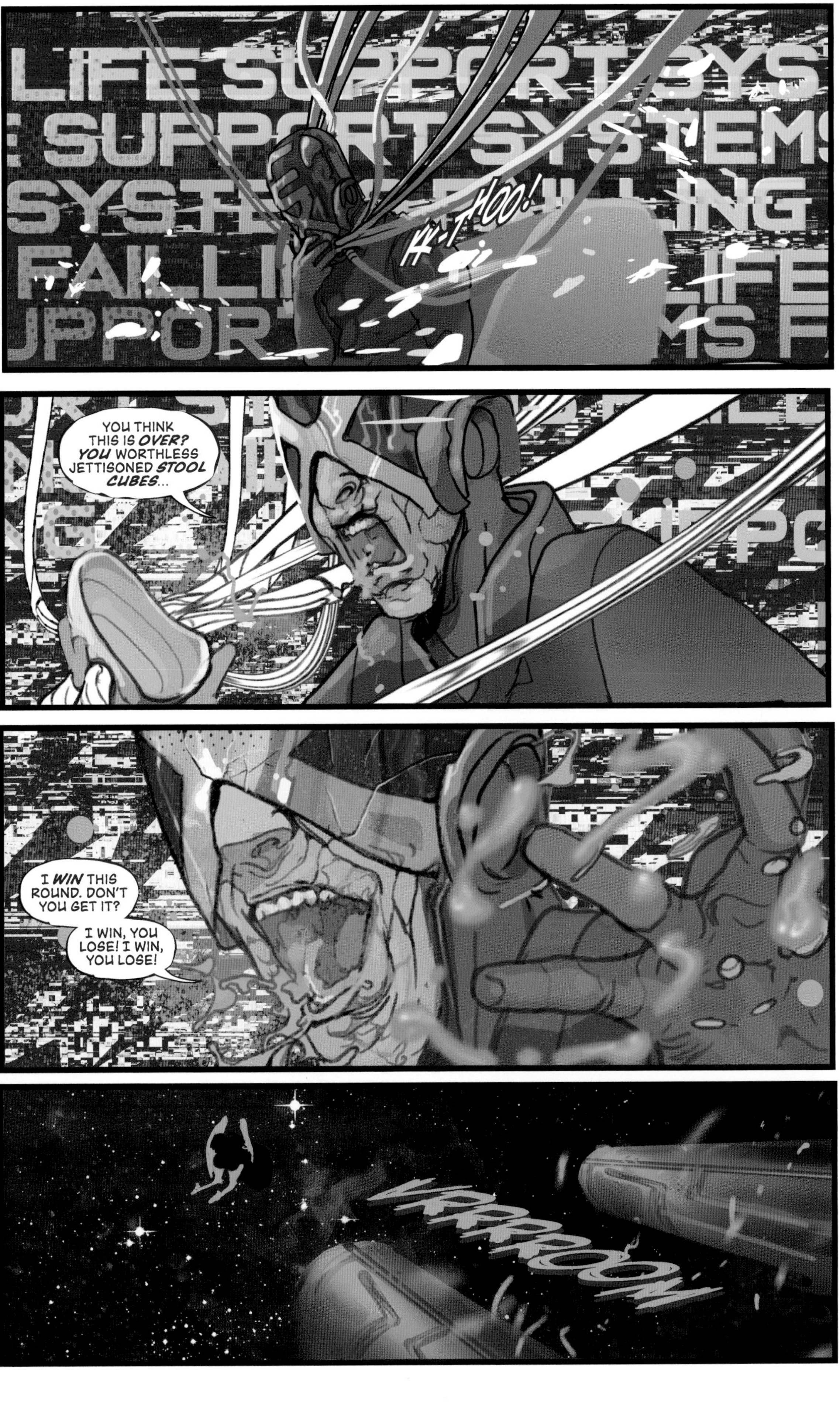
LIFE SUPPORT SYS
SUPPORT SYSTEMS
KK-THOO!
YOU THINK THIS IS OVER? YOU WORTHLESS JETTISONED STOOL CUBES...
I WIN THIS ROUND. DON'T YOU GET IT?
I WIN, YOU LOSE! I WIN, YOU LOSE!
VRRRROOM

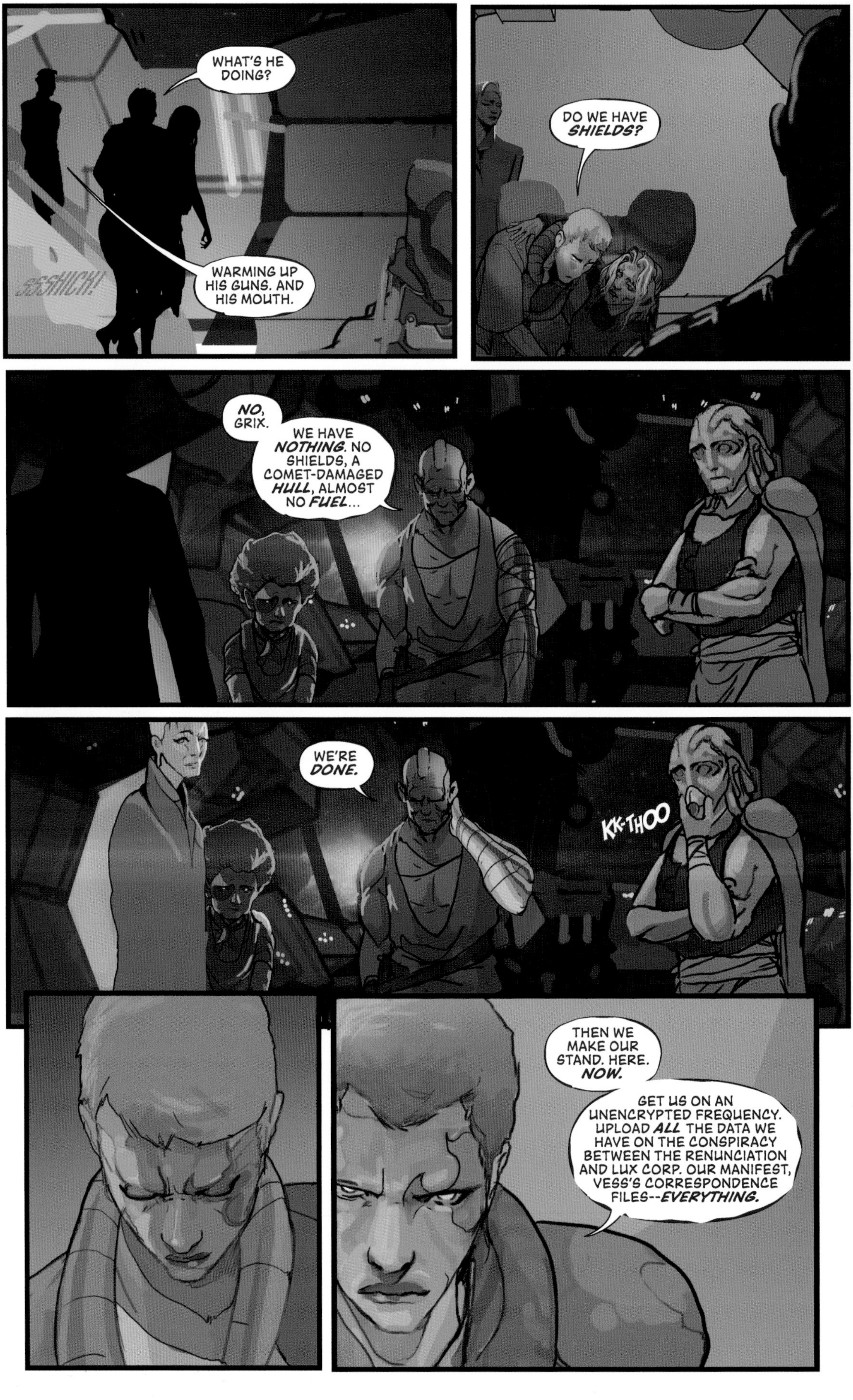
WHAT'S HE DOING?
WARMING UP HIS GUNS. AND HIS MOUTH.
SSSHICK!
DO WE HAVE SHIELDS?
NO, GRIX.
WE HAVE NOTHING. NO SHIELDS, A COMET-DAMAGED HULL, ALMOST NO FUEL...
WE'RE DONE.
KK-THOO
THEN WE MAKE OUR STAND. HERE. NOW.
GET US ON AN UNENCRYPTED FREQUENCY. UPLOAD ALL THE DATA WE HAVE ON THE CONSPIRACY BETWEEN THE RENUNCIATION AND LUX CORP. OUR MANIFEST, VESS'S CORRESPONDENCE FILES--EVERYTHING.

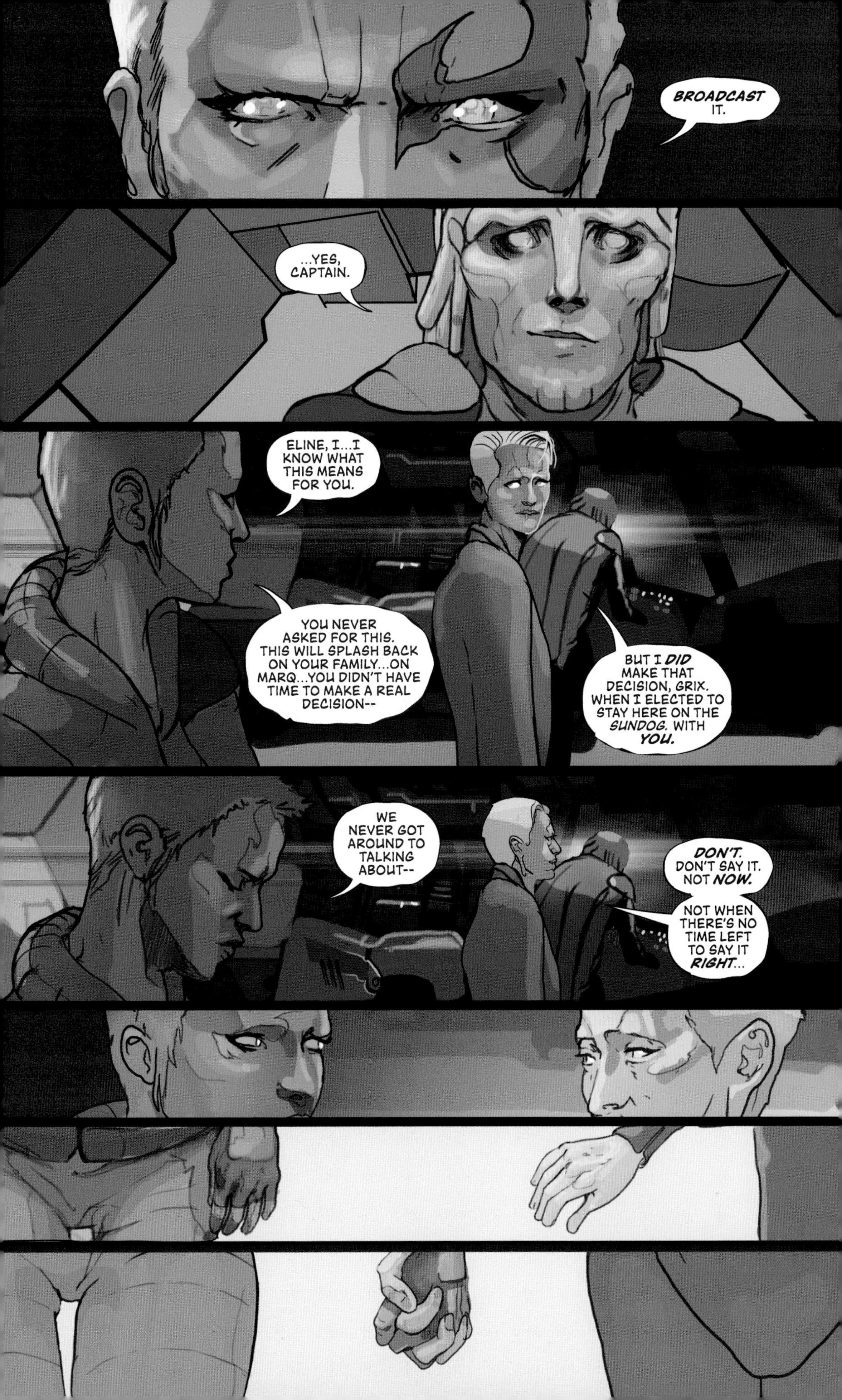
BROADCAST IT.
...YES, CAPTAIN.
ELINE, I...I KNOW WHAT THIS MEANS FOR YOU.
YOU NEVER ASKED FOR THIS. THIS WILL SPLASH BACK ON YOUR FAMILY...ON MARQ...YOU DIDN'T HAVE TIME TO MAKE A REAL DECISION--
BUT I DID MAKE THAT DECISION, GRIX. WHEN I ELECTED TO STAY HERE ON THE SUNDOG. WITH YOU.
WE NEVER GOT AROUND TO TALKING ABOUT--
DON'T. DON'T SAY IT. NOT NOW.
NOT WHEN THERE'S NO TIME LEFT TO SAY IT RIGHT...

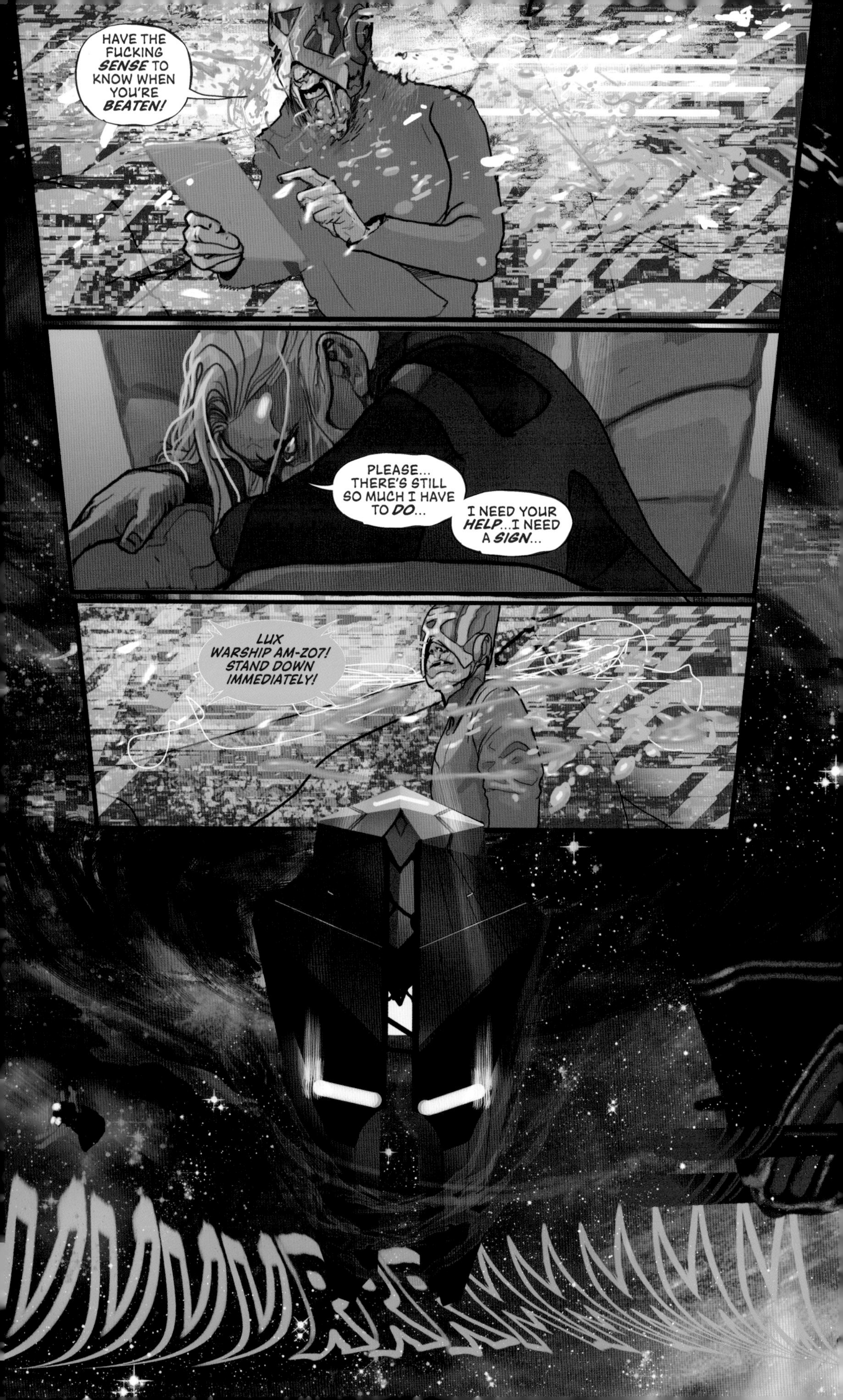
HAVE THE FUCKING *SENSE* TO KNOW WHEN YOU'RE *BEATEN!*
PLEASE... THERE'S STILL SO MUCH I HAVE TO *DO*...
I NEED YOUR *HELP*...I NEED A *SIGN*...
LUX WARSHIP AM-ZO7! STAND DOWN IMMEDIATELY!

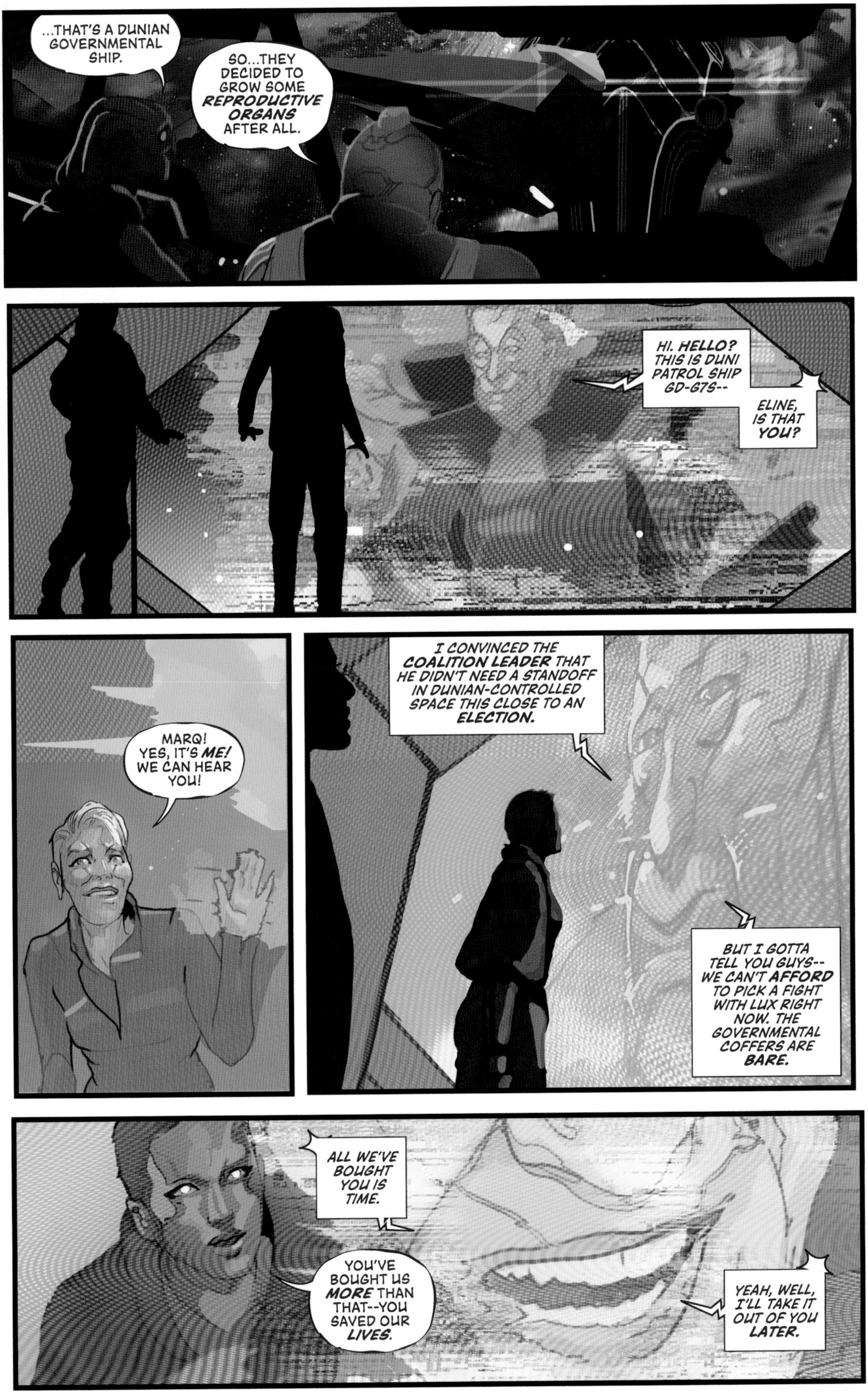
...THAT'S A DUNIAN GOVERNMENTAL SHIP.
SO...THEY DECIDED TO GROW SOME REPRODUCTIVE ORGANS AFTER ALL.
HI. HELLO? THIS IS DUNI PATROL SHIP GD-G7S--
ELINE, IS THAT YOU?
MARQ! YES, IT'S ME! WE CAN HEAR YOU!
I CONVINCED THE COALITION LEADER THAT HE DIDN'T NEED A STANDOFF IN DUNIAN-CONTROLLED SPACE THIS CLOSE TO AN ELECTION.
BUT I GOTTA TELL YOU GUYS-- WE CAN'T AFFORD TO PICK A FIGHT WITH LUX RIGHT NOW. THE GOVERNMENTAL COFFERS ARE BARE.
ALL WE'VE BOUGHT YOU IS TIME.
YOU'VE BOUGHT US MORE THAN THAT--YOU SAVED OUR LIVES.
YEAH, WELL, I'LL TAKE IT OUT OF YOU LATER.

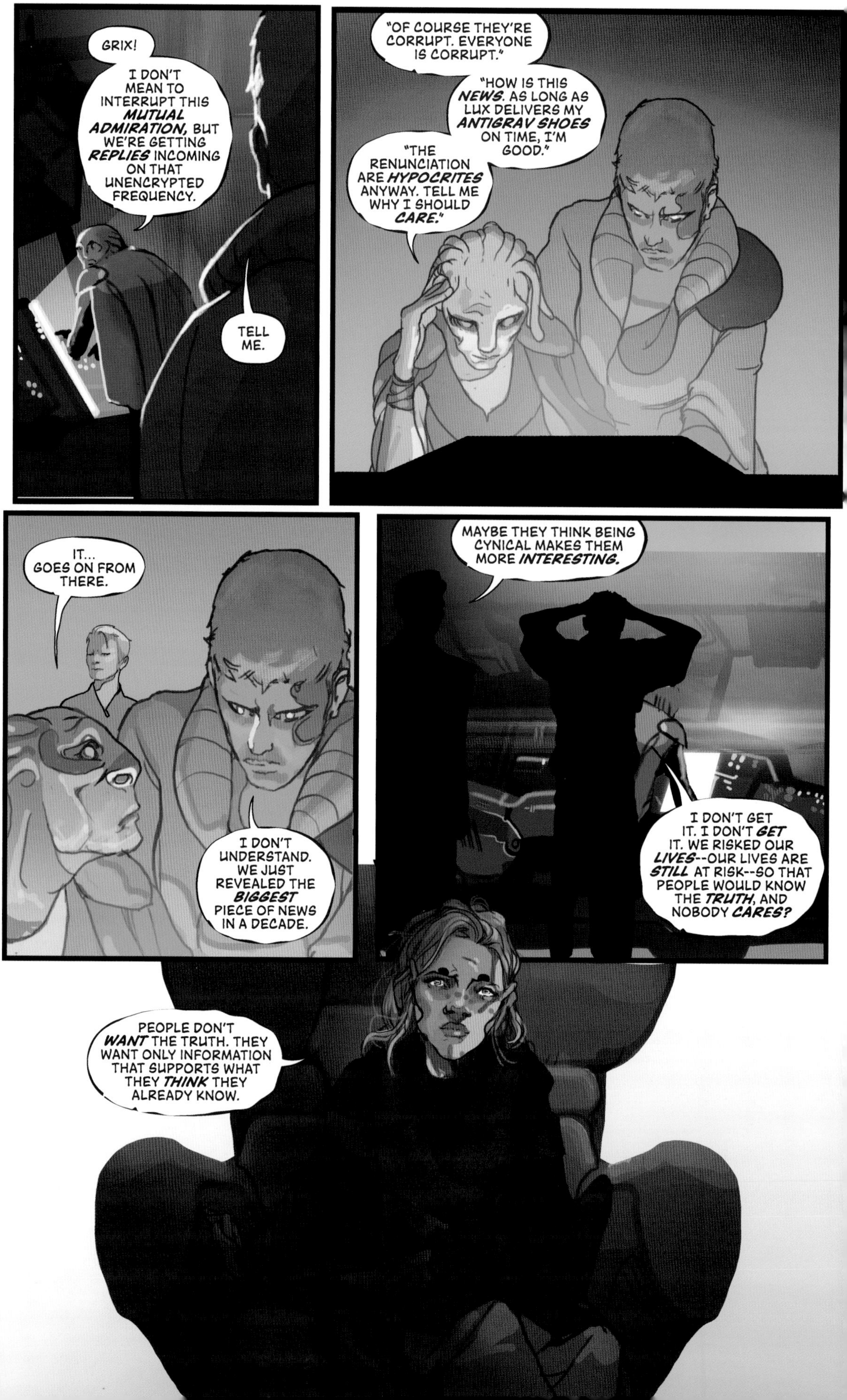
GRIX!
I DON'T MEAN TO INTERRUPT THIS *MUTUAL ADMIRATION,* BUT WE'RE GETTING *REPLIES* INCOMING ON THAT UNENCRYPTED FREQUENCY.
TELL ME.
"OF COURSE THEY'RE CORRUPT. EVERYONE IS CORRUPT."
"HOW IS THIS *NEWS*. AS LONG AS LUX DELIVERS MY *ANTIGRAV SHOES* ON TIME, I'M GOOD."
"THE RENUNCIATION ARE *HYPOCRITES* ANYWAY. TELL ME WHY I SHOULD *CARE.*"
IT... GOES ON FROM THERE.
I DON'T UNDERSTAND. WE JUST REVEALED THE *BIGGEST* PIECE OF NEWS IN A DECADE.
MAYBE THEY THINK BEING CYNICAL MAKES THEM MORE *INTERESTING.*
I DON'T GET IT. I DON'T *GET* IT. WE RISKED OUR *LIVES*--OUR LIVES ARE *STILL* AT RISK--SO THAT PEOPLE WOULD KNOW THE *TRUTH,* AND NOBODY *CARES?*
PEOPLE DON'T *WANT* THE TRUTH. THEY WANT ONLY INFORMATION THAT SUPPORTS WHAT THEY *THINK* THEY ALREADY KNOW.

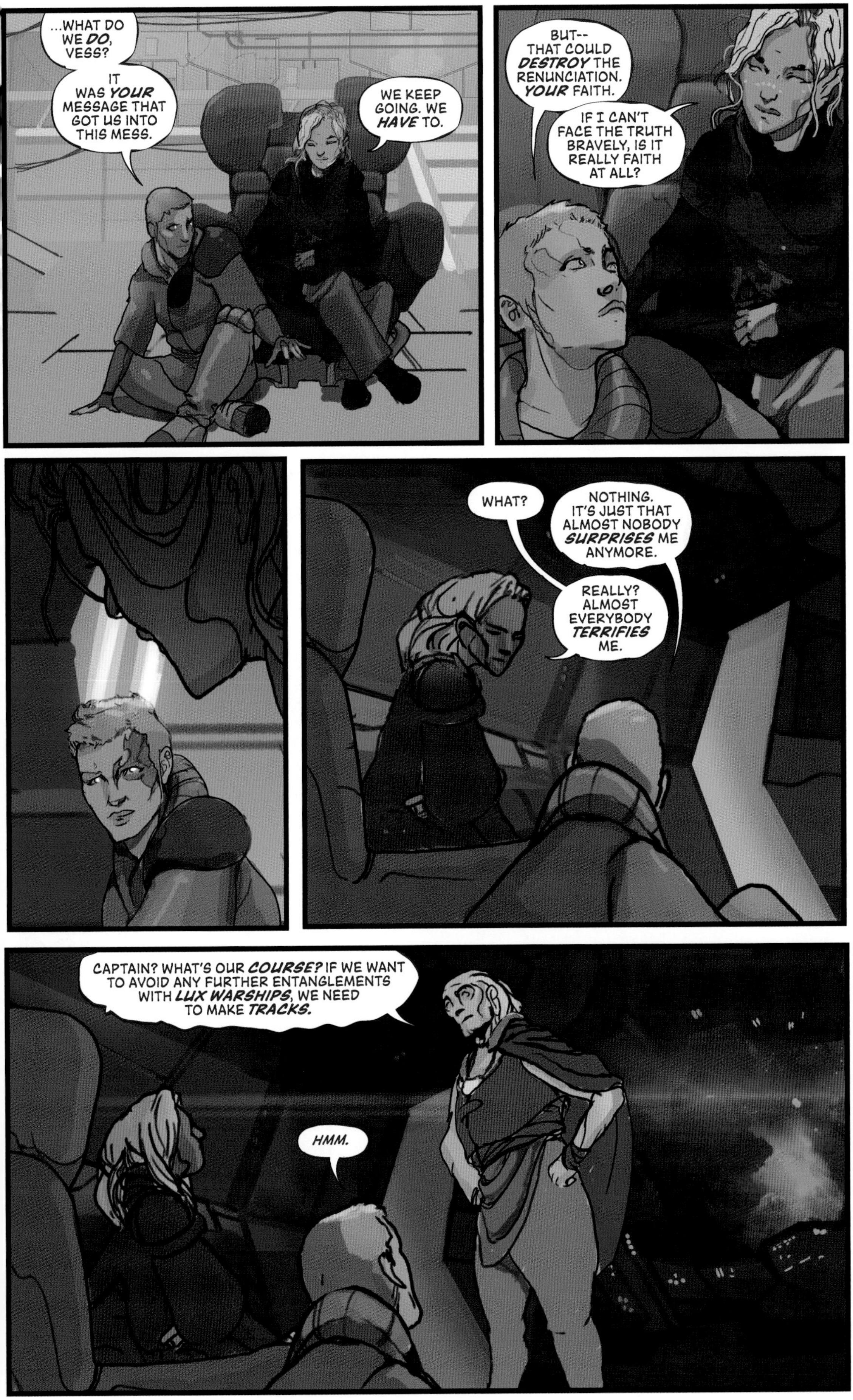
...WHAT DO WE *DO*, VESS?
IT WAS *YOUR* MESSAGE THAT GOT US INTO THIS MESS.
WE KEEP GOING. WE *HAVE* TO.
BUT-- THAT COULD *DESTROY* THE RENUNCIATION. *YOUR* FAITH.
IF I CAN'T FACE THE TRUTH BRAVELY, IS IT REALLY FAITH AT ALL?
WHAT?
NOTHING. IT'S JUST THAT ALMOST NOBODY *SURPRISES* ME ANYMORE.
REALLY? ALMOST EVERYBODY *TERRIFIES* ME.
CAPTAIN? WHAT'S OUR *COURSE?* IF WE WANT TO AVOID ANY FURTHER ENTANGLEMENTS WITH *LUX WARSHIPS*, WE NEED TO MAKE *TRACKS.*
HMM.

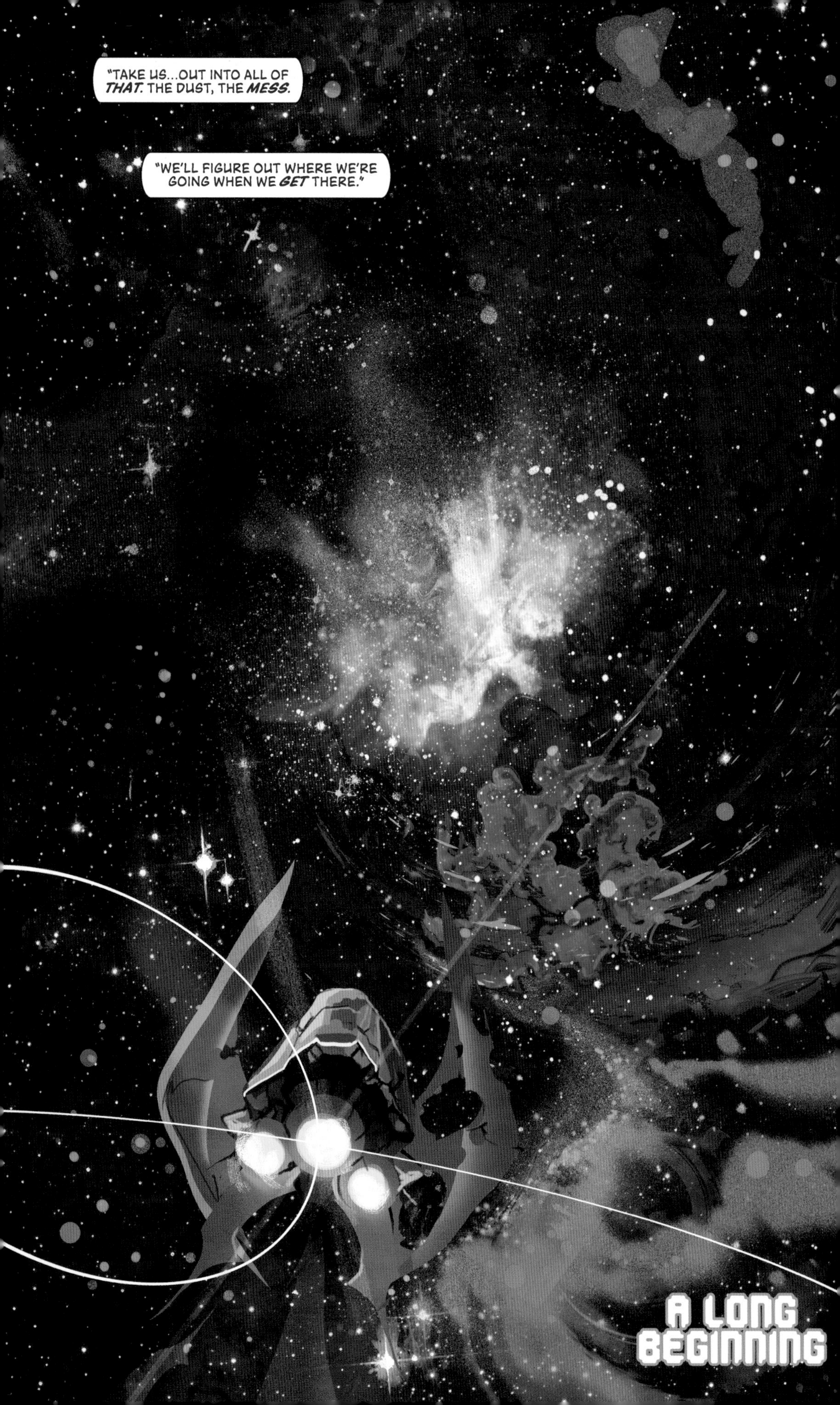
"TAKE US...OUT INTO ALL OF THAT. THE DUST, THE MESS.
"WE'LL FIGURE OUT WHERE WE'RE GOING WHEN WE GET THERE."
A LONG BEGINNING

LUX

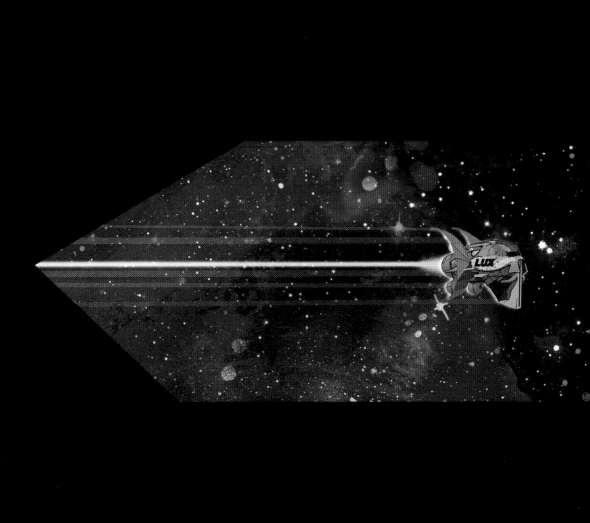

FUTURE, INC.

AT SOME POINT several years ago, I decided that I wanted to write a book about space nuns. I was researching medieval monastic traditions for a different project, and had become fascinated by the tension between secular life and the pull of the unseen—between the messy, complex demands of the material world and the complete renunciation that so many ancient philosophers seemed to find so compelling. At the same time, I began to imagine a sci-fi story about space travel without faster-than-light technology, in which characters move between worlds that are not impossibly far apart, but uncomfortably close together. And living in Seattle, the hub of e-commerce giants, I couldn't help but wonder what life would look like if our ubiquitously-branded packages were being shuttled not between cities, but between planets.

Out of this mental jumble, *Invisible Kingdom* was born. Set in a small solar system comprised of four planets in close orbit, it follows the lives of Vess, a pious, rebellious girl who has run away to join an order of monastic Nones; and Grix, a freighter pilot who once dreamed of putting her skills to use for exploration, not package delivery. When they separately discover evidence that the leaders of the system's dominant religion, the Renunciation, are conspiring with those of its largest and wealthiest corporation, Lux, they are drawn together from their wildly separate walks of life, and must decide whether what they know is worth dying for.

Grix and Vess come from worlds that could not be more different. Grix is from Zith, a searingly hot planet closest to the system's massive, dying sun. Vess hails from Rool, a planet of clouds and water, its inhabitants descended from two symbiotic species that merged to create a single people with four distinct genders. On the system's largest and most prosperous planet, Duni, seat of the Renunciation and headquarters of Lux, both Vess and Grix are outsiders and outliers, chafing at the narrow limits of their own lives.

This is a story that wears its influences on its sleeve: Christian and I have drawn inspiration from the sci-fi and fantasy epics that inspired us as kids and young adults, including *Dune*, *Cowboy Bebop*, and the lush visual world-building of Hayao Miyazaki. Yet we have also consciously made some profound deviations from typical genre fare. The alien peoples in this story resemble human beings only insofar as they are bipedal. At the same time, some elements of the book are drawn directly and pointedly from our own world, and will, I hope, make you laugh. The surreal and the very real intermingle. Christian is at the height of his powers in these pages, creating environments that you feel as though you could step into and inhabit.

This is a story about having faith in what we can't see: the loyalty of our friends, the truth of our causes, and the possibility of change.

Welcome to the Invisible Kingdom.

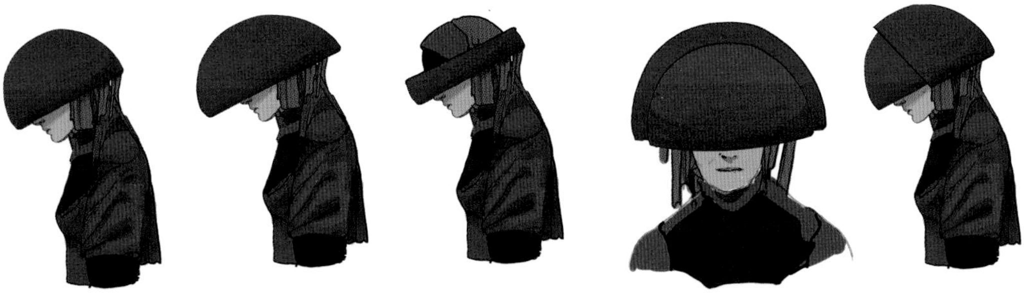

CHRISTIAN WARD

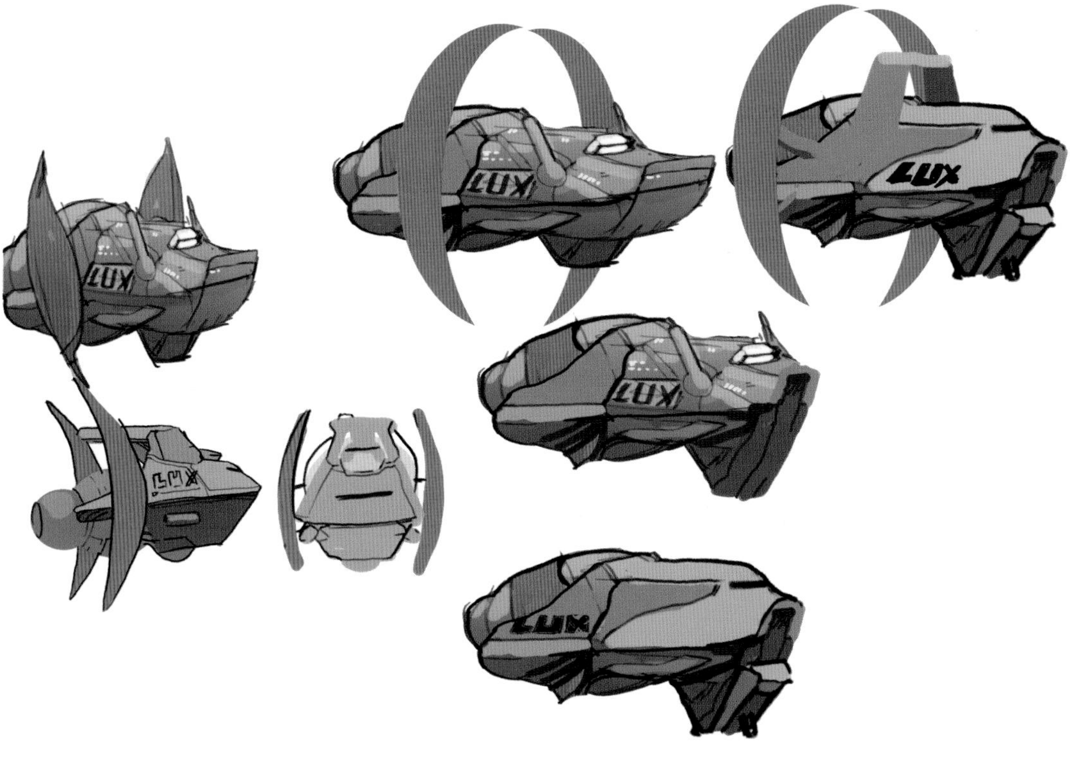
LUX

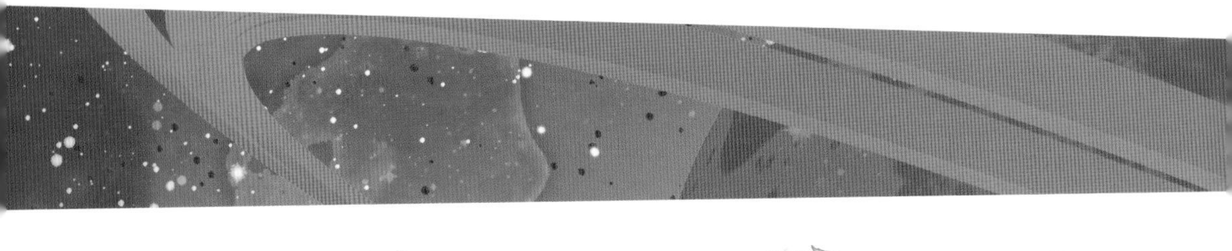

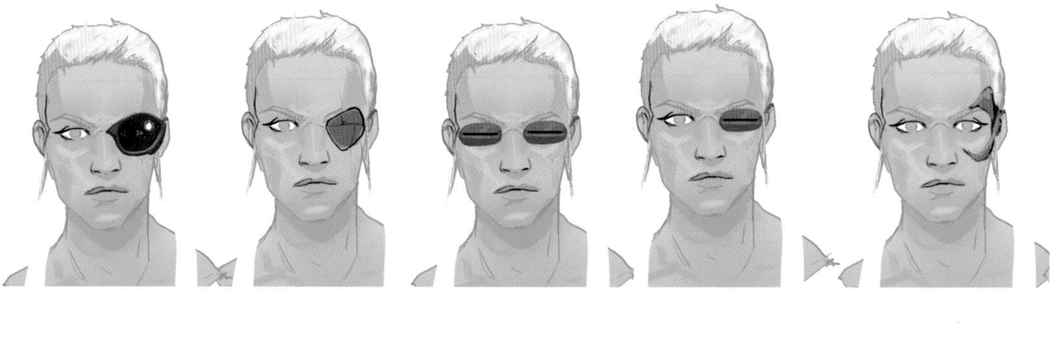

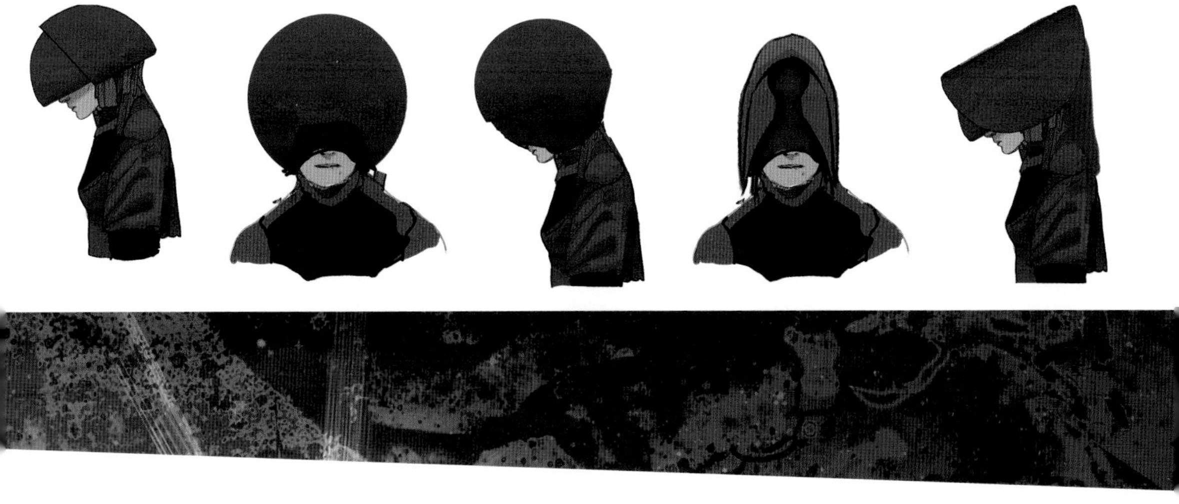

SUNDOG

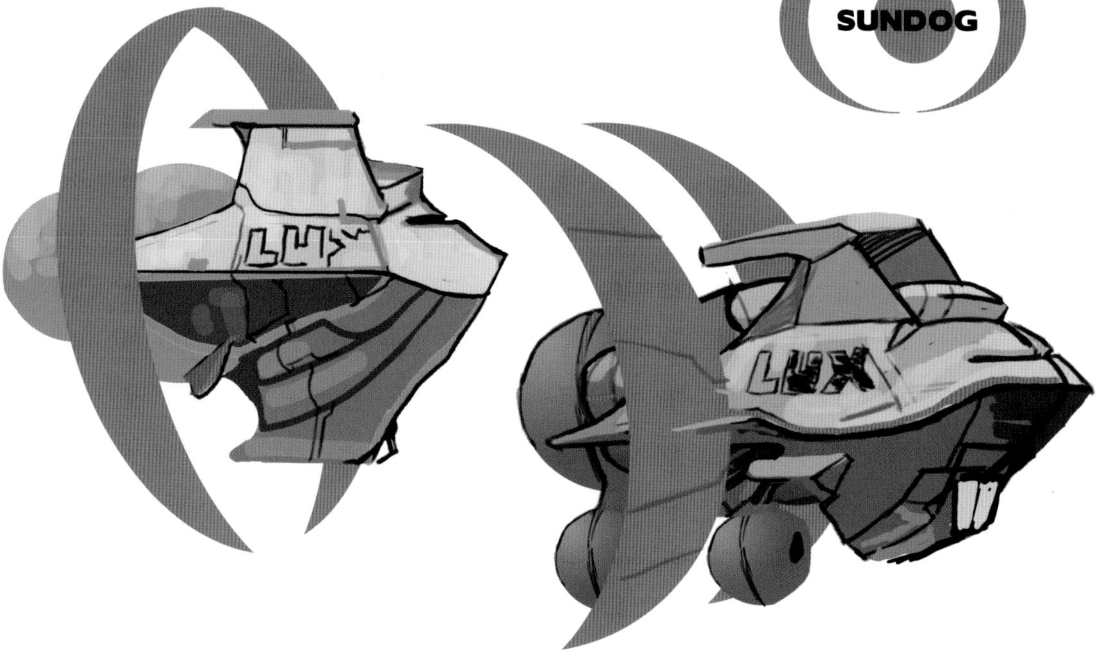
LUX

DEVELOPMENTAL ART

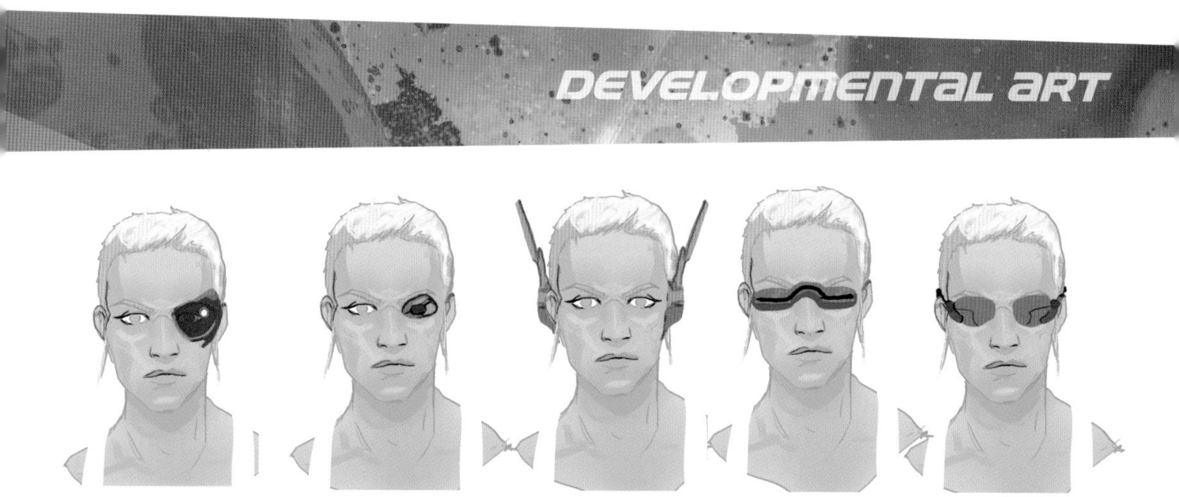

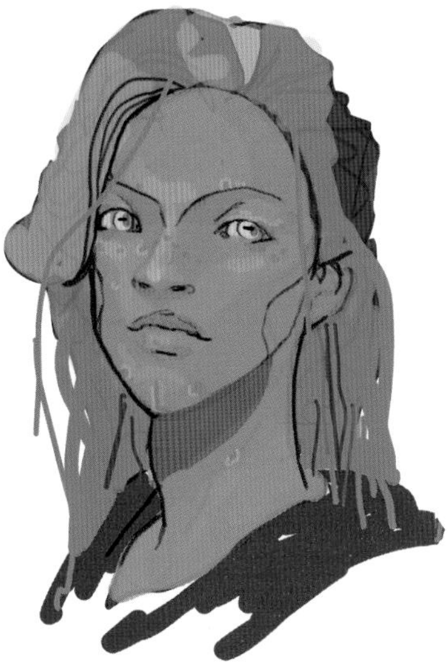
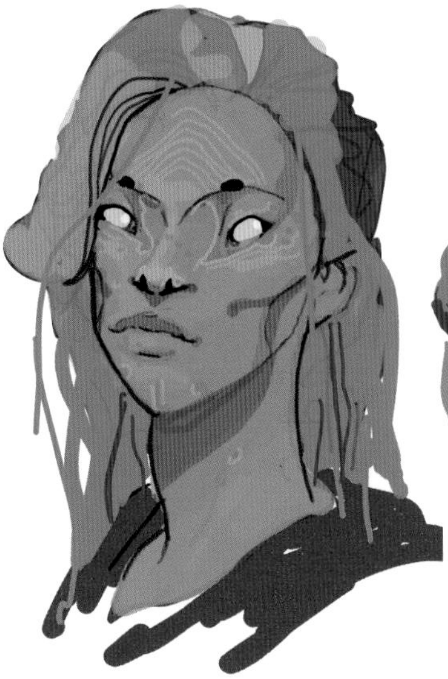
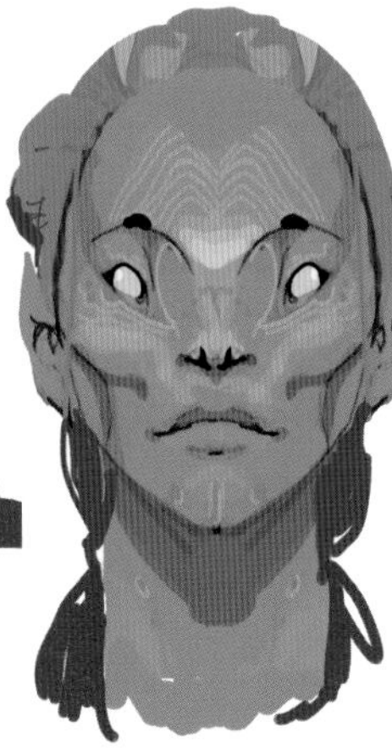
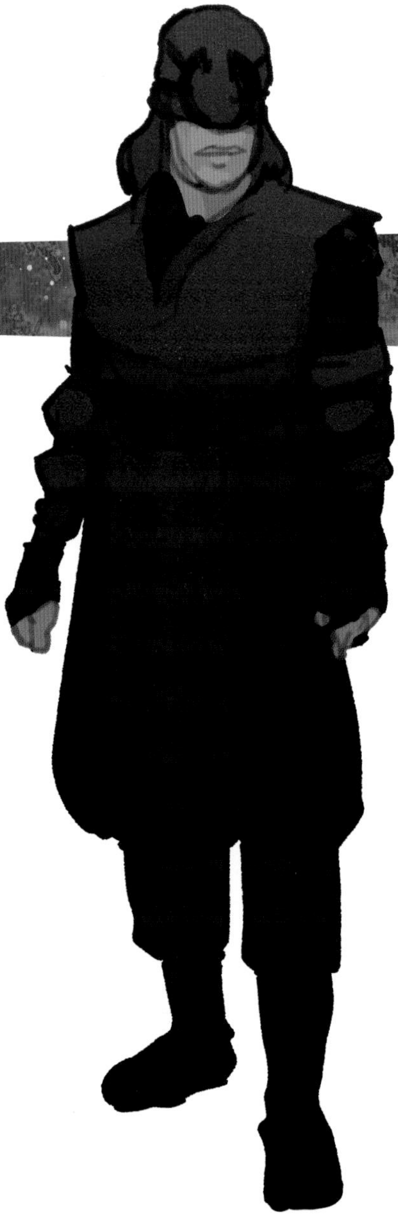
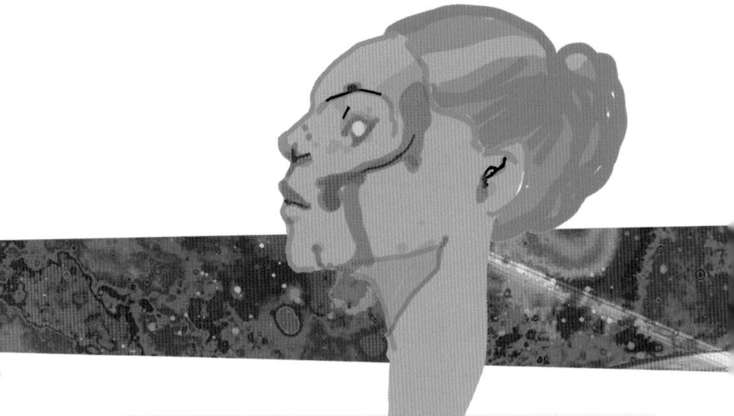
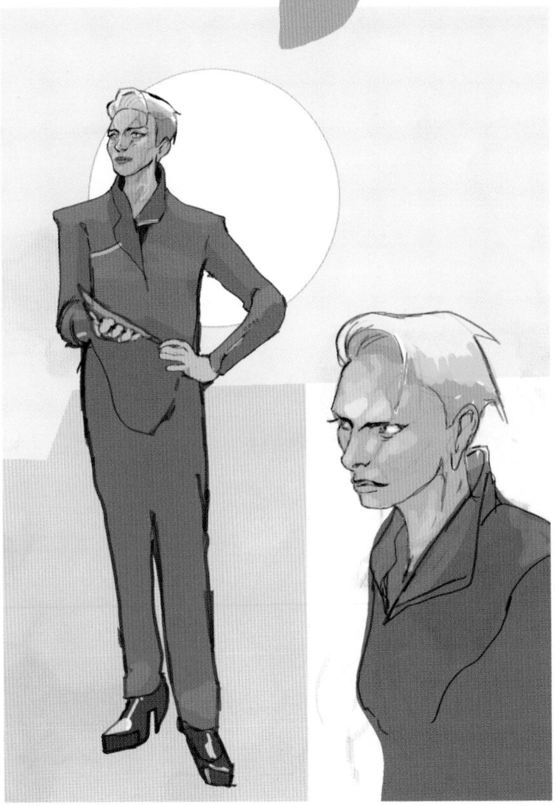

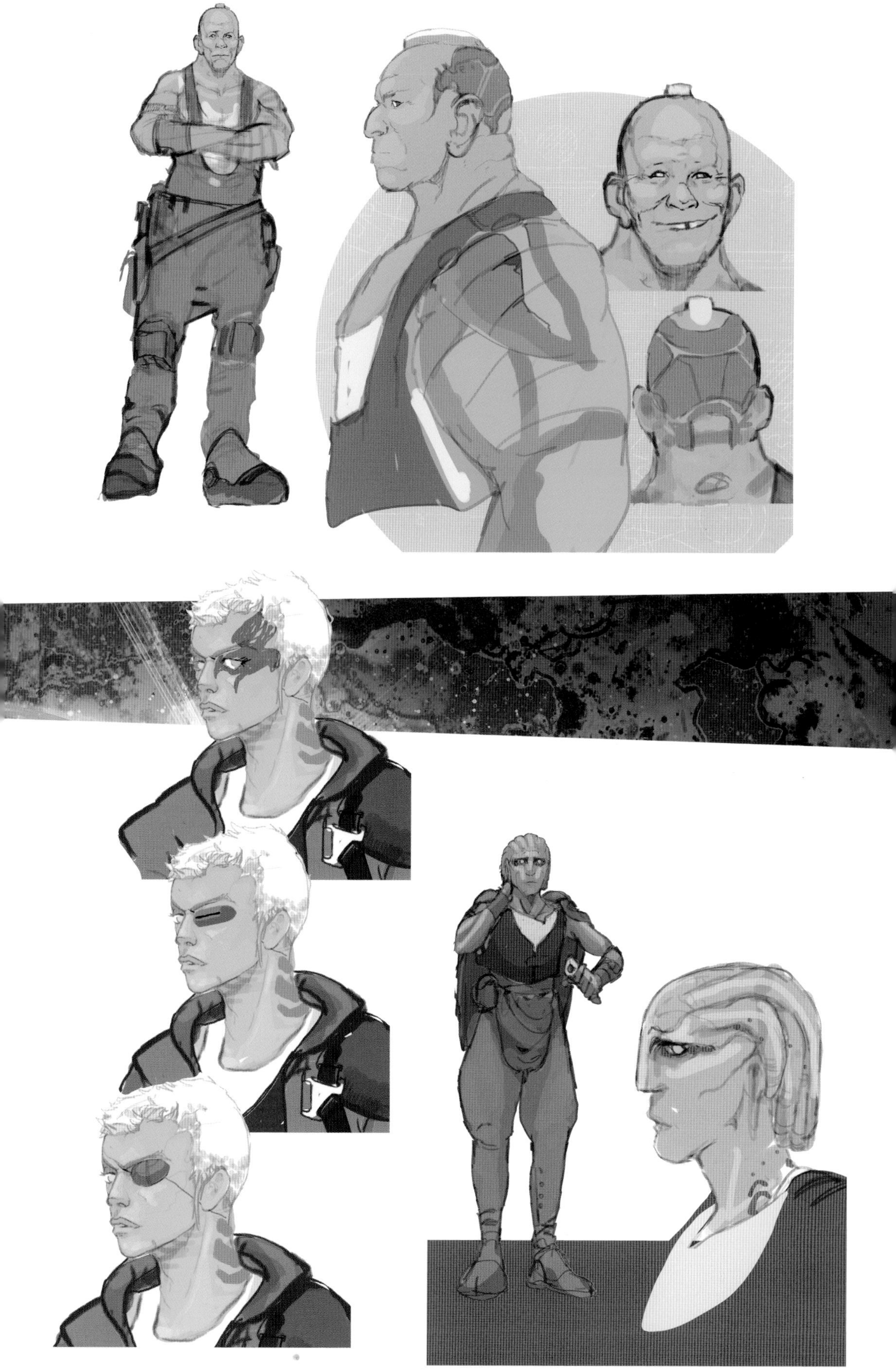

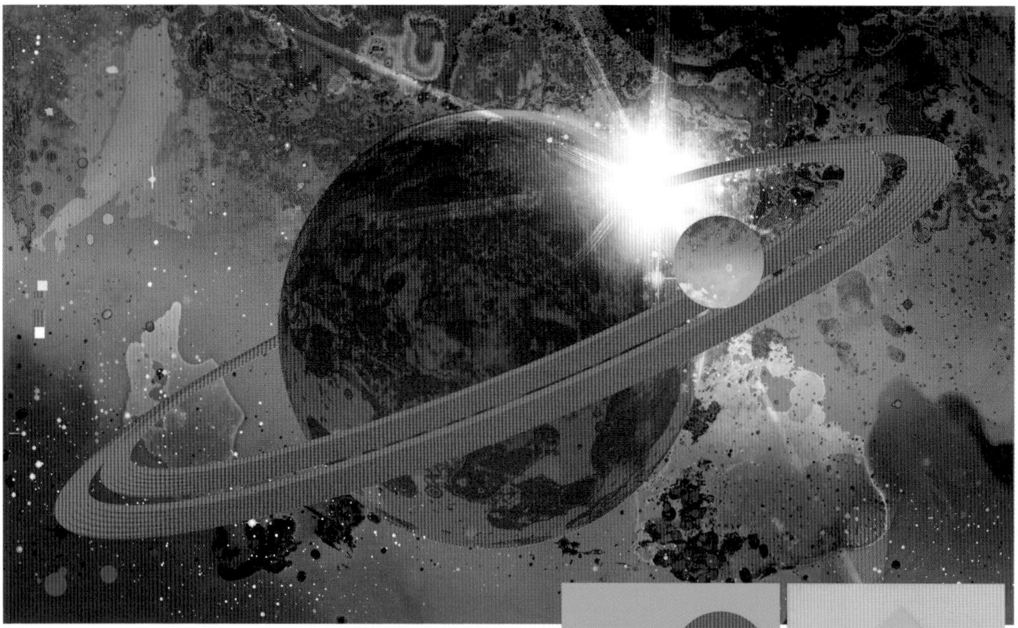

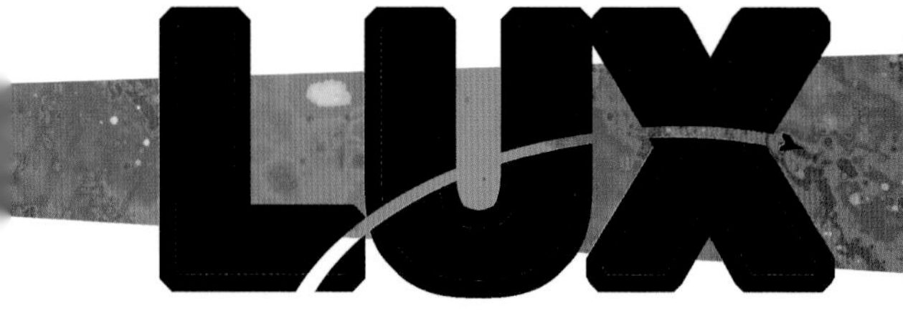
LUX

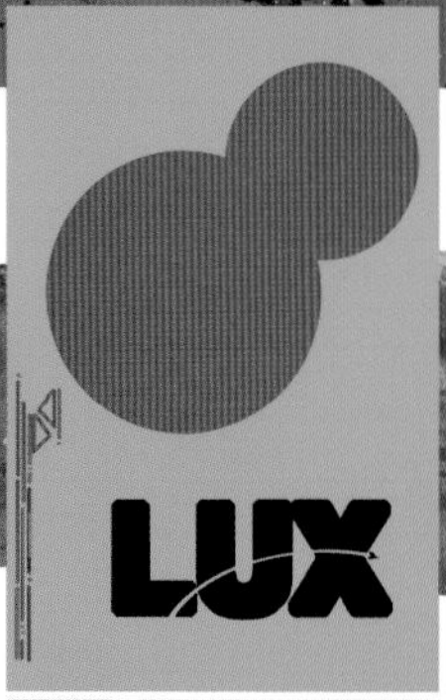
LUX

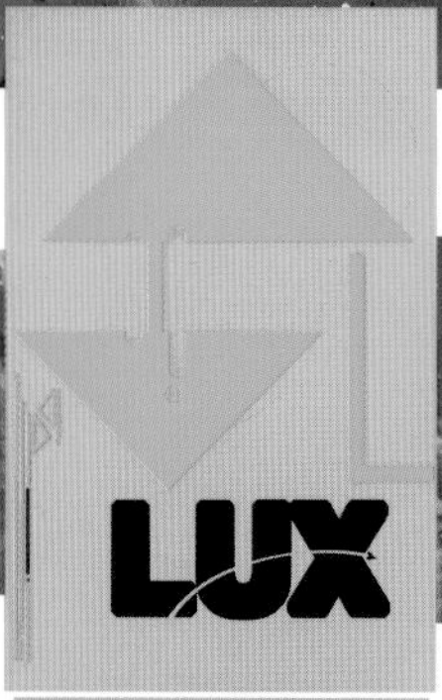
LUX

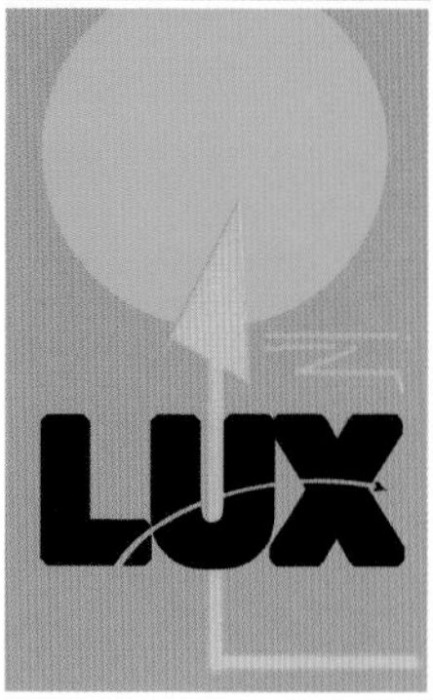
LUX

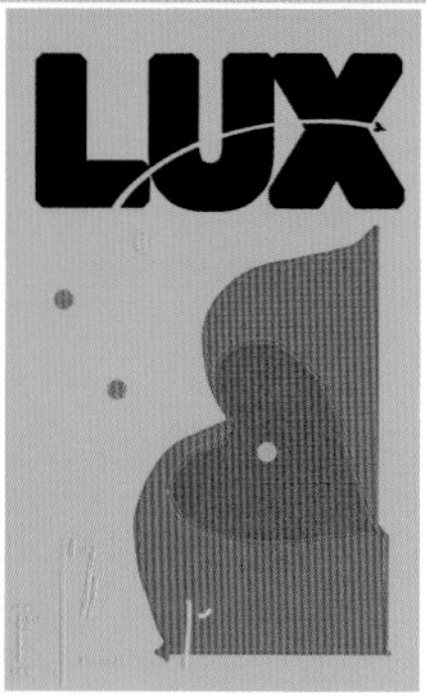
LUX

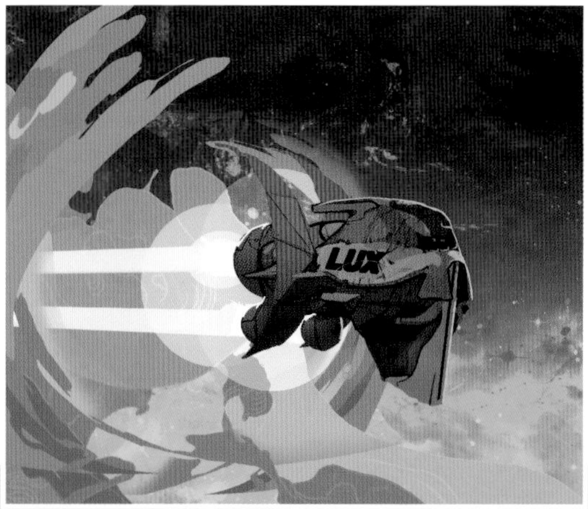
LUX

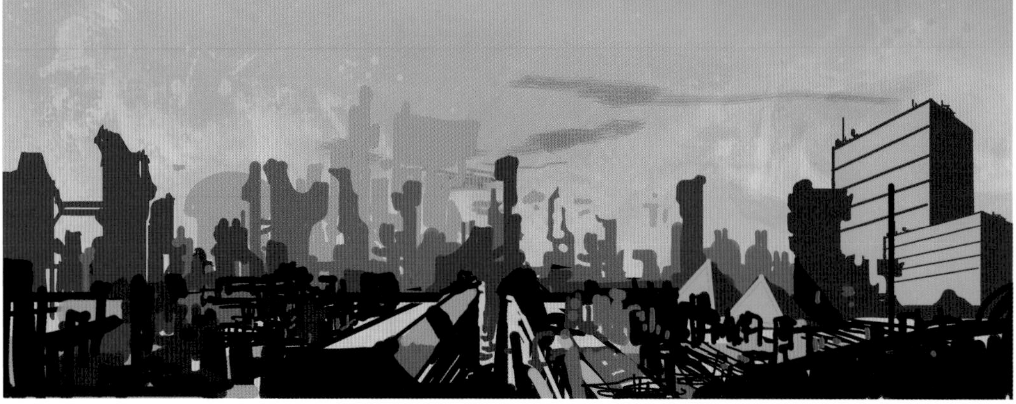

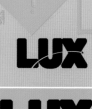

The story continues in **Volume II; "Edge of Everything"**

In an asteroid belt on the furthest reaches of the solar system, the Sundog encounters a group of space-faring privateers called the Riveters...who are only too happy to believe that the system's largest corporation and its major religion are conspiring to defraud the People.

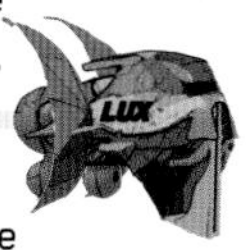
LUX

But when a Lux ship becomes disabled in the asteroid belt and the Riveters prepare to capture it and set the crew adrift to die, Grix and Vess begin to wonder whether these are the kinds of friends they need...

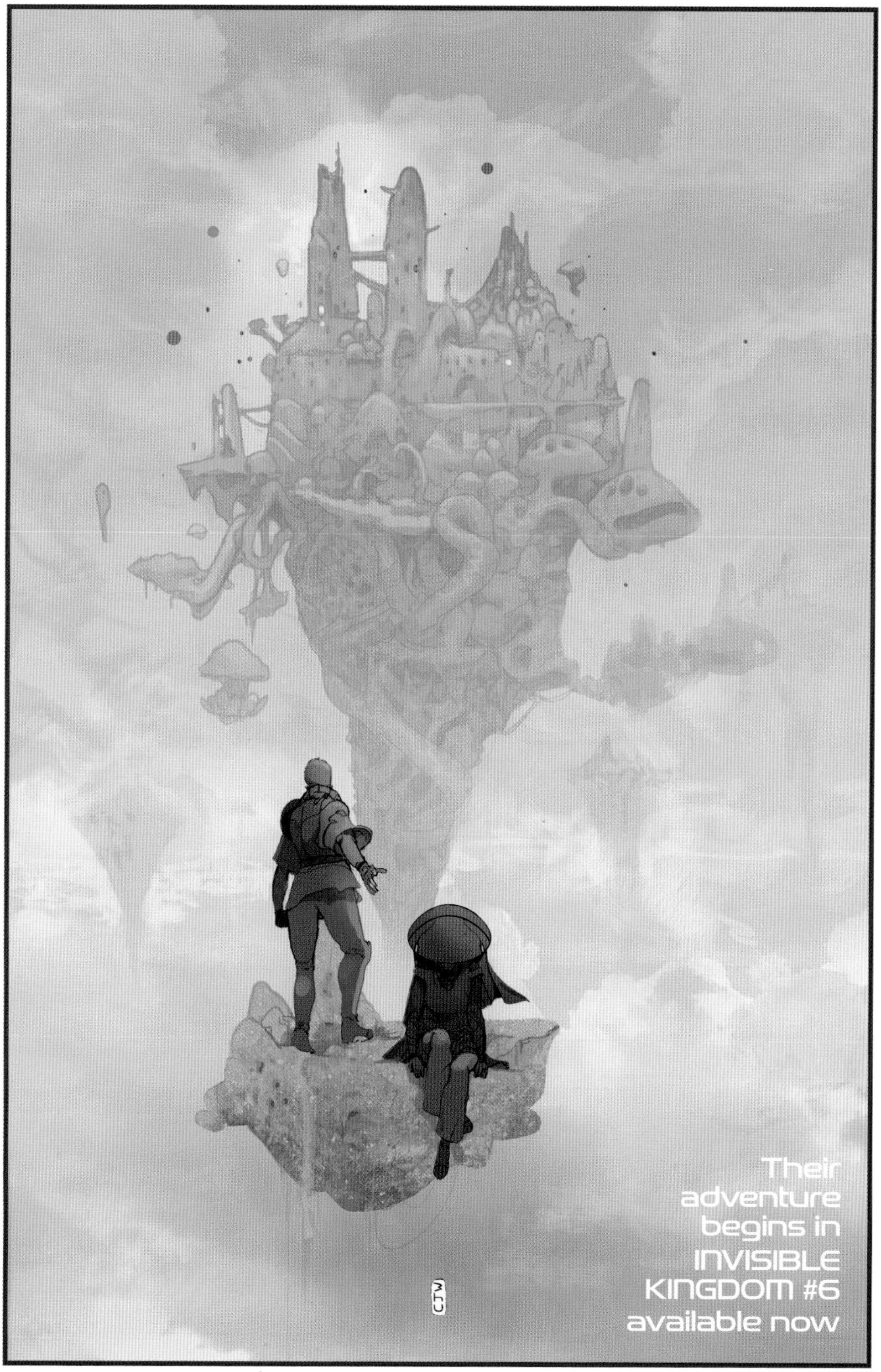
Their adventure begins in INVISIBLE KINGDOM #6 available now

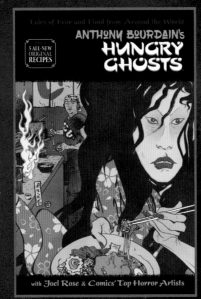

ANTHONY BOURDAIN'S HUNGRY GHOSTS

Hardcover, 88 Pages
$14.99 ◊ ISBN 978-1-50670-669-6

Inspired by the Japanese game 100 Candles, a circle of chefs gather to outscare each other with modern tales of fear and food from around the world—and pray that they survive the night.

Includes original recipes by Bourdain.

SHE COULD FLY
Vol. One: Obsessive Propulsion

Deluxe Softcover, 128 Pages
$19.99 ◊ ISBN 978-1-50670-949-9

A fantastic, unknown flying woman suddenly explodes mid-air. No one knows how she flew, or why. Luna Brewster, a disturbed 15-year-old, becomes obsessed with finding out. Will the truth free her...or shatter her life?

THE ALCOHOLIC:
10th Anniversary Expanded Edition

Deluxe Softcover, 144 Pages
$19.99 ◊ ISBN 978-1-50670-808-9

The heartbreaking yet hilarious tale of a boozed-up, sexually confused, hopelessly romantic writer who careens from one off-kilter encounter to another in a mad search for himself.

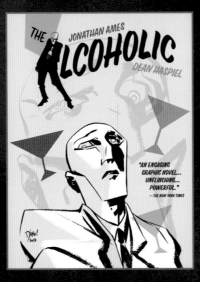

MATA HARI

Deluxe Softcover, 110 Pages
$19.99 ◊ ISBN 978-1-50670-561-3

The unseen side of the notorious exotic dancer and convicted double agent who was executed by a French firing squad in 1917 is explored in this haunting and gripping telling.

INCOGNEGRO: RENAISSANCE

Hardcover, 110 Pages
$19.99 ◊ ISBN 978-1-50670-563-7

A page-turning thriller of racial divide, this story explores segregation, secrets, and self-image as our race-bending protagonist penetrates a world where he feels stranger than ever before.

BERGER BOOKS

The Must-Have Graphic Novel Library

OLIVIA TWIST: Honor Among Thieves

Deluxe Softcover, 110 Pages
$19.99 ◊ ISBN 978-1-50670-948-2

In dystopian future London, teenage orphan Olivia Twist joins a girl gang of thieves to save a new friend.

But Olivia has more power than she knows... and it comes at a great cost.

"Terrifically relevant and of-our-moment." – Jonathan Lethem
OLIVIA TWIST
HONOR AMONG THIEVES
DARIN STRAUSS
NATIONAL BOOK CRITICS CIRCLE AWARD WINNER
ADAM DALVA
EMMA VIECELI
LEE LOUGHRIDGE

THE originals
THE ESSENTIAL EDITION
DAVE GIBBONS

THE ORIGINALS: The Essential Edition

Hardcover, 156 Pages
$29.99 ◊ ISBN 978-1-50670-562-0

An oversized new edition of this Eisner Award-winning story, now with additional material including a large sketchbook section.

In a retro-futuristic city, two childhood friends join the toughest, most stylish gang around – but their dreams are dashed when deadly violence changes their lives.

J.M. DeMATTEIS CORIN HOWELL JAMES DEVLIN
the girl in the bay

THE GIRL IN THE BAY

Deluxe Softcover, 116 Pages
$17.99 ◊ ISBN 978-1-50671-228-4

A supernatural coming-of-age mystery begins in 1969, when Kathy Sartori is murdered– only to reawaken in 2019, where another version of herself has lived a full life. And her "killer" is about to strike again.

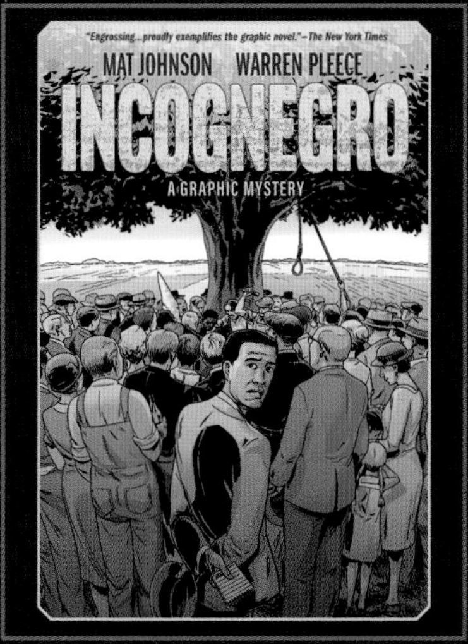

"Engrossing...proudly exemplifies the graphic novel."–The New York Times
MAT JOHNSON WARREN PLEECE
INCOGNEGRO
A GRAPHIC MYSTERY

INCOGNEGRO: A GRAPHIC MYSTERY

Hardcover, 128 Pages
$19.99 ◊ ISBN 978-1-50670-564-4

Reporter Zane Pinchback goes "incognegro", traveling from Harlem to the deep south to investigate the arrest of his brother.

A fast-paced mystery and riveting exploration of race and identity.

Nnedi Okorafor
HUGO & NEBULA AWARD-WINNER
LAGUARDIA
Tana Ford & James Devlin
EQUALITY AND JUSTICE
NO HATE
ALIENS ARE CITIZENS
BABY on BOARD
ALIENS ARE PEOPLE TOO

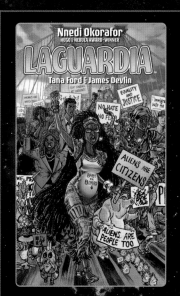

LAGUARDIA

Deluxe Softcover, 128 Pages
$19.99 ◊ ISBN 978-1-50671-075-4

In an alien-integrated world, a very pregnant doctor named Future Nwafor Chukwuebuka smuggles an illegal, sentient plant through LaGuardia International and Interstellar Airport, and their arrival to New York marks the abrupt start of a an amazing new life – for everyone!

Invisible Kingdom Volume One: Walking the Path, October 2019.
Published by Dark Horse Comics LLC, 10956 SE Main Street, Milwaukie, Oregon
97222. Text and illustrations of Invisible Kingdom™ © 2019 G. Willow Wilson and
Christian Ward. The Berger Books Logo, Dark Horse Comics ® and the Dark Horse
logo are trademarks of Dark Horse Comics LLC, registered in various categories
and countries. Berger Books ® is a registered trademark of Karen Berger.

This volume collects Issues #1–5 of Invisible Kingdom.
First Edition: October 2019
ISBN 978-1-50671-227-7
Digital ISBN 978-1-50671-291-8

1 2 3 4 5 6 7 8 9 10
Printed in China

Published by
Dark Horse Books
A division of Dark Horse Comics LLC.
10956 SE Main Street
Milwaukie, OR 97222

DarkHorse.com
ComicShopLocator.com

Names: Wilson, G. Willow, 1982- writer. | Ward, Christian (Christian J.), artist. | Cipriano, Sal, letterer. Title: Walking the
path / written by G. Willow Wilson ; art by Christian Ward ; lettered by Sal Cipriano. Description: First edition. | Milwaukie,
OR : Dark Horse Books/Berger Books, 2019. | Series: Invisible Kingdom ; Volume 1 | "This volume collects Issues #1-5 of
Invisible Kingdom." Identifiers: LCCN 2019019717 | ISBN 9781506712277 (paperback) Subjects: LCSH: Comic books, strips,
etc. | BISAC: COMICS & GRAPHIC NOVELS /   Science Fiction. | COMICS & GRAPHIC NOVELS / Literary. Classification:
LCC PN6728.I574 W55 2019 | DDC 741.5/973--dc23 LC record available at https://lccn.loc.gov/2019019717